W9-AHH-505

ASPERGER'S CHILDREN

Center Point
Large Print

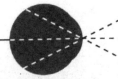

**This Large Print Book carries the
Seal of Approval of N.A.V.H.**

ASPERGER'S CHILDREN

The Origins of Autism in Nazi Vienna

Edith Sheffer

WOODS MEMORIAL LIBRARY
19 PLEASANT STREET
BARRE MA 01005-0489

CENTER POINT LARGE PRINT
THORNDIKE, MAINE

This Center Point Large Print edition
is published in the year 2018 by arrangement with
W. W. Norton & Company, Inc.

Copyright © 2018 by Edith Sheffer.

All rights reserved.

The text of this Large Print edition is unabridged.
In other aspects, this book may vary
from the original edition.
Printed in the United States of America
on permanent paper.
Set in 16-point Times New Roman type.

ISBN: 978-1-68324-946-7

10/18

Library of Congress Cataloging-in-Publication Data

Names: Sheffer, Edith, author.
Title: Asperger's children : the origins of autism in Nazi Vienna /
   Edith Sheffer.
Description: Center point large print edition. | Thorndike, Maine :
   W.W. Norton & Company, Inc., 2018. | Includes bibliographical
   references.
Identifiers: LCCN 2018033889 | ISBN 9781683249467
   (hardcover : alk. paper)
Subjects: | MESH: Asperger, Hans. | Asperger Syndrome—history |
   Child Psychiatr—history | Child Abuse—history |
   War Crimes—history | National Socialism—history | World War II |
   Austria
Classification: LCC RJ506.A9 | NLM WS 11 GA8 |
   DDC 618.92/85883200943613—dc23
LC record available at https://lccn.loc.gov/2018033889

To my son,
Eric

CONTENTS

ASPERGER'S
CHILDREN

Introduction

W hat is the difference between a butterfly and a fly? "The butterfly does not grow up in the room as the fly does," said Harro. This was his intelligence test. Harro chose to talk about the fly:

> It has a completely different development! The fly mother lays many, many eggs in a gap in the floorboards and then a few days later the maggots crawl out. I have read this once in a book, where the floor talks—I could die laughing when I think of it—what is looking out of this little tub? A giant head with a tiny body and a trunk like an elephant? And then a few days later they cocoon themselves in and then suddenly there are some dear little flies crawling out.[1]

Harro and other children were growing up in a room, too, cocooned at Hans Asperger's Curative Education Clinic at the University of Vienna Children's Hospital. Like the curiously shaped larvae, they stuck out. Differences such as theirs had become more objectionable in the Third Reich, and the doctors and nurses on the ward were working to develop the children. Asperger held that with proper "understanding, love and guidance" they could find "their place in the organism of the social community."[2]

Asperger said he valued the unique characters of the children he treated, tailoring his approach to their individual needs. He had a holistic approach. Children at the elegant and open Widerhofer Pavilion engaged in a range of activities, from sports to drama to music. Asperger sat with the children, his tall frame hunched over to connect with them at their level. With his intent gaze, he noted all realms of their behavior in his postdoctoral thesis. Harro was one of the case studies for his new diagnosis: autistic psychopathy.

Harro's school had referred the boy to Asperger's Curative Education Clinic for evaluation. Its report stated that the eight and a half year old seldom did as he was told. Harro talked back, did not do his homework, and complained his lessons were "far too stupid." He was ridiculed by his classmates, and hit and injured other boys over petty issues. Harro was even said to crawl on all fours during lessons and commit "homosexual acts."[3] His teachers maintained that the boy could succeed "if he wanted to." But Harro had failed every subject and was repeating a grade.

He was difficult to test, often uncooperative and unsuccessful in conventional tasks. In certain areas, Harro demonstrated skills beyond his age. With math, for example, he came to solutions in his own way. What is 47 minus 15? 32—"either add 3 and also add 3 to that which should be taken away, or first take away 7 and then 8." Asperger saw such "exceptional originality" as evidence of "special abilities" in many boys.[4]

The problem, as Asperger saw it, was that Harro did not have social feeling. Asperger said Harro went his own way in a group, and "never became warm, trusting or cheerful" in the ward. Harro resisted the "important social habits of daily life." He did not play with other children, but spent much of his time reading in a corner, indifferent. When teased, Asperger held that Harro "lacked any sense of humor." He had a "lost gaze" and "few facial expressions and gestures."[5]

Asperger decided that Harro demonstrated autistic psychopathy. But because of his intelligence, Harro was on the "favorable" end of the autistic "range." That meant he was capable of remediation and joining the community. Children such as Harro could be taught "social integration" and be of "social value" in specialized technical professions.[6] What these promising children needed, Asperger wrote, was individualized care to nurture their cognitive and emotional growth. He sympathized with their challenges, advocated their potential, and celebrated their uniqueness.

This is the benevolent image of Asperger today.

But it represents only one side of Asperger's work. While Asperger did support children he believed to be teachable, defending their disabilities, he was dismissive about those he believed to be more disabled. Deprecatory pronouncements could be a death sentence in the Third Reich. And in fact, some of Asperger's judgments were death sentences.

Although Harro passed Asperger's test, Asperger's label of autistic psychopathy still underestimated the boy. Asperger contended that autistic children "did not really fit into this world" and looked as if they had "just fallen from the sky"—but Harro had not really fallen. Like the fly, he was simply making his own way. Harro explained, "The fly is much more skillful and can walk up the slippery glass and can walk up the wall . . . just yesterday I saw it has teeny weeny claws on the feet and at the ends tiny little hooks; when it feels that it slips, then it hooks itself up with the hooks."[7]

This is not a story about one boy, however. Nor is it about children on the luckier end of Asperger's autistic range. This book is about all the children who faced the Third Reich's diagnosis regime, and how Nazi psychiatry judged their minds and determined their fates. Diagnoses reflect a society's values, concerns, and hopes. As this book uncovers the nightmarish contexts of autism's creation, it reveals how what

14

today appears to be a singular idea rested upon the community that made it. Asperger's diagnosis of autistic psychopathy emerged from the values and institutions of the Third Reich.

THE TERM *AUTISM* was introduced in 1911 by Eugen Bleuler, a Swiss psychiatrist who used it to describe schizophrenic patients who appeared disconnected from the outside world. Hans Asperger and fellow Austrian-born Leo Kanner were the first physicians to introduce the term *autism* as a standalone diagnosis to describe certain characteristics of social withdrawal; others had described similar children, yet referred to them as schizoid. Over the years, a number of psychiatrists became captivated by children who were said to isolate themselves from others and the world around them—and developed different terms to classify them.[8]

Kanner, by then based at Johns Hopkins in the United States (where he would be regarded as the "father" of American child psychiatry) published his work on autism, "Autistic Disturbances of Affective Contact," in 1943.[9] The same year, in Vienna, Asperger presented his postdoctoral thesis, "The 'Autistic Psychopaths' in Child-hood," which he published in 1944. Kanner described children he considered to be relatively similar to one another. He saw them as socially and emotionally withdrawn, and preoccupied with objects and rituals—with repetitive behavior, little to no speech, and severe cognitive impairments. This is now called "classic," or Kanner-type autism. For decades, practitioners in the United States went by this narrower definition. Autism was a relatively rare diagnosis: 1 in 5,000 in 1975. Asperger's definition of autistic psychopathy was much broader, and included those he saw with far milder challenges; the children might, for example, have fluent speech and be able to attend a standard school. Asperger's diagnosis remained little known for decades, until leading British psychiatrist Lorna Wing discovered Asperger's 1944 thesis and publicized the diagnosis in 1981 as "Asperger's syndrome." The idea took off in psychiatric circles and, by 1994, the American Psychiatric Association included Asperger's disorder as a diagnosis in the fourth edition of the *Diagnostic and Statistical Manual of Mental Disorders* (DSM-IV). Because Asperger's disorder has been increasingly understood as "high-functioning" autism, the American Psychiatric Association removed it from the DSM-V in 2013 and subsumed it under the general diagnosis of autism spectrum disorder. But internationally, Asperger's syndrome remains a distinct diagnosis in the World Health Organization's predominant standard, the *International Classification of Diseases, Tenth Revision* (ICD-10).[10]

The introduction of Asperger's work changed the face of autism in the 1990s. Psychiatrists came to view autism as a spectrum disorder that included children with varying characteristics. The diagnosis expanded from Kanner's idea of individuals who he saw as quite disabled, limited in their speech and ability to interact with others, into a personality description that might include math whizzes who were socially awkward.

Rates of autism spectrum diagnoses skyrocketed. While the specific medical, genetic, and environmental causes behind the rise are much debated, most agree that at least some of the increase is due to the widening of diagnostic criteria. According to the United States Centers for Disease Control and Prevention (CDC), the number of children classified with autism spectrum disorders rose from 1 in 2,500 in 1985 to 1 in 500 in 1995. As Asperger's work became mainstream, rates of diagnoses continued to rise from 1 in 150 children in 2002 to 1 in 68 children by 2016.[11] Specialists attribute the increase to a greater sensitivity in recognizing the challenges of children as well as to an objective increase in symptoms.

The American Psychiatric Association's criteria for autism spectrum disorder, while a composite of work conducted by hundreds of psychiatrists, still retains strong echoes of ideas and even language put forth seven decades earlier. As

Asperger wrote in 1944, "the fundamental disorder of autistic individuals is the limitation of their social relationships"; a core criterion in the DSM-V for autism is "persistent deficits in social communication and social interaction." Asperger also defined autistic psychopathy by a "restriction of the self and a narrowing of the relations to the environment"; another core criterion in the DSM-V is "restricted, repetitive patterns of behavior, interests, or activities."[12]

Since Asperger's work wound up broadening ideas of an autism spectrum, many laud him for recognizing and celebrating children's differences. Asperger is often portrayed as a champion of neurodiversity. While the way in which Lorna Wing reintroduced Asperger's 1944 thesis did, indeed, push public discussion toward respecting the uniqueness of individuals, it is time to consider what Asperger actually wrote and did in greater depth, as products of Nazi psychiatry and the world in which he lived.

The aim of this history is not to indict any particular figure, nor is it to undermine the positive discussion of neurodiversity that Asperger's work has inspired. Rather, it is a cautionary tale in service of neurodiversity— revealing the extent to which diagnoses can be shaped by social and political forces, how difficult those may be to perceive, and how hard they may be to combat.

• • •

ASPERGER IS OFTEN depicted as compassionate and progressive, absorbed in his research during the Third Reich and opposed to Nazism. He was a devout Catholic and never joined the Nazi Party. Asperger also has a reputation for defending disabled children from Nazi persecution. Many believe that he emphasized the special abilities of children and their potential value to the state in technical professions in order to protect them from being killed in the Nazi "euthanasia" program. In this view, Asperger was using the autism diagnosis as a psychiatric Schindler's list.[13] After the Third Reich, Asperger himself said he had resisted the regime, that he had risked his life to rescue children from Nazi extermination.[14]

The archival record, however, suggests a different story. Files reveal that Asperger participated in Vienna's child killing system on multiple levels. He was close colleagues with leaders in Vienna's child euthanasia system and, through his numerous positions in the Nazi state, sent dozens of children to Spiegelgrund children's institution, where children in Vienna were killed.[15]

It is difficult to reconcile Asperger's role in the child euthanasia program with his well-known support for children with disabilities. Both are in the documentary record. Delving into Asperger's work exposes a two-sided nature to his actions. Asperger distinguished between youths he believed to be remediable, who had the potential for "social integration," and youths he believed were irremediable. While he offered intensive and individualized care to children he regarded as promising, he prescribed harsh institutionalization and even transfer to Spiegelgrund for children he judged to have greater disabilities. Asperger was not alone. His senior colleagues in Nazi medicine likewise advocated compassionate and first-rate care for children who might be redeemed for the Reich and excision for those they believed to be irredeemable.

The double-sided character of Asperger's actions underscores the double-sided character of Nazism as a whole. The Reich's project to transform humanity involved both treatment and elimination. Depending on the defects, some individuals could be trained to meet Nazi standards, and some were to be eradicated.

It did not take much to define new groups for persecution and death, as inhabitants of the Reich devised and implemented changing labels, rather than a fixed, faceless rulebook, and elastic categories evolved over time. In this diagnosis regime, some people labeled with defects were to be transformed to meet Nazi standards rather than eradicated. Whereas full Jews were written off, for example, certain people with Slavic heritage might be Germanized, or the "work-shy" might be taught to work. Similarly, for Asperger, those on the "favorable" side of autism could be taught "social integration" and even be recognized for "special abilities."[16]

The efforts of the Third Reich to create a homogenous national community meant bringing people in and multiplying and unifying people the regime deemed desirable, as well as cutting people out. Efforts to cleanse the body politic led to the Holocaust—the killing of over six million Jews in the largest genocide in history—as well as to numerous other programs of systematic elimination. The Reich killed over 200,000 people seen to have disabilities, 220,000 "gypsies" (Roma and Sinti), and huge segments of eastern European and Soviet populations, including 3.3 million Soviet prisoners of war.

Nazi officials categorized people for removal according to purportedly scientific principles of racial hygiene, attributing problem traits to inferior heredity and physiology. As the regime biologized categories of belonging and un-belonging, historians have called the Third Reich a "racial state."[17] Certainly, race was an organizing principle of the Nazi regime. But the term can also suggest that Nazi labels and programs were more defined than they actually were.

In reality, expelling undesirables was a process of trial and error. Definitions were elastic, and policies inconsistent—shifting with time, place, and actors. Even Jewishness, which might seem a clear category, had convoluted criteria in the 1935 Nuremberg Laws and, later, in debates over the fate of *Mischlinge*, or half-Jews. Officials were also unclear on how many biologically inferior individuals there were; estimates ranged from one million up to thirteen million, as many as one in five Germans.[18] The identification and persecution of people who could not be considered healthy Aryans was likewise haphazard: the "asocial" and "work-shy" (e.g., criminals, unemployed, homeless, alcoholics, prostitutes), male homosexuals, political opponents (especially Communists and Socialists), and religious dissidents (such as Jehovah's Witnesses). Decisions to arrest, deport, and kill could come down to individual people and agencies making individual classifications.

This book suggests a new lens on the Third Reich—as a diagnosis regime. The state became obsessed with sorting the population into categories, cataloguing people by race, politics, religion, sexuality, criminality, heredity, and biological defects. These labels, then, became the basis of individuals' persecution and extermination. So although National Socialism is typically seen in terms of its violent outcomes, backing up the chain of causation reveals how these outcomes hinged upon the initial act of diagnosis. Nazi eugenics was marshaled to redefine and catalogue the human condition.

Increasing categorization of defects, then, propelled state persecution and murder.[19]

The mind received special scrutiny in the Third Reich. Doctors who lived during the Nazi era named at least thirty eponymous neurological and psychiatric diagnoses still used today.[20] As mental health depended on multiple factors of genetics, health, family status, class, and gender, the mind lay at a crossroads of Nazi eugenics. Neuropsychiatrists also played the largest role of any professional group in the medical cleansing of society, in the development of forced sterilization, human experiments, and the killing of those perceived to be disabled.[21]

Nazi psychiatry became a totalizing approach to the observation and treatment of children. To examine the entire character rather than just discrete symptoms, the psychiatrist required full knowledge of the child's behavior and personality. This meant surveilling youths with ever greater nuance, noting ever milder deviations, which widened the scope for new diagnoses.

What, exactly, was being diagnosed? In Asperger's circles, proper race and physiology were necessary for joining the national community, or *Volksgemeinschaft*. But community spirit was also required. One had to believe and behave in unison with the group. The vitality of the German *Volk*, or German people, depended upon the ability of individuals to feel it. The fascination with social cohesion spotlights the importance of fascism at the heart of Nazism.[22]

As commitment to the national community became a priority in the Third Reich, collective emotions became a part of Nazi eugenics. Sociability evolved into a category of persecution alongside race, politics, religion, sexuality, criminality, and physiology. Asperger and his senior colleagues developed the term *Gemüt* to capture the concept. *Gemüt* was a term that originally meant "soul" in the eighteenth century and, within Nazi child psychiatry, came to signify the metaphysical capacity for social bonds. *Gemüt* was essential to individuals' connection with the collective, a key ingredient for fascist feeling. Nazi psychiatrists began to diagnose children who they said had poor *Gemüt*, who forged weaker social ties and did not align with collectivist expectations. They created a number of diagnoses like autism, such as *"gemütsarm"* [lacking *Gemüt*] long before Asperger described autistic psychopathy in 1944—which he, too, defined as a defect of *Gemüt*.[23]

The history of Asperger's work shows the individual and elastic ways in which new categories of defects were defined within, and because of, the Third Reich's diagnosis regime. The paradigm of a diagnosis regime leads us from looking at the Nazi state through a narrower lens of extermination to a wider lens of perfectibility.

At its core, the Third Reich was about the continual evaluation and remaking of humanity. Beyond racial and physical ideals, Nazism was also about how one thought and felt. It imposed mental and emotional norms—toward a model kind of personality.

While medicine and psychiatry elsewhere in the world in this era shared characteristics, the Reich's diagnosis regime operated under the shadow of death, and it included death as a treatment option. Proliferating diagnoses radicalized into the killing of those deemed unfit for the *Volk*, as "life unworthy of life." This was called euthanasia, although the term is inaccurate; the vast majority of individuals killed in the program were physically healthy, neither terminally ill nor physically suffering. They were regarded as disabled. Many children were targeted for behavioral or social concerns—especially at Spiegelgrund in Vienna, where Asperger and his colleagues referred youths. In Nazi psychiatry, a child needed to demonstrate conformity, "educability," and "ability to work" for community competence [*Gemeinschaftsfähigkeit*]. Family and class factors also played a role. Chances of death were greater if the child was born out of wedlock, had an absent father, or a mother suspected of being unable to cope, with other children at home. In other words, the child euthanasia program came to medicalize social belonging, incorporating social concerns as eugenicist criteria.

Child killing was the Reich's first system of mass murder. It lay at the transition from racial hygiene measures, such as sterilization of the "hereditarily ill," to mass extermination. Child euthanasia was conceived as a legal, permanent feature of Reich health care, unlike other forms of Nazi extermination that would emerge. For example, adult euthanasia, conducted until 1941 under the T4 program (named after the address of its headquarters on Tiergartenstrasse 4 in Berlin) and then unofficially thereafter, was a far more indiscriminate process that killed over 200,000 people. By contrast, child euthanasia was to involve lengthy observation and deliberation of individual cases. The program was smaller; it killed between 5,000 and 10,000 youths, including 789 at Spiegelgrund, the Reich's second largest child killing facility.

The child euthanasia program reveals an intimate dimension to extermination. Doctors personally examined the children they condemned. Nurses personally fed and changed the sheets of children they killed. They knew the children's names, voices, faces, and personalities. Killings were typically done in the children's own beds. Death came slowly, painfully, as children would be starved or given overdoses of barbiturates until they grew ill and died, usually of pneumonia. While Nazi extermination is often told as separate stories of how Nazis killed versus how victims suffered, in child euthanasia these were not parallel experiences, but interactions—which affected how the killings unfolded and escalated as they did.

Where, if anywhere, can one draw lines of complicity for ordinary people in a criminal state? In marginal and major ways, conscious and unconscious, people became entangled in systems of slaughter. Asperger was neither a zealous supporter nor an opponent of the regime. He was an exemplar of this drift into complicity, part of the muddled majority of the populace who alternately conformed, concurred, feared, normalized, minimized, repressed, and reconciled themselves to Nazi rule. Given these inconsistencies, it is all the more striking that the accumulated actions of millions of people, acting for individual reasons in individual circumstances, added up to a regime so thoroughly monstrous.

It is difficult to separate the murderous and nonmurderous aspects of the Nazi state. Complicity in the Reich's thirty-seven child euthanasia wards extended far beyond just medical professionals. Staff, maintenance crews, cooks, and cleaners made the killing centers possible; accountants, insurers, drug producers, and city officials facilitated them; truck drivers, railroad workers, local vendors, and food sellers sustained them. These people had families and neighbors with whom they would discuss what was happening. Parents whose children were kept in institutions could know of the program, too. Some rescued their children from the killing wards; some delivered their children to them.

Because child and adult euthanasia killings unfolded inside the Reich, many ordinary citizens knew what was happening. People in their daily lives could smell the stench of human ashes from the crematoria of the killing facilities. Hundreds of thousands learned of the deaths of friends and loved ones under suspicious circumstances; healthy individuals would die of supposedly natural causes within weeks of admission.

Widespread public knowledge of euthanasia led to a public outcry—especially under the leadership of Bishop von Galen of Münster—to the point where Hitler officially ended the adult euthanasia T4 program in August 1941.[24] The T4 effort was the only program of mass murder that Reich citizens broadly protested during the Nazi period. While courageous, the public dissent also had disturbing implications. After all, people were protesting the killing of members of the Reich, not the extermination of those presumed to be outside the national community. Moreover, Hitler's official cessation of T4 suggests that popular protests of other Nazi initiatives might have had some effect. Still, the decentralized killings of supposedly disabled adults continued under greater cover, continuing to claim hundreds of thousands of lives.

Other forms of systematic murder pervaded the Reich. Nazi camps of undesirables dotted German-occupied Europe: more than 42,000 in all. There were 980 concentration camps, 1,150 Jewish ghettos, 500 forced brothels, 1,000 camps for prisoners of war, and 30,000 labor camps. This was in addition to unknown thousands of detention and transport centers.[25] To do the math is staggering. If only one hundred people were involved in the operation and support of each of these 42,000 camps (an implausibly low estimate), that would involve over four million people. This book shows the creep of murderous thought and practices into medicine and society. In following Asperger and his associates, the cascade of microsteps exposes how history happened.

Asperger, like others in the Third Reich, improvised his decision making: he could staunchly defend youths he believed might be able to join the national community, even as he transferred those he deemed on the other end of the spectrum to Spiegelgrund. The linkage of help and harm renders the seemingly contradictory roles and intentions of ordinary people more intelligible, and speaks to the power of diagnosis in deciding one's destiny in the Nazi state.

• • •

THIS BOOK TRACES how the values and events of the Third Reich shaped Asperger's concept of autistic psychopathy. It examines the long lineage of the diagnosis, linking Asperger's thoughts and actions to the broader world in which he lived. To recognize Asperger within the swirl of events around him is to expose both the origins of Nazi psychiatry and the origins of Nazi mass extermination in the child euthanasia program. This history unsettles the aura of inevitability and mystery around autism, destabilizing its hold on our imaginations. The diagnosis did not arise fully formed, *sui generis*, but emerged bit by bit, shaped by the values and interactions of psychiatry, state, and society.

Understanding these connections can shed new light on the idea of autism and help us reflect on its cultural ramifications for the twenty-first century.

1

Enter the Experts

HANS ASPERGER BELIEVED he had unique insight into the minds of children, as well as a calling to shape their characters. He sought to define what he called youths' "innermost essence."[1] His daughter said Asperger often likened himself to Lynceus, the tower warden in Johann Wolfgang von Goethe's *Faust*, who sings alone at night as he surveys all before him:

> *Born to see,*
> *appointed to watch,*
> *sworn to this tower,*
> *I enjoy the world.*

Like the warden, Asperger appraised the world from his Curative Education Clinic at the University of Vienna Children's Hospital. Known to speak in quotations, Asperger frequently cited German literature and classics in Greek and Latin, as well as his own dictums. Asperger spoke deliberatively, formally; he would refer to himself in the third person, by name.[2] He was a man of certitude who grasped Lynceus' wisdom and was able to penetrate the "cosmos" around him.

Asperger was born on February 18, 1906, in the heart of the Habsburg Empire. Fifty miles outside Vienna, his agricultural village of Hausbrunn occupied a small valley near the Morava River, a tributary of the Danube that later marked the eastern border of Austria. He was the oldest of three children. His middle sibling had died after birth, and his brother Karl, four years younger, would be killed in the Soviet Union during World War Two.

As a child, Asperger said he was raised "with much love, indeed self-sacrifice from my mother, and great strictness from my father." His father, Johann Asperger, was from a long line of farmers; he had gone to Vienna for vocational training but, as a bookkeeper, was frustrated that he could not go further with his education. Asperger felt that his father demanded flawless grades and behavior because he wanted Asperger to fulfill his own dashed dreams. Though Asperger lived up to those high expectations, he disapproved of the harsh parenting later in life. "I have not been that way with my children or any of my patients," he later reflected.[3]

With a more romantic approach toward life than his father, Asperger called himself a "wild reader" as a child, with special talents in languages, literature, classics, history, and art. As an adult, he said he had collected ten thousand books in his library at home. This voracious reading, he maintained, brought him "to progressive spiritual maturity." Over time, language "radiantly reveals its meaning, one could also say, it comes to one, or it overtakes, or one overtakes it."[4]

The German youth movement, which brought Asperger from the austerity of home and school into the outdoor camaraderie of boys' groups, also exerted a kind of spiritual influence. Asperger relished hiking and mountain climbing with the Wandering Scholars of Bund Neuland, an organization of politically conservative Catholic youth groups that he would support throughout his life. His experiences of intense fellowship shaped his later ideas of childhood and social bonds. As he later recalled: "I was molded by the spirit of the German youth movement, which was one of the noblest blossoms of the German spirit." In 1959, Asperger praised the Hitler Youth, too, as "widely fruitful, formative."[5]

He maintained his love of outdoor excursions. Asperger hiked his entire life: on short trips, long trips, up the Matterhorn, and as a guide to boys' troops, often recording his thoughts on small notes as he went. While mountain climbing, he even met his wife, Hanna Kalmon, with whom he had five children.[6]

Indoors, however, Asperger was reportedly socially awkward, cool, and distanced. Today, people debate whether Asperger had Asperger's—if he had traits of the syndrome that later bore his name. As will become clear, it is problematic to assess anyone by the criteria Asperger set forth in his 1944 definition of autistic psychopathy, let alone retrospectively. That said, it seems highly unlikely that Asperger would define himself by his own diagnosis, given the harsh critique it contains. Yet he did suggest he might share at least one of its characteristics; success in science, he asserted, required a "dash of autism."[7]

Asperger claimed his moment of scientific calling came at a young age. He described his experience dissecting a mouse's liver at school in the third person:

> There was a small white mound on the surface. The pupil cut it—and to great astonishment a two-centimeter long worm-like parasite crept out. But that fascinated the pupil, who was I . . . how life was living in another life, how both existed together in close mutual relations. Should one not take up the path? . . . And at that moment it became clear, you must pursue studies, that it must continue. That was very unusual at that time, that someone in the second year of Gymnasium knew he would study medicine.[8]

With great ambition, then, Asperger left his small town of Hausbrunn at age nineteen, in 1925, for his medical studies at the University of Vienna. A tall, lanky young man with an angular face and wire-rimmed glasses, he wore his light hair wavy on top and cropped close on the sides. Living in Vienna, Asperger would experience—and become shaped by—a metropolis undergoing extraordinary change. After defeat in World War One, the city had become a cauldron of social upheaval, political strife, and economic catastrophe. Asperger's approach to child development was forged in this tumultuous environment, and his story begins with Vienna's transformation.

VIENNA HAD BEEN the cultural capital of Europe at the turn of the twentieth century—the birthplace of modernism where cafés, salons, and schools brought together art, society, and science like nowhere else. Its great achievements, ironically, arose from deep cultural pessimism, with figures such as Sigmund Freud, Gustav Klimt, Egon Schiele, and Arthur Schnitzler responding to widespread fears of moral decay, the ravages of industrialism, and state collapse.[9]

These fears then all came true in interwar Vienna. The city did fall into economic, political, and social ruin. Vienna had suffered greatly during the First World War. Although it did not face a direct military threat, the population faced mass hunger, food riots, and widespread unrest. As the war ended, hundreds of thousands of refugees and former soldiers flooded into Vienna from across the Habsburg Empire, many injured, sick, and malnourished. The influx aggravated already severe food and housing shortages. Diseases raged, especially tuberculosis and the Spanish flu.

Austria's shaky government was ill-equipped to handle the crisis. After the Habsburg monarchy collapsed on November 11, 1918, the National Assembly proclaimed Austria a democratic republic. The new state faced daunting challenges, and it was not clear it would even be viable. War settlements reduced the population of Austria to one-eighth of the empire's former size; it was limited to just its German-speaking portion, with 6.5 million people, and barred from uniting with Germany.[10]

Moreover, leftist and cosmopolitan Vienna, with one-third of Austria's population, was detached from the rest of the rural and conservative country. In the first municipal elections of May 1919, voters swept Social Democrats into city government in a landslide, with an absolute majority—making Vienna the only European city of over one million people to elect a Socialist government. The city thus earned the moniker "Red Vienna." The Social Democrats' creed of Austro-Marxism was democratic, and sought to build socialism and reshape the populace through steady governance rather than violent revolution.

Yet Austria's progressive capital and conservative countryside went in opposite political directions. Neither wanted interference from the other, and Vienna split off into its own federal province. This empowered the Socialist city government to run the metropolis as a state within a state.

Despite a solid Social Democratic majority and a fixed goal to forge a democratic society, Red Vienna saw mounting strife. Economic failure and hyperinflation destroyed individuals' savings and plunged many into poverty. The value of the Austrian krone fell from six to the dollar in 1919 to 83,000 krone in 1922; things were even worse in Germany, where the mark went from 8.2 marks to the dollar in 1919 to 4.2 trillion in 1923. Politics was turbulent, too. Beyond ongoing conflict with the Christian Social Party, there was an angry "Black Vienna" that sought destruction of the republic. Representing a virulent form of reactionary and authoritarian clericalism, its proponents were antidemocratic, antisocialist, and anti-Semitic.[11] Opposing political parties established paramilitary groups that drew on disaffected war veterans and hoarded stocks of weapons. Marches, demonstrations, and clashes turned bloody on Vienna's streets.

As Vienna's inhabitants worried about the political viability of the new republic, they also worried about the physical viability of its inhabitants. A weakened, war-torn populace seemed unlikely to overcome crises and disintegration—with gaunt women in long food lines and street children with rickets. Building a healthy and vital nation required healthy and vital citizenry.

To nurture citizens for the new Socialist society, Vienna's city government launched a vast and daring experiment in public welfare.[12] Julius Tandler, the leading city councilor who headed Vienna's Public Welfare Office, talked of forging "new people." In his view, an orderly and hygienic milieu would improve people's constitutions, so that the state could promote the strength of the nation through shaping the conditions and care of its people.

The "Vienna system" was admired as one of the most progressive welfare programs in Europe and the United States. Tandler was internationally acclaimed, and traveled widely to disseminate Vienna's theories and practices. So although democracy had come to Vienna in the worst circumstances imaginable, the city's programs—against all odds—became renowned.

Vienna's approach to welfare drew on eugenics, which was seen as a scientific approach to population management and was popular in many countries at the time. Eugenics had support across the political spectrum, from leftists to conservatives to clericalists to feminists. Tandler himself was Socialist and Jewish. Eugenics promised that the dislocations of modern society might be conquered by rational programs and planning—and underpinned fledgling welfare systems across Europe and the United States. These efforts included "positive" as well as "negative" eugenics. The former meant promoting the health and reproduction of segments of the population that were desired; the latter meant reducing the number of people who were not, either by discouraging reproduction, withholding social services, or more extreme measures. Both impulses were present in 1920s Vienna.

For positive eugenics, Vienna's city leaders sought to regenerate the population on multiple fronts. The government offered citizens hygienic and material improvements, such as salubrious public housing for working-class people living in unsanitary and overcrowded conditions. It built over 380 apartment complexes between 1923 and 1934 that held 220,000 people, one-tenth of Vienna's population. Massive "superblocks" offered modern plumbing, neat kitchens, ample light, and green courtyards. Rents ran around 4 percent of a working-class income. The city also combatted rampant disease through health clinics and free medical examinations in kindergartens and schools. Since tuberculosis and rickets were especially common, officials offered children daylight and fresh air in new playgrounds, new public sports facilities, over twenty new outdoor public swimming pools, and new summer camps in the countryside. To educate children and keep them off the streets, officials offered daycare, after school programs, and more than doubled the number of kindergartens to fifty-five in the city. Government aspirations were breathtaking. Though implementation proved more complicated than utopian goals, the municipal government achieved many of its aims.

Darker currents ran alongside these efforts, however. Austrian eugenics is often regarded as more positive than many movements elsewhere in Europe—not least because of Catholic constituents who opposed measures such as forced sterilization. And Red Vienna is seen apart from the authoritarian measures that would come with the Austrofascism of the mid-1930s and eventually the Third Reich. But the architects of these different systems shared many of the same social goals, and there is a continuity in their eugenicist models.[13]

Julius Tandler, for example, envisaged the forced sterilization of what he called "the inferior," which included people deemed to have heritable diseases, physiological or mental impairments, and some criminals. Tandler also talked of the "extermination" of "life unworthy of life" as an idea for consideration, using vocabulary the Third Reich would invoke for the killing of adults and children believed to be unfit.[14] In other words, eliminationist ideas were in circulation among city leaders long before the Nazis came to power.

The spread of eugenicist welfare efforts in the 1920s medicalized social anxieties. Vienna, as an unusually large metropolis in an unusually rural country, exposed what people feared most about modern society. Welfare sought to redress the ills of urbanization—of poverty, cramped houses, dirty streets, and unruliness—by regulating families, bodies, and behavior.[15] Public initiatives recast the working class as a pathology to be cured. The state set and enforced new norms of living according to middle-class standards. And the state increasingly intervened in the private lives of its citizens.

RED VIENNA'S MOST radical and eugenicist undertaking was arguably in social work, as state officials became ever more involved in the oversight and rearing of children. Welfare reached beyond providing youths with physical and material support into the realms of upbringing and character. Asperger's approach emerged from these far-reaching ambitions—in which a network of clinics, special schools, reformatories, and children's homes sprung up to supervise child rearing. Certainly, not everyone agreed on approaches and ideologies. But most government officials, educators, physicians, psychoanalysts, and psychiatrists accepted that modern welfare would be multipronged and interventionist.

Before World War One, approaches to social work had been piecemeal. Poor relief run by Catholic Church organizations and private charities had focused on ameliorating living conditions, while government offices and courts removed supposedly problem children from society into prisons and asylums. Later welfare efforts moved beyond such countermeasures and disciplinary actions, into more preventative care.[16] With a new army of specially trained and certified social workers, welfare was to support the whole life of the child in a cohesive system, where no one would fall through the cracks.

State involvement in reproduction and child-rearing began from day one. Upon the birth of a child, social workers visited the home to offer advice on feeding and care, as well as to inspect living conditions. Since less fortunate babies were often swaddled in newspapers, social workers gave all mothers a layette of clean clothing and diapers. Mothers would receive maternity benefits and ongoing advising and medical checks, at home and in clinics.

Social workers tracked family relations. Children born out of wedlock, or a mother absent at work, were special causes for concern. Also, if a district social worker caught word that a child's family might be negligent, or learned of problem children from regular Youth Office school reports, city officials would conduct repeated family visits and inspections. The state gained increasing power to determine what was normal, in children and in their homes. If something was deemed amiss, children might be removed from their families, placed in foster care, institutionalized in a children's home, or imprisoned. Social work was an expanding system with expanding effects.

Thirty-four-year-old Erwin Lazar, an idealistic pediatrician at the University of Vienna Children's Hospital, grew concerned about the hastiness of government procedures. He felt that city officials and delinquency court judges were too arbitrary in their decisions about children's fates, making recommendations without fully understanding their behavior. Lazar wanted city offices to consult experts in child development before institutionalizing or incarcerating youths. He aimed to integrate specialists into Vienna's sprawling bureaucracy in order to give child welfare decisions a scientific basis. Lazar sought to create a clinic at the University of Vienna Children's Hospital—which Asperger would inherit—to issue these expert opinions.

Lazar was bold. He aimed to found a new field of child development: *Heilpädagogik*, or curative education. Lazar said curative education would integrate numerous disciplines, creating "a novelty, whose establishment would represent a long striven-for goal of [combining] pedagogy, psychology, and scientific medicine in equal measure."[17] This approach would consider all aspects of a child's health, psyche, and family circumstances, offering sweeping assessments. While Lazar called his work curative education, it differed from established *Heilpädagogik*, which was a pedagogical approach to special education in Germany, Switzerland, and Austria that dated back to the mid-1800s.[18] Lazar's staff physician Georg Frankl was dismissive of this tradition, led by Theodor Heller in Austria, claiming that "curative education as a science was not much more than concept and name."[19] Lazar wanted to move the approach away from special education into something more like medical and holistic psychiatry.

The University of Vienna Children's Hospital.

Lazar's vision of *Heilpädagogik* is somewhat difficult to translate. There are various possibilities: orthopedagogy, therapeutic pedagogy, remedial education, or special education. For Lazar and, later, Asperger and his associates, "curative education" perhaps fits best, conveying their totalizing ambitions. The word *curative* takes the prefix *Heil*, or "healing," seriously. The approach was more biological than those named above. And *healing* also conveys its spiritual overtones, which distinguished it from mental hygiene or child guidance movements in the United States. Indeed, Asperger's colleagues described their mission as the "care of souls."[20]

To establish curative education, Lazar sought support for his vision from a visionary, Clemens von Pirquet. Internationally acclaimed for his advances in immunology, Pirquet headed the University of Vienna Children's Hospital from 1911–1929 and turned it into a leading pediatric facility in the world. One colleague said Pirquet's rounds "had the attraction of a show," and drew so many foreign visitors that the hospital considered including a multilingual guide.[21] Pirquet was also a leader in social causes. After World War One, as Vienna's children suffered hunger and malnutrition, Pirquet headed Austria's unprecedented food program under the American Relief Administration that provided up to four hundred thousand meals a day. Many at the time

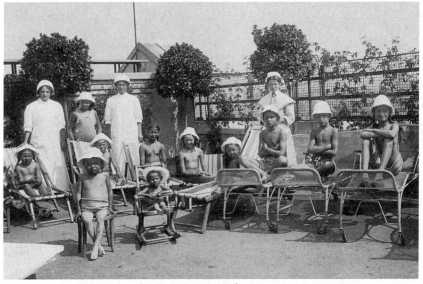

The rooftop "Open Air Department"
at the Children's Hospital, 1921.

even envisaged Pirquet as president of Austria.[22] He was progressive, open to international collaboration and to the advancement of women and Jews. He welcomed experimentation; he turned the roof of his hospital, for example, into an "Open Air Department" where children could play and gain strength exposed to the elements, in rain, snow, or shine. So when Lazar came to Pirquet in 1911 with his unusual idea for a Curative Education Clinic, Pirquet was receptive.[23]

Curative education fit squarely within Vienna's multidisciplinary approach to social work, and became central to it. Lazar's ward developed into one of three major diagnostic clinics in Vienna— along with the Psychological Service of Vienna's

Municipal Youth Office and the Pedagogical Service of Vienna's Municipal Education Authority. Schools, welfare offices, and courts would refer problem children to Lazar's clinic, and staff would issue recommendations for youths' treatment, institutionalization, or detention. Though the Curative Education Clinic was located inside the University Children's Hospital, Lazar received state funding for it from the Imperial Ministry of Education's section for elementary schools. And the clinic advertised its services in school newspapers. This was an ambitious concept: creating a network among state institutions with the expert physician at the center.[24]

Lazar worked tirelessly to integrate curative education into state structures. His clinic taught courses for social workers, teachers, and physicians. It also became a model within Vienna's welfare system, as the city incorporated "Curative Education Wards" in other children's homes that would temporarily house, observe, and diagnose children to be placed.[25] Employed by several city offices, Lazar reorganized children's homes, drafted juvenile criminal legislation, and consulted for the Health Office of the new Ministry for Public Health from 1918–1925. He campaigned to end corporal punishment in state children's institutions, at the time a common practice.[26]

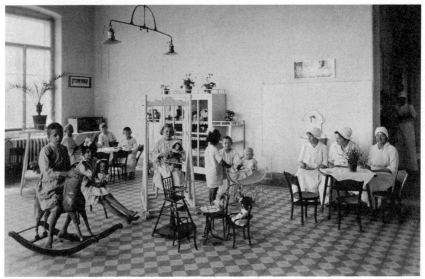
A playroom at the Children's Hospital, 1921.

Curative education dovetailed with the main goal of welfare efforts, which was to socialize children. Approaches varied, but most sought to foster children's "community competence" [*Gemeinschaftsfähigkeit*]. This meant preempting dereliction and criminality, assuring that children would lead economically productive and law-abiding lives. It also meant instilling a sense of group obligation, norms, and integrity—an emotional, educational, behavioral project.

Lazar was particularly interested in "dissocial" youths who had fallen afoul of the law. He felt it important to differentiate what he called endogenous and exogenous causes—between children whose dissociability stemmed from internal factors (physical or psychiatric) versus external factors (illness or milieu). In endogenous

48

cases, Lazar boasted that his Curative Education Clinic was "the first attempt" to distinguish between "the mental and physical defects of the wayward and criminal."[27] Committed to physiological detail, for example, Lazar would examine the genitals of a child "right away," and send boys whose testicles had not dropped to a surgeon.[28]

According to clinic staff physician Josef Feldner, Lazar possessed an uncanny ability to "see people" instantaneously, in their entirety, grasping their "life's arc from beginning to end." With "surprising certainty," Feldner said, Lazar judged "as many children as humanly possible" in his clinic—thousands of children over two decades. Yet some officials in the welfare and juvenile court systems worried about the accuracy of Lazar's "snap diagnoses," which prejudged a child's "essence, potential behavior, and future."[29] During Lazar's directorship, the Curative Education Clinic diagnosed around a third of the children it evaluated with "dissociability," a fifth with "learning and achievement disorders," and around 30 percent with "disciplinary disorders." For all his purported idealism, Lazar could be damning in his judgments. As his coworkers put it, "He was not sentimental," and would pronounce children "morally" damaged, "degenerate," or even "waste."[30]

The Curative Education Clinic under Lazar had

both liberal and authoritarian elements. Lazar was seeking to improve the care of children but, in so doing, unwittingly expanded a system that in time would ultimately control and condemn "dissocial" children.

Lazar's terminology followed trends in interwar child development that conflated social and medical judgments. Eugenics offered a biological lens on social organization, and pervaded Viennese welfare practices in myriad forms, from psychological screening tests to sterilization.[31] As social workers more frequently consulted perceived experts about children in their case loads, experts' prescriptions increasingly pathologized behavioral deviations. Fuzzy terminology helped to blur the distinction between social and medical concerns. Labels such as "neglect," "endangerment," "asociality" or "learning difficulties" encompassed a range of issues. The child might be sick, misbehaved, badly parented, cognitively impaired, or simply poor. Lacking "community competence" became a sociomedical condition. These labels had serious practical consequences, too. Social workers used them in the title lines and gridded forms of their reports, formalizing them into medical histories and diagnoses.[32]

These pronouncements, then, followed a child through rounds of expert testing and evaluation at clinics and children's facilities. The most significant consequence was removing a child from his or her home, which became increasingly common. By 1936, an average of twenty-one children a day were removed from families into Vienna's Child Foster Care Service, the Child Intake Office (*Kinderübernahmestelle*, or KÜST).[33] Depending on the evaluation, youths might enter foster care or face institutionalization in one of Vienna's many children's homes, remedial schools, or detention facilities. Though many child development workers were well intentioned, state homes offered dismal, often abusive, conditions. Even if not subjected to violence by their caretakers or other youths, children suffered hunger or neglect. And they, and their families, found that new people in new professions now had breathtaking power to shape their lives.

The politics of child development work were knotty, entangling the rights of the child, the family, and the perceived good to society. But state-supervised child rearing had support across the political spectrum. Professionals from varied backgrounds experimented with methods that included both liberal and authoritarian practices, and both positive and negative eugenics. Many progressives and socialists saw government care and education of children essential to building a stable and democratic society; many middle-class moralists sought to instill bourgeois norms among the poor; and many Catholic and conservative practitioners focused on promoting reproduction and traditional religious ideals of the family.[34] Vienna had become a crucible of ideas, where an abundance of educators, pediatricians, psychiatrists, and psychoanalysts brought different theories to bear in schools, courts, clinics, and a burgeoning welfare system.

Whatever the political aims, though, it is clear that state intervention had both the potential to help children and, as Austria slid into fascism and the Third Reich, the potential for catastrophic harm.

A PREEMINENT AREA of child development work in this period was Viennese psychoanalysis. The city had a surfeit of psychoanalytic pioneers who were eager to help Vienna's youth in need, such as August Aichhorn, Charlotte Bühler, Helene Deutsch, Anna Freud, Hermine Hug-Hellmuth, and Melanie Klein. As Anna Freud explained, "Back then in Vienna we were all so excited—full of energy: it was as if a whole new continent was being explored, and we were the explorers, and we now had a chance to change things."[35]

Sigmund Freud himself sounded the call to social action. In his speech to the Fifth International Psychoanalytical Congress in 1918, Freud proclaimed, "The poor man should have just as much right to assistance for his mind as he now has to the life-saving help offered by surgery."[36] At Freud's instigation, psychoanalysts opened twelve free outpatient clinics in the 1920s and 1930s throughout Europe, in cities ranging from Berlin to Zagreb to London.

While psychoanalysis might conjure up images of privileged individuals reclined on sofas, its practitioners developed a strong social mission to help Vienna's disadvantaged. Vienna's Ambulatorium, founded in 1922, provided free services as well as a training program. Affiliated psychoanalysts donated a fifth of their time to the Ambulatorium, aiming to transform society through restoring individuals' mental well-being. Some of the leading figures who pitched in were Alfred Adler, Bruno Bettelheim, Helene Deutsch, Erik Erikson, Anna Freud, Erich Fromm, Carl Jung, and Melanie Klein.[37] There were numerous other initiatives, too. For example, August Aichhorn worked with delinquent and troubled youth, and established a state-funded home for them in 1918 at Oberhollabrunn, where he overlapped with Lazar. Alfred Adler started child guidance clinics throughout Vienna, helping not just children, but also advising their teachers and families.[38]

This ferment of experimentation encouraged exchange between Viennese psychoanalysts and psychiatrists. Certainly, the disciplines had different theoretical approaches: psychoanalysts tended to focus on individuals' interior lives and the relationship between their conscious and unconscious, while psychiatry aligned itself with physiological sciences, particularly neurology.[39] Yet Vienna's tight-knit institutions allowed for considerable formal and informal interactions. People regularly moved in and out of each other's schools, clinics, and organizations, and also intersected at their work for the city's welfare institutions. In time, psychoanalysis formed tighter social networks and attracted more Jewish practitioners; some even called it a "Jewish science." But it is impossible to imagine the evolution of either psychiatry or psychoanalysis without interaction with the other.[40]

A major site of exchange between Vienna psychiatry and psychoanalysis was the University of Vienna Psychiatric-Neurological Clinic of Nobel laureate Julius Wagner-Jauregg.[41] Though a psychiatrist who personally disapproved of psychoanalysis, Wagner-Jauregg fostered a vibrant and inclusive environment. As psychiatrists rotated through his hospital early in their careers, they gained exposure to psychoanalysis, developmental psychology, and pedagogy in addition to psychiatry and neurology. Inspired, a number of people then left psychiatry to pursue the trendier path of psychoanalysis. The regular flow of psychiatrists into psychoanalysis kept the two fields in dialogue.[42]

Erwin Lazar had trained at Wagner-Jauregg's clinic, and he was part of this mixing for a short time. When Lazar founded his own Curative Education Clinic, he even had the sponsorship of Otto Pötzl, Wagner-Jauregg's prominent successor as director of the Psychiatric-Neurological Clinic; Pötzl was one of three signatories who vouched for Lazar's clinic to the University of Vienna medical faculty.[43]

But Lazar's practice of curative education sat rather uneasily with Viennese psychoanalysis. Despite Lazar's claim that his work engaged intensively with Freud's and Adler's theories, many psychoanalysts saw little resemblance and were dismissive. Lazar's staff physician Georg Frankl wrote several articles defending the ward against psychoanalysts' accusations that curative education was "methodless" and "unoriginal," a mere "mosaic made from countless splinters of other sciences."[44]

Helene Deutsch, an eminent psychoanalyst, had only negative things to say about her time working at Lazar's clinic in her early career. She complained that Lazar's free-flowing approach to child assessment was a "jumble of topsy-turvy testing" with an "anarchistic mood," where "things are pitsch-patschi." Deutsch also said that "the atmosphere stinks" and "Lazar is a ridiculous caricature."[45]

Notwithstanding fraught ties with Vienna's

mainstream circles of psychoanalysis and psychiatry, Lazar and his clinic still intersected with them. Under Asperger's directorship, the Curative Education Clinic would grow more isolated from the city's prominent figures and operate apart from the networks for which Vienna was renowned. The divergence began as the University of Vienna Children's Hospital veered away from the progressive idealism of the 1920s and moved toward authoritarianism.

THE TRANSFORMATION OF the Children's Hospital started in 1929, when Clemens von Pirquet, widely acclaimed for turning it into a world-class facility, was found lying in bed in a close embrace of his wife of twenty-five years, both of them dead from potassium cyanide. The double suicide was a shock; Pirquet had struggled with depression, but, at fifty-four, he was at the pinnacle of his career.

Given Pirquet's fame as a statesman and potential successor to Austrian President Michael Hainisch, his unexpected death led to a high-stakes leadership battle over the Children's Hospital. The search committee tasked with his replacement was fractious. Overseen by the University of Vienna, which was riven by political clashes that could turn violent, the committee's members ranged from Otto Pötzl, a member of the (largely Jewish) Vienna Psychoanalytical

Society, to extreme right-wing and anti-Semitic Franz Chvostek, whose clinic at the university was known as the "swastika clinic."[46]

A number of stellar candidates were put forward, including Pirquet's own students. But Chvostek backed the lesser-known pediatrician Franz Hamburger, who shared Chvostek's political views. At fifty-four, Hamburger had helped found Graz's society for racial hygiene in 1924, and was from the University of Graz, a hotbed of right-wing radicalism.[47] Chvostek, exploiting divisions among the other search committee members, was able to advance Hamburger's name to second position on the committee's candidate list. The university administration rejected the inclusion of Hamburger, however, due to his "personal character" and lack of scientific achievement. But the Ministry of Education interceded and upheld Hamburger as second choice. So when first choice Meinhard Pfandler turned down the job, Hamburger became director of the Children's Hospital.

The selection of Hamburger sparked widespread surprise and anger. Hamburger had nowhere near the medical stature of Pirquet, and had even had sharp disagreements over immunological research with Pirquet, who was the leader of the field. The newspaper *The Evening* lamented that the appointment of Hamburger, a "hundred percent reactionary," was "a grievous insult to the dead."[48]

Hamburger's leadership had profound consequences for the Children's Hospital. Following Nazi ideology, Hamburger promoted a eugenicist vision of women as breeders and children as physical specimens. He believed in the biological superiority of the German *Volk*, though his son later said that when Hamburger was a ship doctor as a young man, he had enjoyed his encounters with "aboriginal and exotic" corners of the world, "especially India, China, and Japan." Hamburger's son also said that Hamburger, with his intense stare and firm countenance, was "a strict but compassionate father, a role model for his relentlessness."[49]

Notorious among his critics for his "anti-scientific attitude," Hamburger cut ties with international research and visiting scholars, and moved the University of Vienna Children's Hospital away from cutting-edge biological research under Pirquet into medicine driven by social utility. Hamburger wanted his physicians to practice more primary care rather than pursuing medical specialties. He reportedly made his lectures "easy to understand, with simple logic, for the practical activities of the physician."[50] Doctors at the hospital were to serve public health through rotations in curative education and mother advising. Doctors were also to provide spiritual healing. Hamburger proclaimed, "The medical practitioner's most important daily work is the care of souls."[51] In effect, Hamburger was deprofessionalizing one of the top-notch pediatric facilities in the world.

He was likewise amassing greater power from his position at the Children's Hospital, organizing and manipulating Vienna's professional associations, such as the Society for Pediatrics, toward the extreme right. Hamburger enjoyed authority, fealty, and grandiosity. An image of one 1931 memorial ceremony spotlights him inside a conspicuous sunbeam, surrounded by a throng of children and nurses, the girls with festive bows in their hair.[52]

With this growing dominance, Hamburger transformed the staff at the Children's Hospital. He purged many Jewish and liberal faculty, and pressured others to resign. After 1930, virtually all of Pirquet's Jewish coworkers left. Erwin Lazar remained, but died in 1932.[53] Hamburger installed his own supporters and students in their stead.

In hiring, Hamburger prioritized his assessment of character over intellectual qualification; ideology was paramount, and would become increasingly so. His staff tended to lack the hard science backgrounds of Pirquet's staff, and tended to be on the far right. Certainly, many of Hamburger's protégés went on to be Nazi enthusiasts and leaders in the euthanasia program.

One of Hamburger's first hires was twenty-five-year-old Hans Asperger, who had just finished his medical studies on March 26, 1931, at University Medical Clinic III under Franz Chvostek, the man who had maneuvered Hamburger into power the year before. Chvostek was known for training National Socialist doctors and for barring women from his lectures, which was against the law at the time.

Asperger gushed over his first meeting with Hamburger, saying it felt "like fate." The interview, according to Asperger, was "not a rigorous test, but an almost confidential conversation between an older and younger man, which was a great deal of fun for me, and obviously also for Professor Hamburger."[54] Delighted with his monthly salary of 120 schillings, as his father had earned only 50, Asperger began as Hamburger's postdoctoral advisee on May 1, 1931. He was enthusiastic about Hamburger's new vision for the Children's Hospital, eager to contribute to the "bustling construction, reconstruction of the hospital," as well as to "rectify the errors" of Pirquet's leadership.[55]

As one of Hamburger's prized students, Asperger came to revere Hamburger. He repeatedly hailed his mentor for shaping his outlook on medicine and remained loyal to him through the postwar period, even after Hamburger had been discredited. In 1962, Asperger explained that working for Hamburger at the Curative

Education Clinic had "fatefully fulfilled" what the German Youth Movement had "invested in me in my teens"—his "passionate interest in people" and "striving to help and treat" them. In 1977, Asperger still spoke of Hamburger in adulatory terms: "He encompassed all pediatric knowledge at one time. He was a teacher of great charisma. Most of what I learned from him still holds."[56]

Soon after Asperger began at the Children's Hospital in May 1931, Hamburger placed him in the Curative Education Clinic in the fall of 1932. A year and a half later, despite Asperger's relative youth and inexperience among seasoned staff, Hamburger installed Asperger as director of the clinic.[57]

Hamburger also accepted Erwin Jekelius as one of his first postdoctoral students at the Children's Hospital. Hamburger appointed the twenty-six-year-old to the Curative Education Clinic in 1931, where Jekelius worked until 1936. During the five years Jekelius and Asperger worked together at the ward, the last two of which Asperger was his director, Jekelius was a Nazi enthusiast. He joined the party in June 1933, when it was still essentially a terrorist organization in Austria, and even signed up for the Nazis' paramilitary unit, the SA (Stormtroopers).[58] Under the Third Reich, Jekelius would become the most prominent figure in child and adult euthanasia in Vienna, directing the killing centers of Spiegelgrund and Steinhof.

In the 1930s, Jekelius was viewed by his associates as eager and industrious, receiving positive evaluations from internships in 1933 and 1934. Senior physician Emil Mattauschek wrote that Jekelius "had great zeal, great devotion, great skill, and great persistence in his work." Heiman Schlesinger said Jekelius was "a very hard-working and conscientious physician [. . .] His winning and humane demeanor won the affection of doctors and patients." He was certainly dashing—tall, with dark hair slicked back from his angular face. Jekelius's purportedly kind bedside manner is certainly ironic, given his deadly convictions about racial hygiene and later role directing bedside killings.[59]

Political allegiances became more important in Vienna over the 1930s. Austria, like elsewhere in central and eastern Europe, was turning toward authoritarianism. Depression had sent the nation into crisis, leading to unemployment rates over 25 percent by 1932. Street clashes among Socialist, Communist, Nazi, and Christian Socialist para-military groups increased. Armed units regularly marched through Vienna in uniform, intimidating the populace and provoking brawls, sometimes fatal.[60]

In 1933, as Hitler and the National Socialists consolidated power in Germany, a new national government headed by 39-year-old Engelbert Dollfuss and the Christian Social Party consolidated power in Austria. Dollfuss banned all demonstrations except those of the conservative Christian Social Party's paramilitary organization, the *Heimwehr* (Home Guard). But this did not calm the situation; Nazis, forbidden from wearing their brown shirt uniform on the streets, simply strutted around Vienna without shirts at all, donning silk hats.[61] Parliament became unmanageable. Following a major showdown, Dollfuss, encouraged by Benito Mussolini, suspended parliament on March 4, 1933, and began to rule by emergency decree.

Austrian Nazis resorted to terror tactics, seeking to weaken the national government through violence. After one hand grenade attack in June 1933, Dollfuss banned the Nazi Party. Austrian National Socialists fled to Bavaria and founded the Austrian Legion, a paramilitary force of around ten thousand. Based in camps just over the German border, Nazis made constant incursions into Austria, attacking cafés, shops, and streets with tear gas, dynamite, and handmade bombs. There were around 140 attacks in the first weeks of January 1934 alone.[62]

Franz Hamburger joined the Nazi Party that year. This was a fringe position in Austria, especially as the party was illegal—and 1934 was an extraordinarily tumultuous time. In February, a so-called civil war erupted as the Dollfuss government cracked down on Social Democrats.

The right–left clash lasted only four days, but the violence had spread throughout the country. At least 1,500 people died and 5,000 were wounded. After the government defeated the left, it outlawed the Social Democratic Party, imprisoned and executed opponents en masse, and passed a new constitution May 1, 1934, that effectively made Dollfuss dictator. Austria became a single-party state led by the Fatherland Front, a nationalist, clerical, corporatist, and authoritarian successor to the Christian Social Party that was supported by Mussolini.[63]

Nine days later, on May 10, 1934, Asperger joined the Fatherland Front and supported the new Austrofascist regime.[64] The Austrofascist government shared ideological elements with Nazism but, committed to Austrian independence, opposed a Nazi takeover by Germany and remained locked in a battle with Austrian National Socialists. Nazi insurrectionists attempted a coup in July 1934 and, while the Austrian army easily defeated them, insurgents wounded Dollfuss and he died shortly thereafter. Despite a continued ban of the National Socialist Party under the chancellorship of Kurt Schuschnigg, Nazis became more vocal and visible. They shifted tactics for undermining the government and, rather than relying on terrorism, managed to infiltrate state and police positions.

Asperger had solid far-right-wing credentials,

holding memberships in several antiliberal, anti-socialist, antimodern, and anti-Semitic organizations. In addition to the Fatherland Front, Asperger joined the Association of German Doctors in Austria in 1934, which promoted German nationalist objectives. To reduce the role of Jews in medicine, for example, it sought to impose quotas for Jewish students and compiled lists of supposedly non-Aryan doctors that were later used for Jewish purges under Nazi rule.[65]

Moreover, Asperger was a devoted member of Bund Neuland, an extreme nationalist Catholic youth association with anti-Semitic leanings. He was also secretary of the eighty-member Saint Lucas Guild, an organization that promoted Catholic eugenics through lectures and courses within Vienna's medical community. Like many doctors at the time, Asperger was a self-proclaimed eugenicist. The Catholic variant common in Austria focused more on the "positive" rather than the "negative" side, as it sought to encourage reproduction among people considered desirable, and to discourage reproduction among those deemed undesirable through voluntary abstinence, rather than through contraception, forced sterilization, or abortion. Then again, the Saint Lucas Guild was open to more Nazi attitudes, as the organization accepted National Socialist members in the mid-1930s when the party was still banned and engaged in acts of terrorism.[66]

While Asperger's memberships in the Fatherland Front and Association of German Doctors in Austria might be unremarkable for an ambitious physician in Vienna in the 1930s, his dedication to the Saint Lucas Guild and Bund Neuland suggests a genuine commitment to far-right-wing positions.[67]

Meanwhile, Asperger appears to have had hardly any connection with the mainstream Viennese milieu of psychiatry and psychoanalysis, confining his professional circles in Vienna to Hamburger and his associates at the Curative Education Clinic. Arguably, he could have sought out broader networks, but did not. He did serve a three-month internship in the summer of 1934 with Otto Pötzl, who, as the head of the Psychiatric-Neurological University Clinic from 1928 until 1945, was perhaps the best networked figure in Viennese psychiatry and psychoanalysis. Pötzl trained neurologists and Freudians alike, and his work ranged from aphasia to optical-agnostic disorders to dream analysis. Pötzl had even joined the Vienna Psychoanalytic Society in 1917, an unusual move at the time for a neurologist and psychiatrist of his stature, since psychoanalysis was still regarded as an unconventional and controversial field in traditional academia. Yet Asperger appears neither to have valued his time at Pötzl's clinic nor been influenced by Pötzl's work. He did not credit or cite Pötzl in his subsequent publications, even as he lavished praise on others. In fact, Asperger had harsh words for Pötzl's practice, calling Pötzl a "fearsome examiner" whose method of "stereotypical questions" and "prescribed agendas" for patients was "an abomination."[68]

AS ASPERGER AND his colleagues distanced themselves from the preeminent Viennese networks of psychiatry and psychoanalysis, the renowned Vienna system of the 1920s morphed into an instrument of authoritarianism in the mid-1930s. The interventionist and eugenicist strains that had always underlaid Viennese child development efforts increasingly came to the fore. In this new political context, the Third Reich's diagnosis regime would not be simply imposed by National Socialist officials but would be a joint collaboration with preexisting supporters in Vienna.[69] And from these foundations of Nazi child psychiatry in Vienna, Asperger's definition of autistic psychopathy would emerge.

2

The Clinic's Diagnosis

ERWIN LAZAR HAD been a busy man, dividing his time between his work for the city and for his Curative Education Clinic. Nurses and physicians on his ward largely forged the new field of curative education in his absence. They were a tight-knit community, occupying the grand Widerhofer Pavilion at the Children's Hospital with spacious, high-ceilinged rooms, black-and white-checked floors, and scenic wall trimmings. The department was unlike other clinics of its time, as its daily therapies were unusually flexible, empathetic, and playful. Close and collaborative, the staff shared weekly dinners and "round tables" at one another's homes to exchange ideas.[1] This all continued as Hamburger, their boss, led the University of Vienna Children's Hospital toward Nazism.

Asperger called the ward's staff a "small, select group" whose discussions were formative for him. "The wonderful debates at the Curative Education department are an inextricable part of my being," he reminisced in 1958, and "decided my scientific and personal fate."[2] Indeed, clinic doctors and nurses were dedicated to Lazar's progressive vision, and developed concepts in dialogue— including what would become Asperger's idea of autistic psychopathy.

The ward was relatively egalitarian, with women holding prominent roles. Photographs of the clinic highlighted nurses in positions of leadership, heading tables of attentive and well-behaved children. The department revolved around one woman in particular: nurse and educational director Viktorine Zak. She ran daily life on the ward for thirty years and generated many of its theories and techniques. Known for her compassion and open-ended approach, Zak developed play-based interventions that are still in use today.

Zak outlined her philosophy in an article, "The Development of Clinical Curative Education in Vienna," that she published for *The International Council of Nurses* in 1928. It contains an image of her sitting at a desk next to a boy, looking over his shoulder as he works. Zak urged caregivers to recognize the uniqueness of all children through evaluating their "characters." Because "the personality shows itself in small things," Zak maintained, staff should focus on minute observations and "minute diagnoses." Rather than issuing blanket labels for behavior, practitioners would describe children as individuals, paying attention to unconscious acts in how a child played, ate, walked, and talked. Zak called this the "psychology of non-essentials."[3]

In her 1932 article, "The Curative Education Department Under Lazar," Zak illustrated how children at the Curative Education Clinic were to live without "superficial constraints." After 1926, the ward had stopped keeping children in beds all day—a common practice at the time—so that youths could be in the ward "as at home, usually more peaceful than at home." The ward, Zak hoped, would then become their actual "home."[4] Moreover, Zak emphasized the clinic's inclusivity. She said that personnel neither quantified nor pathologized children, and "never talked smugly of curing." They used "no equipment, no statistics, no methods [. . .] no buzzwords and no formulas." The aim was to "experience the child's thought process empathically."[5]

Asperger called Zak "the tradition, the living conscience of the department" and the "soul of the ward." While clinic doctors and nurses disagreed over the shape of curative education, holding "debates and battles," Asperger explained, "What remained was only what nurse Zak felt was right."[6] She engaged youths in the clinic's unique form of play therapy through fairytales, adventure stories, dances, songs, and theatrical pieces. She had a "magical influence on children," Asperger reflected, and "held them all under spell." She could unify them "with every look and word, with the beat of tambourine." Zak devised activities in the moment, recreating an "enchanted forest with astonishing, amusing and scary adventures" or impromptu plays with "fantastic robes and swashbuckling finery."[7] Asperger also gushed about Zak's "youthfulness," "feminine spirit," and "flashing eyes and physical agility." He held that her "thoroughly feminine powers" helped "guide the male intellect."[8] And Zak, "motherly" toward the children, went all out for Christmas and other celebrations, turning the clinic into a "true home" [*Heimat*].

Zak, Asperger contended, established an empathetic approach to children in the clinic. "It was never the goal to simply break resistance, to 'dispense with' a child, but to bring him to obey, to integrate properly, because it brought him joy to do what was asked." Asperger recollected that when one "raging psychotic boy" threatened the other children with a large kitchen knife, the child was soon "overcome by her gaze, her considered, calming words, so that he lay it down by himself and let himself be led to his room."[9]

The clinic staff carried on this compassionate philosophy after Lazar died in 1932 of heart failure following a gallbladder operation. Dr. Valerie Bruck ran the ward for two years following Lazar's death. Asperger downplayed Bruck's role in his later publications, suggesting more of a continuity between his own subsequent directorship and Lazar's.[10] But Bruck had standing at the hospital, having copublished with Pirquet on rickets prophylaxis, and she was a strong supporter of Lazar's approach—admiring how Lazar "grasped the whole character of a person" and treated the child with "assistance and recovery," not "atonement and punishment." Bruck emphasized that Lazar never felt "arrogant disdain for 'the inferior.' "[11] Ward physician Georg Frankl also stressed the clinic's tradition of inclusivity. In his 1932 article, "The Sphere of Medical Curative Education," Frankl defended "children who are stamped and thus cast aside" because people deemed them "imbeciles, criminals, malicious, or crazy." He pleaded, "As one gets to know them better, they prove human beings with feelings and desires and hopes and pain." Frankl maintained, "What looks like malice is often nothing more than weakness."[12]

Franz Hamburger installed Asperger, his student, as head of the Curative Education Clinic in May 1934, over the heads of other long-time staff physicians. At age twenty-eight, Asperger had only worked in the ward for a year and a half. He had not published in curative education, but rather published biomedical articles on ultraviolet irradiation, enuresis, leucine and tyrosine in the urine in pulmonary tubercles, and melanin reactions in human urine after exposure to sunlight.[13]

Asperger himself acknowledged his newness to the field. After the war, he credited the long service of Georg Frankl in the ward and recognized staff physician Josef Feldner—who had already worked at the clinic for fourteen years when Asperger took over—as having played "a special role as my teacher."[14] But presumably, Hamburger felt more comfortable with Asperger as department head than with Lazar's veteran staffers. Also, senior physician Georg Frankl was Jewish.

Initially, Asperger's appointment seems to have had little effect on the day-to-day operations of the ward. He even appears to have been somewhat of a nonentity. Staff publications from the 1930s did not reference Asperger, though he was clinic head, but continued to pay tribute to Lazar. This wasn't just department politics. When in 1935 Boston psychiatrist Joseph Michaels wrote an extensive article for the *American Journal of Orthopsychiatry* detailing operations of the Curative Education Clinic—from the times of morning toilet to gymnastics—he recognized the importance of the "Lazar regime" and Viktorine Zak in the text, and Georg Frankl and staff psychologist Anni Weiss in the references, but did not mention Asperger, the titular director.[15]

In his article, Michaels described the department's work much as had Zak in 1928, seven years earlier. He was surprised to find curative education "more of an art than a science." Since children during this period typically faced standardized tests and invasive examinations, Michaels marveled that the Curative Education Clinic "stands somewhat apart" from "this 'age of technocracy' with its overemphasis on technical procedures."[16]

Michaels admired the free-flowing observations at the Clinic's Outpatient Consultation Department, which assessed around sixty youths a week who had been referred by schools, juvenile courts, and children's homes. And he admired inpatient care even more. The clinic had beds for twenty-one children, who usually stayed four to six weeks, and ranged in age from toddlers to teenagers. The staff, Michaels relayed, attempted to recreate "natural" life, as youths were to "live in the hospital as though they were at home and going to school."[17] Children had consistent schedules: up early, breakfast at 8:00, exercise from 9:00 to 10:00, lessons from 10:30 to 12:00 (math on Mondays, reading on Tuesdays, orthography or composition on Wednesdays, geography or history on Thursdays, nature on Fridays, and handwork or drawing on Saturdays) lunch at 12:00, and free time in the afternoon.[18]

Although Michaels did not include the voices of actual children in his article, he stressed the individuality of staff observations. For example, while one child was writing, staff noted "the screwing and writhing of the muscles around the mouth." And, as Zak informed Michaels, "movements may even occur down to the very toes of the child."[19] Clinic personnel paid especially close attention to children's social interactions, detailing youths' responses to group play. A child might "behave as a total stranger" or join the groups in an "intellectual manner, but without genuine spirit"; others might play "passionately, losing themselves and their self-control."[20]

Due to these personal idiosyncrasies, Michaels stressed that the Curative Education Clinic rejected standard diagnoses in favor of individual assessments. It avoided the "classifications of medicine, neurology, psychology and psychiatry." Michaels also underscored that department staff rejected ideas of "normal and abnormal" as "unclear, and practically of no great importance."[21]

Through their attention to socialization, staff of the Curative Education Clinic appear to have crafted a collective definition of autistic characteristics. Department nurses and doctors had used the term *autistic* in the 1930s but did not consider it a pathology, and used nonnormative language to describe it. Asperger himself pointed to their common usage. In one letter to the department from Germany, Asperger described how "we express concepts in a jargon that an outsider would not understand (think of 'autistic'!)."[22]

Michaels also suggested the staff's casual and shared use of the term *autistic* in his 1935 article. He described their concept of "artistic children." Assuming "artistic" is an English mistranslation of "autistic"—since art is nowhere near his reference—Michaels describes how "artistic children may require special personal guidance" because they have difficulty joining the "group," as "frequently their attention and feelings are elsewhere."[23]

Two staff members of the Curative Education Clinic, physician Georg Frankl and psychologist Anni Weiss, published articles about children with such autistic characteristics. In 1934, Frankl described those who, when "surrounded in a group of children," "do not sense the atmosphere, and so cannot adapt." Frankl believed this was due to the youths' "poor understanding of the emotional content of the spoken word." Frankl insisted that one must be forgiving of the children's shortcomings. Contrary to Asperger's later opinions, Frankl held that one should not see "malice" in children with social difficulties, that their challenges had nothing to do with "character or morals."[24]

In a 1937 article, Frankl stressed that the youths' detachment and disobedience did not represent their true emotions behind their "masklike face[s]"—which could "frequently lead to severe misunderstandings." Frankl argued that these characteristics did not amount to a pathology: "No illness has been described here, rather just a dysfunction that may occur in various illnesses and may be accompanied by various other dysfunctions." He distinguished the children he was describing from those who he saw as much more impaired, who had "extreme *autism*" (*Autismus*; emphasis in original) or were "autistically locked."[25] Frankl listed several conditions that might lead to milder social idiosyncrasies, but emphasized that half of the cases of half of the ten children he studied had unclear causes, with features developing in early childhood and remaining stable.

In 1935, Anni Weiss devoted a lengthy article to children with social challenges. She made the same observations that Asperger would three years later, though she expressed far more compassion. Weiss focused on a case study of nine-year-old Gottfried K., whose grandmother brought the boy to the Curative Education Clinic because of "his extreme nervousness and his queer and helpless behavior in his intercourse with other children." According to his grandmother, the boy was scared of numerous aspects of daily life, from dogs and loud noises to darkness and clouds.[26] Gottfried was successful at school, but "children laughed at him and called him 'the fool.' "[27]

Weiss described Gottfried as tall, "frail," and "awkward." He had "beautiful dark eyes" and an "over-emphatic and monotonous way of speaking" with a "sing-song tone." Although Weiss stated at the beginning of the article that Gottfried's face showed "extreme laxity and want of expression," she repeatedly stressed his joy in pleasing adults around him, with his "angelic countenance" and "radiant face." While the boy might sometimes stare in front of himself, Weiss noted, Gottfried could become "merrily excited" and begin "happily jumping about." And even though he did not "attach himself especially to any person at the institute" during the weeks he stayed in the ward, Weiss held that Gottfried was content to talk to clinic staff and eager to fulfill their requests.[28]

Gottfried's engagement became clear during testing, Weiss recalled, as he followed the clinic's Lazar system of evaluation—which included copying stick patterns, beaten rhythms, digits, and syllables, as well as arithmetic, free word association, retelling a story, and creating a narrative out of pictures. Gottfried demonstrated some quirks, such as beginning every answer to object comparisons with "Well, good gracious." In relating the difference between a child and a "dwarf," for instance, Gottfried returned, "Well, good gracious, that the dwarf has a long beard and a cap. One day I saw a dwarf and he was smaller than a three-year-old child." Although Weiss said the staff was "puzzled at first" by Gottfried's "careless and somewhat disrespectful" answers, they decided that the boy "does not want to be rude." Rather, his social irregularities sprang from a "naïve unconsciousness" and "no one could take that amiss."[29]

Weiss portrayed Gottfried sympathetically. "He is good," she concluded, "He never has a spite against anyone; never feels hate or jealousy. He has perfect trust in mankind." She found that Gottfried simply "cannot grasp what is happening around him with any fine shade of feeling," elaborating how "what others perform naturally in the social machinery—perceiving, understanding and then acting—does not function in him as it ought to." Like Frankl, Weiss emphasized the boy's inherent integrity. Gottfried was "a pure, innocent person, beyond any doubt," she claimed, without "hard-heartedness or brutality." She even invoked tenderness in the reader: "He is just like a baby feeling comfortable or uncomfortable without knowing the exact cause."[30]

Toward the end of her article, Weiss mentioned that youths like Gottfried could have unusual skills. "In this type of child," she held, "some special talent may be found which, although limited as to extent, often surpasses the capacity of average men." Weiss suggested these traits in the context of helping the child feel successful later in life. She gave children with narrow interests—"calendar experts, jugglers of figures, artists of mnemonics"—credit for "assiduity and reliability," as well as for "capacity for order and classification."[31]

Weiss's praise followed in the tradition of the eminent Swiss psychiatrist Moritz Tramer, whose 1924 article, "One-Sidedly Talented and Gifted Imbeciles," called people with such calendar and mathematical skills "memory artists." Tramer admired those whose ability to detach from their environment "freed" their mind for areas of greatness.[32] Asperger, however, would frame Weiss's and Tramer's observations in terms of social worth, saying in 1944 that useful "special abilities" made some autistic children superior, while others, such as "calendar people," were "mentally retarded people who show highly stereotyped automaton-like behaviour" and "have crackpot interests which are of no practical use."[33]

There were notable similarities between Weiss's and Frankl's articles. Both described children who had difficulty integrating into groups and forging emotional connections with others. Both stressed the fundamental naiveté of the children's character and morals, and advocated benevolent care. Neither proposed a diagnosis for their behavior nor pathologized their traits. And neither mentioned Asperger as a collaborator in their work, although he was the director under whom they worked while doing the research described in their articles; Weiss credited Lazar, who had died six years earlier.

Frankl and Weiss were both Jewish and, facing growing anti-Semitism in Austria, emigrated to the United States. Weiss left Vienna in 1934 and found a position as an associate in Child Guidance at Columbia University's Teachers College, where she worked for three years.[34] Frankl left in 1937 with the help of Leo Kanner, a preeminent Austrian-born American child psychiatrist who was assisting hundreds of Jewish physicians to emigrate from Germany and Austria. Frankl, with Kanner's personal sponsorship, obtained an entry visa and began working at the Johns Hopkins' Harriet Lane Children's Home in Maryland. Frankl and Weiss married, and Weiss, as a psychiatric social worker, came to lead the Habit Clinic for the Child Welfare Society in Washington, D.C.[35]

Weiss and Frankl's connection with Leo Kanner is an intriguing chapter in how autism was conceived in the United States.[36] Leo Kanner, renowned as the founder of American child psychiatry, was the first in the country to define autism as a standalone diagnosis. Kanner was born in 1894 in Klekotow, a small town in the east of the Habsburg Empire. He had dreamed of becoming a poet since childhood but found little success. After attending school in Berlin and service in the Austrian army in World War One, Kanner completed his medical studies at the University of Berlin in 1921 and worked for a time as a cardiologist. He decided to leave for the United States in 1924 and landed at the State Hospital in Yankton, South Dakota. There, Kanner taught himself pediatrics and psychiatry on his own, obtaining a fellowship in 1928 at the Henry Phipps Psychiatric Clinic of Johns Hopkins Hospital. He made a name for himself and, in 1930, was asked to establish the first department of child psychiatry in the United States at Johns Hopkins. Soon thereafter, in 1935, Kanner published his landmark textbook, *Child Psychiatry*; the first such book in English, it was translated into four languages and remained an authoritative volume for decades.[37]

Kanner published his seminal article on autism, "Autistic Disturbances of Affective Contact," in *The Nervous Child* in 1943. Based on observations of eleven children since 1938, it defined the diagnosis by what Kanner saw as children's social withdrawal, restricted emotional relationships, repetitive language and behavior, limited speech, preoccupation with objects, and preference for routine. What Kanner called "early infantile autism" shared characteristics Asperger pointed to in his description of autistic psychopathy in a talk he gave in 1938, "The Mentally Abnormal Child" (discussed at length in the following chapter), though Asperger described the children he saw as far less impaired.

Because of the similarities between Kanner's and Asperger's work, some have speculated that Kanner was familiar with Asperger's 1938 lecture and appropriated ideas without crediting Asperger.[38] While Kanner was, indeed, familiar with German-language scholarship, it is unlikely that he would have been receiving regular issues of the nonspecialist weekly in which Asperger's talk was reprinted, the *Viennese Clinical Weekly*. The publication was already espousing the sharp racial policies of the Third Reich—such as, by 1939, the "elimination of the Jews." In fact, Asperger's paper on autistic psychopathy was followed in the same issue by an SS doctor's "training" lecture that extolled forced sterilization.[39] Moreover, Asperger's 1938 paper was not published as a scholarly treatise; it was a reprint of a talk that was obscure even among his colleagues in Austria and Germany.

There is another reason Kanner might not have cited Asperger: the idea of autism was not considered to be Asperger's. It may well have been Georg Frankl and Anni Weiss who brought the Curative Education Clinic's idea of autism across the Atlantic. Weiss and Frankl were reportedly in Kanner's "inner circle" during the years Kanner formulated his diagnosis of autism, with Frankl "one of Kanner's top clinicians."[40]

Frankl and Weiss had both described the typology in more well-known scholarly publications than had Asperger—in 1934, 1935, and 1937—and Kanner cited Weiss and Frankl in his publications.[41] In fact, Kanner based his first and most prominent case study of autism, that of Donald Triplett, on Frankl's research. In his article that introduced autism, Kanner relied on Frankl's notes on Donald's development, written with Eugenia Cameron at the Child Study Home of Maryland, quoting entire paragraphs verbatim in the third and fourth pages.[42]

Kanner's theories also dovetailed with Frankl's, as both men focused on "affective contact" as a core trait in children. Kanner's article, "Autistic Disturbance of Affective Contact," was paired in the same issue of *The Nervous Child* with Frankl's article, "Language and Affective Contact." Frankl had submitted his paper to the periodical first, and Kanner voiced his excitement about Frankl's approach. As he wrote to the journal's publisher, Ernst Harms, in January 1943: "The more I read [Frankl's paper], the more I am impressed by it and the more I realize what a gem it is." Kanner added that he was working on "my own paper on autistic disturbances of affective contact."[43]

Frankl, in his 1943 article, was again generous in his judgments of children, explaining that their social differences might have various causes. After classifying "parkinsonian" and "aphasia" groups of socially atypical children, Frankl proposed a "third group." He did not give this group a label, but suggested that he had seen a number of "cases of this type," and that the youths "have in common the disruption of the affective contact." The children in this group, Frankl wrote, "vary in intelligence from idiocy to the astonishing and peculiar performances of a certain type of child prodigy."[44]

He presented an in-depth case study of Karl K., who Frankl believed "ranked at the lowest end" of the "series of cases" he had seen. Frankl allowed that the boy was "a rather poor example" of the condition he described, and that he suffered from tuberous sclerosis and seizures, but felt that Karl's characteristics were nonetheless revealing. Frankl noted that Karl seemed uninterested in personal connections. The child understood language yet would not speak. His "expression remained blank, he did not look into the calling person's face." Neither did Karl play with other children, but wandered "through their groups and circles without interest." As Frankl put it, Karl "seemed not even to notice them" and, "even when amid a crowd of people, behaved like a solitary person."[45]

Karl, in the absence of structure, was reportedly at loose ends in the hospital. Staff kept him "in a closed bed in which he seemed to feel quite happy." When they opened the bed, Karl allegedly "sped in incessant motion around the large ward." According to Frankl, the boy moved among objects and children indiscriminately, grabbing a toy, grabbing a girl's hair, and then moving on. "In this manner he went on incessantly and at breathtaking speed." Frankl did not attribute malicious intent to Karl's actions, though, observing that even when Karl might destroy something, "One never knew whether this was mere incident or an act of deliberate destructiveness." In general, Frankl argued, children with disturbances of affective contact, or " 'poker face[s],' " were still having emotional responses to people, and one should not project "negative qualities" onto them as "indifferent or apathetic," with "impertinence or defiance."[46]

Frankl, Weiss, and other personnel at the Curative Education Clinic did not pathologize the social traits they were observing. They collectively developed a term to describe the children—autistic—but did not feel the youths' behaviors merited a diagnosis. Their work and words are manifest in Asperger's eventual description of autistic psychopathy (though he did not credit anyone from the department), but diverged in one important way. Asperger's diagnosis would be steeped in the principles of Nazi child psychiatry.

3

Nazi Psychiatry and Social Spirit

IN NAZI GERMANY, child psychiatrists were noting similar characteristics of social withdrawal in children as the staff at Vienna's Curative Education Clinic in the 1930s, but they described them in much harsher terms and saw the traits as more problematic for society. The preeminent figure in shaping the Nazi approach to child psychiatry was Paul Schröder, with whom Asperger interned in Leipzig in April and May 1934. This was a little over a year after Hitler had come to power in Germany, and Asperger was struck and intrigued by the breathtaking unity of the National Socialist vision. As he described in his diary:

> an entire people going in a single direction, fanatically, with a narrow range of vision—certainly—but also with enthusiasm and dedication, in tremendous training and discipline, with formidable power. Now soldiers, soldier's thinking—ethos—Germanic paganism."[1]

The Nazi state aimed, above all, to create a spiritually united, strong, and racially pure

German *Volk*, which meant rearing children to be devoted to the regime, steadfast, and physically superior.[2] These qualities required more than simple conformity. They required children's capacity to feel a sense of national belonging, which the regime sought to instill through collective organizations. As Hitler outlined in an address to district leaders in Reichenberg in 1938, the Third Reich had strict standards:

> These youths learn nothing else but to think as Germans and to act as Germans. These boys and girls enter our organizations at the age of ten and get a little fresh air, often for the first time; then after four years of the Young *Volk* they go on to the Hitler Youth, where we keep them for another four years [. . .] then we take them immediately into the Party, the Labor Front, into the SA or the SS, into the NSKK [National Socialist Motor Corps], and so on. And if after two and a half years they are still not real National Socialists, they'll go into the Labor Service for another six, seven months and be polished there.

According to Hitler, it depended, ideologically, on individuals forging collective bonds:

Then the *Wehrmacht* will take over further treatment [. . .] and then, after they return in two or three years, we take them immediately again into the SA, SS, etc. so that they don't backslide in any way; they won't be free again their entire lives, and will be happy about it.[3]

The Third Reich schooled children in communal life from a young age. The Nazi regime moved to control education as it came to power in 1933. It issued new textbooks and purged teachers, requiring them to join the National Socialist Teachers League. Nearly a third of teachers joined the Nazi Party itself. Each day, schoolchildren sang Nazi songs, learned about the historical and racial exceptionalism of the German *Volk*, and stared at the portraits of Hitler that hung in every classroom. Children were taught total commitment to the national community.

Racial science was an important part of the curriculum. Instruction was theoretical, about the superiority of Nordic and other "Aryan" races versus the inferiority of Jews, Slavs, and non-Europeans. And it was practical, teaching children how to identify racial features. Youths were surrounded by visuals such as posters featuring children with hair ranging from light blonde to dark brown, from straight noses to hooked noses. Children also learned about biological and physiological defects. These were harder to quantify, as estimates of Germany's genetically unfit extended from 1 percent to 20 percent of the population.[4] But youths got the message that problem people were lurking among them, dragging down the *Volk*. One math word question, for example, asked, "An idiot in an institution costs around four Reichsmarks a day. How much would it cost if he has to be cared for there for 40 years?" Another question was more direct: "Why would it be better if this child had never been born?"[5]

Genetic fitness went hand in hand with athletic fitness. Schools increased the time spent on physical education, up to two hours a day, with boxing compulsory for boys. Fitness was about much more than cultivating the individual body, though; it was to bolster collective consciousness. According to the Reich's 1937 Guidelines for Physical Education in Schools for Boys, "Physical education is education in community. By demanding obedience, coordination, chivalrous conduct, a comradely and manly spirit [. . .] without regard to person, it trains them in those virtues which constitute the foundations of the Reich."[6]

Certainly, strength and obedience were prerequisites for national belonging, central to Nazi ideals of the *Volk*. One reader for third and fourth graders in 1937 featured Hitler's admonishment to youth:

We want
The *Volk* to be obedient,
And you must train yourselves in obedience! [. . .]
You must learn to be tough,
To assume hardship,
Without ever breaking down.[7]

Community spirit was also taught in textbooks. Children were barraged with images of zealous youths committed to the *Volk* even to the point of frenzy. One assignment in a 1936 fifth- and sixth-grade reader extolled the ecstasies of the fascist crowd, describing the Horst Wessel "storm" at the Nuremberg Rally in 1929:

> The call came in the evening: join the torchlight procession! The streets were jammed with people. Eventually the line started to move, a huge and endless serpent of fire. On both sides of us a wild, cheering crowd. [. . .] We marched, dizzy and rapturous in the glowing torchlight, to greater and greater cheers. We went past the *Führer* in tight lockstep. Music, singing, jubilation. It was too much at once. You couldn't take it all in.[8]

In reality, however, not all children found rapture in the collective, or even community spirit. Being in the *Volk* could be taxing. Fifteen-year-old

Mascha Razumovsky of Vienna was not alone in her complaints about the regime's unceasing demands. She wrote in her diary on March 27, 1938, about her relief in getting out of another parade, "Thank God, I got out of a jam. I didn't have to greet Göring. That would have been something, if we had to stand for X number of hours in knee socks and only a windbreaker in the freezing cold."[9]

To make collectivist life more fun, the Nazi regime organized children into youth groups. Boys and girls aged ten to fourteen joined the German Young *Volk* and German Girls [*Deutsches Jungvolk* and *Jungmädel*]. Boys and girls aged fourteen to eighteen joined the Hitler Youth and League of German Girls [*Hitler Jugend* and *Bund Deutscher Mädel*]. As membership in these groups became mandatory in 1936 and then strictly enforced, by 1939 around 8.7 million youths participated—98 percent of the Reich's children.[10] Nazi youth groups appealed to many. It was a way children could get out of the house, out from under the thumb of their parents. They could enjoy games, sports, and socializing after school, as well as weekend camping trips, hiking, and bonfires. Youths could also feel important, wearing a uniform, marching through streets, and leading community efforts such as Winter Aid collections.

The regime had very different objectives for

boys' and girls' groups. Boys were to become aggressive, tough, and obedient soldiers. They shot rifles, learned combat tactics, played war games, and brawled. They marched to song lyrics like "Jewish blood spurts from the knife" and "heads roll, Jews howl."[11] Girls, meanwhile, were to become healthy wives and mothers, prolific breeders of Aryan children for the *Volk*. Patriarchal and eugenicist approaches to reproduction were widespread in early twentieth-century Germany, Austria, and elsewhere in Europe and the United States.[12] But the Third Reich invested inordinate state effort in shaping girls' identities and mentalities from a young age. The regime taught girls homemaking and child rearing, in addition to collective physical exercises meant to strengthen them for pregnancy.

Plenty of youths chafed against Nazi regimentation and domination of their lives. Reich schools and organizations saw low-level disobedience and rebellion—though coordinated political dissent such as that of the White Rose in Munich, led by the Scholl siblings who gave their lives, was scarce. There were some groupings like the Edelweiss Pirates, Meuten, and Swing Youth, who defied laws, rejected the Hitler Youth, and formed their own, distinct subcultures. In Vienna, the *Schlurfs* were mildly criminal adolescents who rebelled against Nazi socialization through slick fashion, smoking, drinking, hanging out on the streets, and dancing to swing music (similar to Swing Youth elsewhere in the Reich). Police would arrest *Schlurfs* for unruliness and brawling with Hitler Youth, who might cut male *Schlurfs'* long hair.[13] The Nazi regime took these dissident groups very seriously, and punished with an iron fist the youths they caught. Authorities would send them to juvenile detention centers or even the SS proto-concentration camps in Moringen and Uckermark, where youths might find themselves sterilized and, upon turning eighteen, sent to concentration camps for adults.[14]

Nazi officials and child psychiatrists deemed many nonconformist youths to be "asocial" or "unreformable" due to "exogenous" factors—unfavorable upbringing and environment. Yet youths' lack of integration could also stem from endogenous factors—supposed biological or mental defects. Children seen to have "exogenous" problems might be remediated, placed in institutions ranging from labor camps to reformatories, whereas children seen to have endogenous problems were not so lucky. They might be institutionalized indefinitely, or, starting in 1939, meet their deaths in the Reich's child euthanasia program.

In the Nazi state, the lines between the two categories were blurry. It was up to Nazi child psychiatrists such as Asperger to diagnose a child's character against regime norms. Children who did not meet Nazi standards—in mind, body, and spirit—might face any number of labels. While ideals multiplied, definitions of defects multiplied; they were two sides of the same coin in the Reich's diagnosis regime.

As Nazi child psychiatry made progressively grandiose claims about the spirits and value of children, fitness for the *Volk* was not just about the body, it was also about the mind. One had to feel and behave as part of the collective, with social feeling, a condition of biosocial belonging both racially and socially. After all, fascist collectivism lay at the core of the National Socialist project.

CHILD PSYCHIATRY HAD an important place in the Reich's ambition for a unified, homogenous national community. Germany, with its highly developed academies of science and medicine, had long been a place where aspiring doctors and researchers from other parts of Europe went to study or pursue advanced degrees. For child psychiatry, a premier institution was Leipzig University's psychiatric hospital, where Paul Schröder was director from 1925–1938. He had been among the first in Germany to create an independent department, clinic, and a professorial chair for child psychiatry, building an "Observation Ward for Juvenile Psychopaths" in 1925 and an outpatient counseling center.[15]

Schröder did not cut an imposing figure; he had

a pulpous face and, as one colleague described him, was "medium-sized, slope-shouldered, and pot-bellied, with his knock-knees leading to buckling, flat, splayed feet." Others said he was "reclusive, grumpy, and introverted," and had "great trouble with other people."[16] But he gained international stature, known for seeking to establish child psychiatry as its own discipline rather than as a mere offshoot of adult psychiatry, neurology, pediatrics, or special education.

Asperger trained with Paul Schröder in the spring of 1934, taking a leave of absence from the Curative Education Clinic. Schröder, formerly a German National Conservative, was increasingly taking up National Socialist themes in his positions on eugenics, the hereditarily ill, and homosexuality. He served as a medical assessor to the Hereditary Health Court in Leipzig from 1934 to 1937, evaluating individuals for forced sterilizations. And he was known for anti-Semitic statements, at one point boasting that he had hired only one Jew in twenty-two years of practice.[17]

Schröder became a powerful proponent of curative education. In Germany, the discipline had been primarily organized through the Society for Curative Education and the *Journal of Child Research*. Both institutions were robust: the society drew 1,200 attendees to its 1930 meeting, and the journal published well-regarded volumes. With the advent of the Third Reich, the leaders of these organizations were sidelined and persecuted. Three of them—Robert Hirschfeld, Max Isserlin, and Franz Kramer—were classified as "non-Aryan" and lost their positions. Others left their posts, and one, Ruth von der Leyen, committed suicide. By 1936, the long-standing leadership of curative education in Germany was gone.[18]

They were replaced by German child psychiatrists who supported the regime. Figures like Paul Schröder, his student Hans Heinze, and Werner Villinger—who had been more peripheral to the field—were appointed to leadership positions. They had powerful sponsors; Ernst Rüdin, a leading force behind the Reich's racial hygiene measures and the first forced sterilization law, supported Schröder, while Hans Reiter, President of the Reich Health Office, supported Villinger, who was swiftly promoted from an occasional contributor to the *Journal of Child Research* to its editor.[19] These men steered German child psychiatry and curative education into a direction that can be called Nazi child psychiatry.

Asperger would later claim that Schröder's approach was formative to his thinking; in 1942 he called himself a Schröder student with "pride and reverence."[20] As commitment to the *Volk* became a priority in the Third Reich, Nazi child psychiatrists like Schröder and his colleagues increasingly noted children they believed forged weaker social bonds and did not align with the group. This new paradigm led a number of practitioners to develop diagnoses for children who lacked community connectedness, which resembled and preceded Asperger's definition of autistic psychopathy.

Nazi child psychiatrists used the term *Gemüt* to express their ideas of social feeling. *Gemüt* is one of the German language's famously untranslatable words, and its meaning changed dramatically over time. For Nazi thinkers, *Gemüt* referred to one's fundamental capacity to form deep bonds with other people. It had metaphysical and social connotations. Good *Gemüt* was essential to one's worth as an individual, and to the health of the *Volk*.

The term *Gemüt* emerged in the eighteenth century as synonymous with soul, or *Seele*.[21] As ideas of the soul secularized and people paid increasing attention to personal emotions, *Gemüt* became a favored term in German culture. Philosopher Immanuel Kant saw *Gemüt* as the seat of one's "transcendental faculties," animated by *Geist*, or spirit. In the Romantic period *Gemüt* became the innermost layer of the soul—more elemental, emotional, and irrational than one's *Geist*. Music, in particular, was supposed to stir one's *Gemüt*. It was such a popular trope that the venerated writer Johann Wolfgang von Goethe complained in 1826: "Germans should not utter the word *Gemüt* for thirty years; it might then regenerate itself. For the moment, it indicates merely an indulgence with weaknesses—of one's self and of others."[22]

The meaning of *Gemüt* did, indeed, regenerate by the mid-nineteenth century. In everyday conversation, it lost some of its existential and artistic flavor and became more about positive personal and social emotions. Having *Gemüt* meant possessing a rich internal life, strong bonds with family and friends, and a warm and friendly temperament. With the common usage of "*gemütlich*"—cozy or homey—it also encompassed casual, everyday sociability. But in philosophy, the arts, literature, and other intellectual fields, it retained more metaphysical connotations.[23]

While working in Leipzig, Asperger became particularly enamored of the Leipzig school of holistic psychology, which focused on individuals' *Ganzheit*, or "wholeness." Crucial to their "characterology" was *Gemüt*, which signified an all-encompassing quality that connected feelings, experience, consciousness, and character.[24] One's *Gemüt* reflected the value of one's self. Indeed, when Felix Krueger, one of the leaders of the Leipzig school, became chair of the German Society for Psychology in 1933, his first address praised Hitler's "depth of *Gemüt*" [*gemütstiefe*].[25] (Likewise, propaganda minister Joseph Goebbels swooned over Hitler's "wonderful vigor, his verve, his zeal, his German *Gemüt*.")[26]

Asperger, who also met psychologist and philosopher Ludwig Klages in Leipzig in 1934, liked Klages's emphasis on emotion over intellectualism, which he would later acknowledge as central to his thought. Klages contrasted the idea of the Germanic "soul" with the more rational, Western "mind," and his work would become important to Nazi ideology.[27] At the same time Nazi holistic psychologists emphasized the superior attributes of the German soul—employing "anthropological" psychology based on race—Marburg Nazi psychologist Erich Jaensch established the dominant racial typology of the "Northern integration type" (J type) as the superior opposite of the "Jewish-liberal dissolution type" (S type), or "antitype" [*Gegentyp*]. Though Asperger would cite others sparsely in his seminal postdoctoral thesis on autistic psychopathy in 1944—referring to only nine authors in sixty-one pages—he twice noted Jaensch's anti-Semitic typology, with apparent endorsement.[28]

Gemüt was a central concept for psychiatrists who specialized in criminology. Asperger would highlight German psychiatrist Kurt Schneider's definition of psychopathy in his 1944 thesis, which warned about "*gemüt*-less psychopaths" [*gemütslosen Psychopathen*] who had "defective altruistic, social, and moral feelings," without "compassion, shame, honor."[29] Nazi psychiatrist Friedrich Stumpfl, a leading figure in hereditary and racial biology, likewise stressed the genetic and felonious dangers of *Gemüt*-less psychopaths and the "*Gemüt*-lessness of the autistic cold."[30]

While *Gemüt* had held a nationalist character for centuries (Germans claimed that they possessed more *Gemüt* than other Europeans, particularly the petty and rational French), under National Socialism, *Gemüt* became racialized. Meyer's 1938 dictionary defined it as "a term peculiar to the Germans and not translatable into any other language, involving the feeling of inwardness of the soul with which the German man experiences himself and his entire being, rooted deeply in his racial feelings and values."[31] Heinrich Himmler, head of the SS, agreed. In Himmler's infamous speech advocating the "extermination of the Jewish race," Himmler argued that it was "basically wrong" to think Germans should "infuse all of our own inoffensive soul and *Gemüt*, our *Gemütigkeit*, our idealism, into foreign peoples."[32]

In the Third Reich, the interiority of *Gemüt*—the deepest part of oneself—increasingly connoted a social quality to be developed for the good of society. The Nazi-era edition of *Herder's Dictionary* said a person with *Gemüt* would "endow the environment with a spiritual quality" and "feel a cosmic empathy for, and to integrate himself into, the natural and human world that envelops him."[33] *Gemüt* enabled individuals' fusion with the collective, a key ingredient for Nazism.

Nazi psychiatry defined *Gemüt* in more social terms than did other fields, and Nazi child psychiatrists aimed not to cultivate youths' *Gemüt* as an end in itself, but as a way to strengthen the community, to properly socialize children. *Gemüt* was instrumentalized, an individualist means to a collectivist end.

Paul Schröder held that *Gemüt* signified "love of humanity." Stressing the importance of children's "readiness to serve the community" and "incorporation into this national community" [*Volksgemeinschaft*], Schröder maintained that *Gemüt* was essential to success of the collective. "*Gemüt* is the necessary precondition for the possibility of the coexistence of people in communities." Schröder concluded, then, that *Gemüt* determined one's worth to society. "The degree of one's richness of *Gemüt* is one of the most important determinants of the practical usefulness and social value of a person," he said.[34] Defective *Gemüt* was dangerous for the *Volk*: Schröder recommended that some youths "lacking *Gemüt* [*Gemütsarmen*]" be placed "in detention under strict control."[35]

Asperger was deeply influenced by Schröder's approach to the human character, emphasizing in his diary Schröder's focus on "the essence, the richness of the spirit."[36] While Asperger felt that Schröder enumerated aspects of the personality rather systematically for his taste, he noted that "much pivots around" *Gemüt* for Schröder, and he liked the idea. He wrote in his diary that "there is a lot there, it is quite a good concept."[37]

Indeed, Asperger would later describe children with autistic psychopathy much as Schröder described children who lacked *Gemüt*. The children, Schröder asserted, "know no tenderness, and have neither an understanding for nor a need for it; they do not form close attachments and have no friends." Youths lacking *Gemüt* might even be "hardened, spiteful, withdrawn." Schröder called attention to adult features that Asperger would also note, how the children preferred the company of adults and were "very often peculiarly unchildlike, matured, and precocious."[38]

Asperger arrived in Leipzig just in time to meet Schröder's most eminent protégé in *Gemüt*, Hans Heinze, who had worked closely with Schröder from the beginning of his directorship in 1925 until May 1934. The thirty-eight-year-old Heinze, a sharp contrast to Schröder with his shaven head and wireless glasses, authored the clinical cases for Schröder's seminal work, *Childhood*

Characters and their Abnormalities. A month after Asperger's internship ended, Heinze left Leipzig to head child psychiatry at the University Clinic in Berlin and the State Mental Hospital in Potsdam, where he would rise to become one of the top figures in the Reich's adult and child euthanasia killings. Almost twenty years later, in 1962, Asperger would still fondly recall the "Leipzig Station under Schröder and Heinze."[39]

Heinze's 1932 publication, "On the Phenomenology of *Gemüt*," became a touchstone of Nazi psychiatry. Asperger himself featured it in his 1944 thesis on autistic psychopathy.[40] In it, Heinze disdained children with insufficient *Gemüt*, especially the "intellectually gifted," denouncing "their lack of devotion, their lack of respect for personal and material values, their lack of sense of community, their lack of compassion and sympathy." After all, he said, asocials and criminals—even socialists and communists— lacked *Gemüt*. Still, Heinze advocated a nuanced approach to assessing and treating children's *Gemüt*. He said children fell along a wide spectrum of *Gemüt* and intellectual capabilities, as Asperger would also argue.[41]

Schröder trained other students in the importance of *Gemüt*. Heinz Schultz, for example, focused on the deficient *Gemüt* of "hypomanic" children. Anna Leiter developed a diagnosis of "lacking *Gemüt*" [*gemütsarm*] that would later gain traction.[42] Schröder fiercely defended his school of thought. When the former leaders of curative education—Franz Kramer, a Jewish physician, and Ruth von der Leyen, a welfare reformer—doubted the importance and heritability of *Gemüt* in their 1934 article in the *Journal of Child Research*, Schröder published a letter to the editors blasting the pair. Kramer's and von der Leyen's article on the "Development of 'Emotionless, *Gemüt*-less' Psychopathy in Childhood" had even put the *Gemüt* in quotes, as though it did not really exist. Schröder questioned their research sample and accused them of misinterpreting his and Heinze's idea of *Gemüt*.[43]

Kramer and von der Leyen responded to Schröder's charges in one-and-a-half pages, but did not have the opportunity to prove their findings: von der Leyen took her life that year, and Kramer emigrated to the United States with another Jewish colleague, Hans Pollnow. Kramer and Pollnow would go on to define a condition now recognized as a forerunner to attention deficit and hyperactivity disorder (ADHD).[44] In contrast to Nazi psychiatry's emphasis on *Gemüt* in the idea of autism, Kramer resisted the idea of *Gemüt* in his description of ADHD.

Through their institutional dominance, Schröder and Heinze and their followers generated a dizzying number of *Gemüt*-centered psychiatric terms: children might have improper *Gemüt*, with *Gemüt*-defect or cold-*Gemüt* (*Gemütsdefekt, gemütskalt*). Or they might have deficient *Gemüt*, being *Gemüt*-less, *Gemüt*-lacking, or with a *Gemüt*-shortage (*gemütlos, gemütsarm, Gemütsmangel*). Inadequate *Gemüt* was no longer an abstract quality but a quantifiable pathology. Failings of *Gemüt* were supposedly heritable and predicted children's future value, or danger, to society. There were numerous terms for good *Gemüt*, too. Achieving healthy *Gemüt*, with *Gemüt*-depth, *Gemüt*-richness, *Gemüt*-giftedness, or *Gemüt*-life (*gemütstiefe, Gemütsreichtum, Gemütsbegabung, Gemütsleben*) required intensive *Gemüt* cultivation, of *Gemüt*-care or *Gemüt*-education (*Gemütspflege, Gemütsbildung*).

Many figures developed theories of defective *Gemüt* in the 1930s, diagnoses of social disconnection that matched, and predated, what Asperger would call autistic psychopathy. In other words, the idea of autism as a pathology already pervaded Nazi child psychiatry in Germany—and Asperger would name it after Nazism came to Austria.

ON THE MORNING of March 12, 1938, the German Wehrmacht rolled across the border into Austria and met jubilant crowds. Austrians applauded the tanks along their route to Vienna. The intensity of popular euphoria caught most by surprise, including Hitler. Austrians lavished salutes, swastika flags, tears, and cheers on their invaders. Enthusiasm for Nazi annexation spanned all segments of the population, as people hoped for pan-German solidarity, supremacy, triumph over the humiliation of World War One, economic recovery, and an end to political uncertainty.

Prior to the Nazi Anschluss, Austrian Chancellor Kurt Schuschnigg had sought to protect the nation from Reich aggression by appeasing Hitler—accepting foreign policy constraints and allowing National Socialist Party members

Propaganda for the Austrian plebiscite to join the Reich at the Urania educational facility and observatory in Vienna, April 1938.

to hold government positions. By March 1938, Schuschnigg even agreed to appoint the ardent Nazi Arthur Seyss-Inquart as Minister of the Interior. In an effort to preserve something of Austrian autonomy, Schuschnigg sought to hold a referendum on joining the Reich, leaving the decision to the Austrian people. But Hitler blocked the referendum, and Schuschnigg resigned on March 10. Hitler moved immediately to invade Austria.

Asperger, in Vienna, lived at the heart of National Socialist ferment after the Anschluss. Frenzied campaigning for a Nazi-led April 10 plebiscite on joining the Reich kept public life at a fever pitch. Rallies, bonfires, and parades—alongside mass violence and mass arrests of Socialists, Communists, and Jews, who were excluded from the vote—mobilized 99.73 percent of those who did vote yes for incorporation into the Third Reich.[45] With a population of 6.65 million to Germany's 69.3 million, Austria was the Nazi regime's first stop in its expansionist aims to rule the European continent.

In the months that followed, the Third Reich sought to reshape society. Whereas National Socialist transformation had come piecemeal to Germany after 1933, Austrians encountered a full-fledged Nazi government all at once. Ways of talking, thinking, and seeing were to change overnight, as new terminology, acronyms, militarisms, uniforms, and *Heil Hitlers* permeated daily existence. Red swastika banners and flags hung throughout the streets. The party took over, or "coordinated," public and private institutions. Every man, woman, and child was to join some group in the Nazi state—from the National Socialist Women's League to the Hitler Youth. Whether or not one supported the regime, the symbols and practicalities of National Socialism defined one's everyday actions. Both imposed and indigenous, Nazism reconstituted politics, society, economy, and culture. Asperger was living through a revolution.

After the spring of 1938, enthusiasm for the Third Reich cooled somewhat in Austria. German rule did not meet the grandiose expectations of average citizens, economically and politically. Although the rate of unemployment dropped dramatically (22 percent in 1937, 13 percent in 1938, 4 percent in 1939, and 1.2 percent in 1940), the cost of living rose 22 percent. German newcomers had shut Austrians out of the best government and business posts, and Austrian National Socialists felt betrayed. A haphazard handover to the Reich had led to looting and uncontrollable street violence, with disaffected Nazi Party members leading many of the rampages. One-fifth of all those arrested between March to December 1938 were National Socialists.[46]

Violence against Jews in Vienna was especially vicious, regarded by many as the worst in the Reich. People assaulted, beat, and humiliated Jews in the streets. They vandalized, plundered, and desecrated Jews' stores, homes, and synagogues. Vienna had a large Jewish population—around 10 percent, versus less than 1 percent in Germany overall—and a history of pervasive and pernicious anti-Semitism. While Vienna's Jews were a diverse and multi-faceted group, they were stereotyped and widely resented for their disproportionate prominence in business and high-status professions. Up to two hundred thousand Jews lived in Vienna in 1938; Jews owned a quarter of Vienna's businesses (three-quarters of its banks and newspapers) and comprised over half of all doctors and lawyers.[47]

The National Socialist annexation of Austria in March 1938 led to more brutality against Jews than Germany had seen throughout the entire 1930s. It was not just Nazi Party members and paramilitary organizations (the SA Stormtroopers and SS Protective Echelon) who instigated the violence, but also ordinary citizens. The kind of mob terror Vienna saw after the Anschluss in March 1938 was a precursor to the violence that broke out less than a year later, on November 9, 1938, in the Night of the Broken Glass, a Reich-wide pogrom; that night, Viennese despoiled and burned ninety-five synagogues while authorities arrested 6,547 Jews, sending 3,700 to Dachau concentration camp.

Living within this barbarism, Asperger would have walked through anti-Semitic graffiti and the destruction of Jewish property in his everyday life. He would have seen the rapid exclusion of Jews from the public sphere, from Jews losing their jobs to being barred from public spaces. He would have seen "wild Aryanization," the chaotic seizure of thousands of Jewish businesses and homes, and the disappearance of tens of thousands of his Jewish neighbors who were either processed by Adolf Eichmann's emigration machine or deported to camps. One could not *not* know the kind of system one was living under. Brutality and persecution in Vienna in 1938 were more obvious than elsewhere in the Reich.

Asperger, as a dedicated Catholic, would have also witnessed the Reich's persecution of the Church. In July 1938, the Nazi state arrested clergy, took over the Catholic press, and disbanded six thousand church organizations as well as Catholic schools. Although Cardinal Theodor Innitzer had initially cooperated with the regime, by October 7, 1938, Innitzer spoke out against Nazism. His Rosary Mass at St. Stephens Cathedral for Catholic Youth drew six thousand to eight thousand congregants, and escalated into the largest public protest during the twelve years of the Third Reich. The Catholic Church paid for

Inaugural lecture of Eduard Pernkopf, the new National Socialist dean of the University of Vienna Medical School, April 26, 1938.

its disobedience, however, as Hitler Youth raided and desecrated Innitzer's archiepiscopal palace the next day, and wreaked havoc on the streets in massive numbers the following week.

As the new regime unleashed unprecedented violence in Vienna, Asperger acquiesced to the new reality. In a 1974 interview, he seemed to imply that the beliefs he already held made it easier to accept Nazi rule: "The Nazi period came, and it was clear from my previous life, as with many 'nationalists'—in quotes—that one went along with things."[48]

Asperger's professional sphere transformed.

At the University of Vienna, Eduard Pernkopf, a specialist in anatomy who had been an ardent member of the Nazi Party since 1933, was appointed dean of the Medical School. Pernkopf was determined to realign the institution according to National Socialist principles and, four days after his appointment, on April 6, 1938, gave an inaugural address in an SA uniform. In his address, he stressed the centrality of racial hygiene to Nazi medicine, arguing for promoting the "genetically valuable" among the population as well as "the elimination of those who are hereditarily inferior by sterilization and other means."[49]

Pernkopf insisted that all medical faculty swear a loyalty oath to Adolf Hitler and register their bloodline with the administration as either "Aryan" or not. Those who did not swear the oath or were classified as "non-Aryan" lost their positions. While Asperger acceded, his colleagues were purged en masse. The medical school removed 78 percent of its faculty, predominantly Jews, including three Nobel Prize winners. Out of 197 physicians, only 44 faculty remained.[50]

Overall, the University of Vienna removed 45 percent of personnel from its other departments.[51] And two-thirds of all Vienna's 4,900 doctors and 70 percent of its 110 pediatricians lost their positions.[52] Thousands emigrated (primarily to the United States) or suffered deportation. Medicine came to be one of the most Nazified professions in the Third Reich, with around half of all doctors joining the party.[53]

Over three-quarters of psychiatrists and psychoanalysts left Vienna between 1934 and 1940 due to racial or political reasons, leading to a profound transformation of the fields. Vienna's renowned field of psychoanalysis, in particular, was decimated.[54] The membership of the Vienna Psychoanalytical Society was overwhelmingly opposed to the regime, and 84 percent Jewish. The day after Nazi troops moved into Austria, the board of the society met at Sigmund Freud's house and resolved to encourage members to emigrate. An international network was already primed to assist a rescue effort; Ernst Jones, the President of the International Psychoanalytical Association, and French psychoanalyst Marie Bonaparte personally traveled to Vienna to facilitate arrangements, while others abroad provided their Viennese colleagues with funds, contacts, jobs, visas, and affidavits. The majority of Viennese psychoanalysts were able to emigrate within one or two months and begin successful new practices elsewhere in Europe or the United States. Eighty-two-year-old Sigmund Freud and his daughter Anna reestablished an influential circle in the United Kingdom.[55]

Of the 124 former and current members of the Vienna Psychoanalytical Society who lived through the Anschluss, 106 faced persecution due to their religion or political opposition to the regime. The vast majority left the country; ten perished in ghettos or concentration camps. Only five remained in Austria, most notably August Aichhorn and Otto Pötzl. Aichhorn continued to practice but withdrew from public life. Privately, he led a small group of psychoanalysts from his home who were opposed to National Socialist rule and its political goals of psychotherapy. Some of this circle were involved in resistance activity and killed by the regime. Pötzl had joined the Nazi Party in 1930 and continued to run Vienna's University Clinic of Psychiatry and Neurology until 1945.[56]

Purged of Jews, the Berlin Psychoanalytic Institute was absorbed by the German General Medical Society for Psychotherapy— the brainchild of M. H. Göring, the cousin of Reichsmarschall Hermann Göring. In contrast to the "Jewish science" of psychoanalysis, the Nazi variant of psychotherapy was to orient individuals' mental health around regime values, directing patients to concerns of the present, rather than psychoanalysts' excavations of the past. Psychotherapists were put to practical use as consultants to Nazi organizations such as the Hitler Youth and the League of German Girls. The German General Medical Society for Psychotherapy expanded its use for leadership profiling in military and professional occupations. Despite its Nazi mandate, however, in reality Göring's Institute was a big tent that included Jungian, Adlerian, and Freudian psychoanalysts.[57]

The Nazi annexation devastated two branches of curative education in Austria that had been distinct from the approach practiced at Asperger's Curative Education Clinic. Theodor Heller, the leader of traditional educationally based *Heilpädagogik* in Austria, was Jewish and committed suicide upon the Anschluss. Socialist Karl König, who was born Jewish and disabled, with two club feet, believed in sharing a communitarian life with people whom others saw as severely disabled. König and his associates emigrated to Scotland and founded the utopian Camphill residential community, promoting "the encounter of a self with another self" in a non-judgmental way to "counteract the threat to the core of humanity" he saw in authoritarian regimes.[58]

Hamburger's Children's Hospital and Asperger's Curative Education Clinic survived the Anschluss and subsequent purges and reorganizations unscathed. The regime deemed Asperger and his clinic personnel sufficiently reliable; the Jewish staff members, Anni Weiss and Georg Frankl, had already emigrated. This is not to say that Asperger agreed with all of the state's policies. He remained a practicing Catholic and did not join the Nazi Party. But he did ensure his position by joining other Third Reich organizations in rapid succession: the German Labor Front (DAF) in April 1938 and the National Socialist People's Welfare Organization (NSV) in May 1938. While such memberships might be expected for someone in his position, Asperger went above and beyond the usual affiliations. In May 1938, Asperger began to work for the Nazi state as a psychiatric expert for the city's juvenile court system. He also applied to consult for the Hitler Youth, and applied in June 1938 to the National Socialist German Physicians' League (NSDÄB), which was not a straightforward doctors' professional association, but a lead "fighting organization" of the Nazi Party that sought to coordinate physicians according to party principles and was involved in the persecution of Jewish doctors.[59]

Asperger and his colleagues not only survived but thrived during the Third Reich.[60] The expulsion of so many Jewish physicians and psychoanalysts created a vacuum that expanded their opportunities. Asperger and his associates, and curative education as a whole, gained prominence under the Nazi state. As Hamburger instructed in a ceremonial lecture after the annexation, a doctor in the Third Reich "must be a true National Socialist. He must be downright saturated with National Socialist principles of conduct in lifestyle and health."[61] In this new climate, Asperger proposed a new way to classify children.

BEFORE THE NAZI annexation, Asperger had warned against creating childhood diagnoses. In October 1937, in the first of two lectures he gave at the University of Vienna Children's Hospital entitled "The Mentally Abnormal Child," and published in the *Viennese Clinical Weekly*, he asserted that "there are as many approaches as there are different personalities. It is impossible to establish a rigid set of criteria for a diagnosis."[62] A year later, in October 1938, in a lecture under the same name, given in the same place, and published in the same journal, he introduced his own diagnosis:

> this well-characterized group of children who we name "autistic psychopaths"— because the confinement of the self (*autos*) has led to a narrowing of relations to their environment.[63]

Why did Asperger reverse himself? His diagnosis of autistic psychopathy certainly befit the times. The Nazi annexation brought with it ideals of how to be. There were new standards for joining the national community—racial, political, and biological. There were also new standards of the mind—children were to conform and fuse with the collective.[64] The open-ended sentences that Asperger wrote in 1937 simply did not apply to Nazi standards of child development in 1938.

Had it not been for the Nazi invasion, Asperger may never have envisioned autistic psychopathy as he did. His 1938 lecture appears less a piece of scientific research than a political and social statement. Written just months after the Anschluss, it can be read as an attempt to navigate the mind-boggling shifts of the Third Reich. Much more than a medical diagnosis, it seems to be a diagnosis of a new reality, solidifying a coherent framework through which he might have viewed a changing world.

Asperger might also have been considering his career on a larger stage. Nazi child psychiatrists had solidified an international reputation. His former mentor Paul Schröder had just been elected the first president of the International Association of Child Psychiatry, which held its first meeting in Paris in July 1937 as part of the World Exposition. The Paris meeting had been a huge event, drawing 350 participants from forty-nine different countries, and was equipped with the latest headphone technology for simultaneous translation. The Reich delegation included Ernst Rüdin and Hans Heinze, while Werner Villinger was listed as a contributor but did not attend. Franz Hamburger was an official representative from Austria. Asperger was not on the roster, but, close to Hamburger, would have heard about the event, and perhaps wished to be among these influential figures.[65] At Paris, the International Association of Child Psychiatry planned for their next conference in the Third Reich under Schröder's leadership, though it was never held.

In the very first sentence of Asperger's 1938 lecture on autistic psychopathy, Asperger hailed the Reich's grandiose ambition to transform society: "We are in the midst of a massive reorganization of our mental life, which has encompassed all areas of this life, not least medicine." Asperger continued with a tribute to Nazi ideals, using overtly pro-regime rhetoric that was neither obligatory nor even customary in Austrian scientific papers in 1938. He recommended in his second sentence the overhaul of medicine according to guiding principles of National Socialism, declaring that the individual was subordinate to the state, and medicine was to serve the national community. As Asperger put it, "The fundamental idea of the new Reich—the whole is greater than the parts, the *Volk* more important than the individual—must lead to profound changes in our entire attitude toward the most valuable asset of the nation, its health."[66]

In his second paragraph, Asperger appeared to accept sterilization policy. He acknowledged that the Reich had changed health practices and that doctors should now play a role in enforcing racial hygiene laws. "We physicians must take full responsibility for the tasks we are now accruing in this area."[67] Asperger invoked the Nazi Law for the Prevention of Genetically Diseased Offspring, the regime's sterilization law. He affirmed Reich doctors' "responsibility" to prevent "the transmission of sick genetic material" which now included the duty to report people with supposedly hereditary conditions for forced sterilization. Asperger did, however, urge doctors to exercise caution when selecting people for sterilization, to judge them as individuals rather than by tests and statistics.[68]

Many readers of Asperger's 1938 article today dismiss his use of regime rhetoric as compulsory and suggest that he subverted Nazi tenets in other portions of the paper. Asperger prefaced his discussion of case studies by cautioning, "Not everything that falls out of line, that which is 'abnormal,' must therefore be 'inferior' [*minderwertig*]."[69] He ended his paper with the admonition, "Never give up the education of abnormal individuals who seem hopeless from the outset." Children might reveal capabilities in the course of therapy "that were impossible to foresee." The doctor had "the right and the duty" to invest intensively and emotionally in each child, Asperger maintained, since children "who fall out of the norm and are difficult need

123

experience, love, and full commitment from the educator."[70] Perhaps Asperger's benevolent words reflected his true beliefs. At the same time, his compassionate statements were consistent with the compassionate rhetoric of his mentor, Franz Hamburger, and of Nazi child psychiatry in general—and warmhearted rhetoric would remain a feature of the field, even at its most murderous.

It is not clear that Asperger's generous sentiments applied to all children. Asperger lauded autistic youths whose intelligence, "astonishingly mature special interests," and "originality of thought" led to "high performance" and "outstanding achievements."[71] Yet Asperger also warned that in many children "autistic originality can be nonsensical, eccentric, and useless." The latter had an "unfavorable social prognosis," even an "inability to learn."[72]

Asperger defined autistic psychopathy as a "disturbance of the adaptation to the environment" that, in Asperger's opinion, caused "failure of the instinct functions: interference of understanding the situation, disruption of relationships with other people."[73] Therefore, Asperger held, autistic children lacked social relationships. "Nobody really likes these people," he stressed, and they "don't have personal relationships with anyone." Autistic youths were "always loners, and fall out of every children's community." In short, Asperger declared, "The community rejects them."[74]

Most striking, though, was that Asperger named the condition a psychopathy, and in his definition of the diagnosis, underscored the idea of children's malice and recalcitrance, which was in keeping with ideas of psychopathy at the time. The diagnosis of psychopathy, born in Germany in the mid-nineteenth century, had originally applied to individuals in asylums and prisons. The term became increasingly widespread in the 1920s and began to signify those who threatened social order—such as "asocials," delinquents, and vagrants. Psychopathy was a slippery psychiatric diagnosis that welfare, education, and criminal justice systems had increasingly adopted to isolate troublesome, ungovernable, and potentially criminal children. Newspapers used the term in articles about juvenile delinquents and welfare.[75]

In psychiatry, the dominant paradigm of psychopathy was that of Kurt Schneider. In Schneider's definition, "psychopathic personalities are those abnormal personalities whose abnormality causes them to suffer, or society to suffer."[76] Psychopaths lacked proper social emotions—civility, morality, altruism, and connection—which could lead to criminality. Under the Third Reich, the term psychopathy expanded in definition and consequences, designating a category of asocial youths who might be institutionalized or incarcerated.[77] Asperger framed his 1938 paper, from the third paragraph on, with this prevailing understanding of psychopaths, aiming to "prevent the burdens of their antisocial and criminal acts on the national community."[78]

This idea of social threat infused Asperger's case study of the unnamed seven-and-a-half-year-old boy whom he presented as an exemplar of the condition. While Asperger surmised that the child's "relations to the world are constricted," as he lacked an "instinctive understanding" of people and environment, Asperger spent much of the case study portraying the boy's supposed meanness. According to Asperger, the youth had displayed "continuous and infuriating disciplinary problems" since early childhood.[79] As a "massive, rough, and hulking" boy, manifesting "gross awkwardness," Asperger remarked that "He does not submit to others' will; indeed, he takes a malicious pleasure in not following other people and annoying them." He was allegedly "extremely malicious against the other children, acting like a red rag."[80] The boy's school could not "control" him. "He upsets the whole class with his trouble-making and tussling." This, according to Asperger, was in keeping with autistic children's "lack of respect for authority, the altogether lack of disciplinary understanding," and "unfeeling malice."[81] These characteristics, Asperger concluded, added up to "a psychopathic personality."[82]

Asperger did not introduce his definition of autistic psychopathy until Nazism controlled his world—and when he did, he defined it in terms of Reich rhetoric and values. Does it matter if Asperger was only signaling regime values superficially to get by, to protect his career, or to advance it? It is Asperger's words, not his innermost thoughts or beliefs, that affect our conception of the autism diagnosis more than seventy years later.

A YEAR AFTER the Nazi annexation of Austria, in July 1939, Asperger attended the First International Congress for Curative Education in Geneva. It brought together three hundred psychiatrists, psychologists, teachers, social workers, and policy makers from thirty-two countries. A young assistant professor at age thirty-three, Asperger did not give a talk at the Geneva conference; he enthusiastically described the participants as "leading child psychiatrists and child psychologists, pioneers of their fields."

Notwithstanding the international cast, speakers from the Reich, including Paul Schröder and Werner Villinger, promoted Nazi tenets and dominated. The top conference organizer, Viennese curative education specialist Anton Maller, boasted about the supremacy of their new values: "The German Reich's seizure of power shattered all principles based purely on compassion and charity—in Austria, too; they are no longer relevant for the national community."

Screening the population mattered most. Because "the decline of the healthy gene pool means the deterioration of the *Volk*," Maller insisted, child care professionals were to ensure that "inferior hereditary material should be eliminated."

Asperger watched and listened as his Reich colleagues set the deadly direction of Nazi psychiatry. Soon, he would begin to participate in programs that implemented their macabre visions.

4

Indexing Lives

IN A PERIOD photograph from Vienna Children's Hospital, a proud young Dr. Heribert Goll, a fellow postdoctoral student of Asperger's under Hamburger, posed in the driver's seat of the Health Car. He was driving to thinly populated areas in the Zwettl District of the Lower Danube region to dispense basic medical care and health advice to mothers. Another photo showed the intrepid Health Car moving through a snowy pass, and another showed a Nazi People's Welfare (NSV) nurse and a robust woman in a dirndl smiling at a healthy toddler.[1]

Motorized Mother Advising was one of Franz Hamburger's signature programs, one that he asked Asperger to help direct—a sign of his trust.[2] Hamburger had participated in a similar outreach initiative in rural Austria through the American Commonwealth Fund in the 1920s, but now adapted his program to Nazi aims. "A university children's hospital in the Third Reich," Hamburger said, "should not just care for sick children, but also for healthy ones." He took this principle to extremes. While his doctors gained "practical" experience with hearty youths in the countryside, they denied medical care to the ailing. Heribert Goll, who Asperger recommended as his replacement in the leadership of the program, stressed that Health Car personnel treated ill children "only in urgent cases."[3]

During Asperger's tenure, between October 1939 and July 1940, Hamburger's Motorized Mother Advising executed seventy-seven trips and examined 5,626 infants and children up to age fourteen. It claimed to have reduced rates of rickets and infant mortality, and fashioned itself as a model for other districts in Austria.[4] Yet Hamburger noted that some locals worried about the Health Car's visits from Vienna, writing of "mothers who initially had a certain mistrust of the new facility."[5]

The mothers were right to be wary. Hamburger's Motorized Mother Advising also acted as the eyes and ears of the Nazi regime. The Health Car was specially fitted with three seats so that a Children's Hospital doctor would always be accompanied by a Reich welfare worker and NSV nurse.[6] They noted children they considered to be disabled or genetically tainted, as well as those whose parents they considered to be socially or financially unfit. Health Car personnel would then coordinate with local Public Health Offices to register "the hereditarily ill, alcoholics, and those with tuberculosis and other infectious diseases."[7] One inspection of 1,137 children in 1940 classified 62 percent with ostensibly problematic conditions such as "severely flat feet" (eight children), "hereditary feeblemindedness" (twenty-four children), and an "alcoholic father" (three children).

This indexing of youths, then, would soon be put to use by the child killing program that began at Vienna's Spiegelgrund institution at the end of August 1940, just a month following Asperger's tenure at Motorized Mother Advising. In one sample of Spiegelgrund medical histories, over a fifth of children who were killed—22 percent— were from the Lower Danube region that included the area covered by Hamburger's program.[8] Marie Fichtinger, for example, was born paralyzed on her right side; Zwettl's district administrator recommended her institutionalization in the summer of 1942, and Marie's father signed the consent form for admission. After senior Spiegelgrund physician Heinrich Gross deemed Marie "deeply idiotic" and "physically considerably backward," her case was forwarded to the Reich Committee for approval to kill the girl. Marie died on New Year's Eve.[9]

AFTER ASPERGER WRAPPED up his work in Hamburger's Motorized Mother Advising, he gave a talk on September 4, 1940, at the forty-seventh annual meeting of the German Society for Pediatrics. In his paper, "On Educational

Therapy in Childcare," Asperger reflected that although there used to be different approaches to child development, he believed there would only be one approach under Nazism. "Previously there were quite a number of philosophical, political, and religious goals for child rearing that competed with one another," he explained. But now, "National Socialism established its own goal of child rearing as the only one with validity."[10]

Asperger went on to say that he "greatly approved" of the Third Reich's "single goal" of child development. The very purpose of special education, Asperger declared, was to "align these children with the National Socialist state."[11]

To "align," Asperger argued that some children required fundamental transformation, even alteration of their characters. Asperger was reversing his opinion from two years before, when he said that doctors should give youths "the confidence that they are not sick, but in charge."[12] Rather, in his 1940 talk, Asperger asserted that "Education can select for desired traits, and offer certain circumstances where you can—within limits of course—achieve a change of personality." He touted his vision of child transformation, devoting the concluding paragraph of his four-paragraph report on the pediatrics conference for *The Neurologist* to describing it.[13]

As Asperger pursued regime positions and

organizational memberships immediately following the Anschluss, his work was shaped not only by Nazi ideals, but also by Nazi institutions. Reich mandates scaffolded his professional world. At the Children's Hospital, Franz Hamburger considered Asperger sufficiently reliable to remain his postdoctoral student, as well as to remain director of the Curative Education Clinic and a director of Motorized Mother Advising. To Hamburger, being a department head was an important responsibility, and signaled fealty to the regime. Hamburger had insisted in a lecture in 1939, "It is necessary that the chief faculty representative of a university department is a convinced National Socialist."[14]

Asperger chose to stay at Hamburger's hospital, where, according to Nazi Party records, every doctor besides himself was a party member.[15] His decision not to join the party could mark him as politically oppositional (indeed, it saved his reputation after the war). But Asperger's choice was also in keeping with the vast majority of his Austrian peers. While around half of all doctors in the Reich overall became party members, two-thirds of doctors in Austria did not. In Vienna, seven in ten physicians eschewed membership.[16]

An offhand comment from one of Asperger's colleagues, Josef Feldner, sheds some light on Asperger's relationship with National Socialism. Upon reviewing one of Asperger's papers,

Feldner recommended that Asperger tone down his pro-regime rhetoric—"It is perhaps a bit too Nazi for your reputation."[17] Feldner's advice suggested it was well known that Asperger was not a Nazi enthusiast; it also suggested that Asperger strove to look like one, to the point of overdoing it. Indeed, Asperger did include pro-regime rhetoric in his papers, and he complied down to small details such as signing documents *Heil Hitler* when it was not required.[18]

Asperger's religiosity did raise some eyebrows among Nazi Party officials, since the Third Reich contested the practice of religion, seeing it as incompatible with and even threatening to Nazi ideology. The regime persecuted and incarcerated priests, desecrated churches, and pressured citizens to cease religious observances. One SS letter in Asperger's party file expressed concern that "Dr. Asperger comes from clerical circles and was staunchly clerical during the *Systemzeit* [1933–1938]." The same document noted that Asperger had been a member of the heavily Catholic Bund Neuland and the secretary of the Catholic St. Lucas Guild.[19] Still, being a practicing Catholic in Nazi Austria did not necessarily signify opposition to the Reich. After all, 90.5 percent of the population was Catholic. It was an umbrella faith that spanned people with a wide variety of political and religious positions. Anti-Nazi Catholic dissidents might attend mass alongside pro-Nazi Catholics who shared the regime's conservative values and anti-Bolshevism. They might be joined by Austrians who had not been religious before the annexation, but who began to attend church as a form of protest. Church participation actually rose after the Anschluss. Even in Germany, where only a third of the population was Catholic, the majority of registered Catholics regularly attended church, dropping only in the war years.[20]

National Socialist officials soon determined that Asperger's Catholicism did not affect his political trustworthiness. One party report from 1939 maintained that while Asperger was "a typical black [Catholic]," he was "not an opponent" of Nazism during the years when it was known for extreme violence and banned in Austria.[21] Another report certified in 1940 that Asperger was "a devout Catholic, but without the political tendencies that accompany Catholicism." Party personnel vetted and cleared Asperger's religiosity, concluding that "he shares no common interests with that political community."[22]

Nazi and state officials became increasingly confident about Asperger's reliability. Asperger's district party file [*Gauakt*] is thin, and its pro forma assessments consistently deemed Asperger loyal to the regime. Party officials confirmed each year that "there are no concerns about his character or politics."[23]

In matters of Nazi racial hygiene, Asperger would also be considered reliable. In one party assessment from November 1940, an SS major assured that Asperger "has never actively committed acts against Nazis, although at the Children's Hospital—which is staffed with only National Socialist doctors—it would be easy for him to procure materials for exposure."[24] As most such documents, the language is oblique, and the possibilities of what might be "exposed" numerous: the hospital's role in the sterilization of children, medical experiments on children, or transferring children to the euthanasia program at Spiegelgrund that had just begun. Asperger certainly proved himself trustworthy in his service to the state, working at the locus of racial hygiene measures in Vienna.

ON OCTOBER 1, 1940, Asperger expanded his collaboration with the Nazi state, applying for the position of medical expert for Vienna's Public Health Office, the central Reich agency that assessed individuals' value to the regime and assigned their fates. Asperger had already begun to work for the Nazi government after the Anschluss in the juvenile justice system and remedial schools, and his clinic had become an important part of government operations. By August 7, 1940, the *New Viennese Daily* (*Neues Wiener Tagblatt*) praised Asperger's Curative

Education Clinic as an "advisory body" for the city of Vienna, treating children with the "closest cooperation with the entire municipal welfare department."[25]

Asperger moved even closer to the heart of government operations two months later, then, with his official "request" to the Public Health Office to become a "specialist physician" in "curative educational and child psychiatric concerns" for the city. Asperger would assess the capabilities of youths from remedial and special education schools for Vienna's Department of Schoolchild Welfare. Once his application was approved by Public Health Office director Max Gundel, Asperger signed up for twelve hours a week, which he estimated to be a quarter of his time.[26] The work paid well; his 1,920 reichsmarks a year was equivalent to the yearly income of a full-time worker in the Reich.[27]

Public Health Offices were key instruments of Nazi eugenics. Just six months after Hitler came to power, in July 1933, the Law on the Unification of the Health Care System restructured and centralized health care through these offices. A total of 739 Public Health Offices dotted the Reich, from large cities to rural areas, with a wide-ranging staff that included SS officials, physicians, nurses, lawyers, and biomedical personnel. Their mandate spanned health services, family planning, and "hereditary and racial care"—overseeing the social, biological, and racial lives of Reich citizens.[28]

Vienna city councilor Max Gundel, a zealous supporter of Nazi racial hygiene who directed Vienna's Department for Care of Health and the Nation, ran the city's Public Health Office, and subsumed municipal health, welfare, and racial hygiene systems under its umbrella. He also led the arrest and deportation of thousands of individuals, making extra efforts to accelerate the transport of Vienna's Jews, and was active in founding Vienna's child euthanasia program. As the first municipal administrator of Spiegelgrund in 1940, Gundel participated in the earliest talks about killing methods with Erwin Jekelius, the first medical director of Spiegelgrund, and Viktor Brack, who designed the Reich's entire euthanasia program.[29]

To the public, the mission of Vienna's Health Office, and indeed all Reich Health Offices, was to provide generous preventative and family care. The offices promoted "positive" eugenics for the well-being and propagation of desirable citizens, offering women medical care during pregnancy, advice on child rearing, instruction on homemaking and hygiene, and even breast milk collection. Positive eugenics often had a darker side, however, with negative eugenics embedded within it. For example, while administering marriage loans to encourage reproduction, Public

Health Offices simultaneously screened individuals for "hereditary diseases." In 1938, Vienna's first year of the program, the city's Public Health Office denied marriage loans to 682 people deemed to be biologically defective—out of a total of 43,000 applicants—and even denied their right to marry at all.[30]

Public Health Offices also managed the Reich's program of forced sterilization. Sterilization had support throughout Europe and the United States at the time—twenty-nine American states involuntarily sterilized over thirty thousand people from 1907 to 1939—yet the Third Reich brought the practice to new extremes. Between 1934 and 1945, the Nazi regime sterilized up to four hundred thousand individuals, 1 percent of people of child-bearing age.[31] The program was smaller in Austria, with six thousand victims, as sterilization came into effect two years after the Nazi annexation in 1940.[32] Since euthanasia killings were beginning around the same time, many Austrians who would have been subject to sterilization were instead killed.

In theory, Public Health Offices targeted individuals for supposedly genetic and discrete conditions such as "hereditary feeblemindedness," schizophrenia, manic-depressive disorder, epilepsy, Huntington chorea, hereditary blindness and deafness, "severe bodily malformation," and alcoholism. Doctors and nurses, as well as teachers and welfare workers, were to report people who they considered defective, and this process was systematized into standard forms for denunciation.[33] While individuals were to fall into medical classifications, informing often had more to do with social prejudices, targeting those in poverty or who failed to meet bourgeois norms. This class dimension is likely one reason sterilization was broadly unproblematic within the Reich population.

Denounced individuals were to appear before one of the Reich's two hundred Hereditary Health Courts, where a three-person panel determined their genetic worth in mere minutes. If found deficient, people were sent to clinics—10 percent had to be brought by police force—and typically subjected to vasectomy or tubal ligation, what some called the "Hitler cut."[34] Many hundreds, mostly women, died as a result of complications.

Estimates suggest that the vast majority of individuals were sterilized for alleged mental defects. In the program's first years, officials labeled over half of victims "feeble-minded," around a quarter with schizophrenia, and the next largest percentage with epilepsy.[35] Since these conditions then became primary categories for killing in the child and adult euthanasia programs, the intent of these efforts might be considered tantamount to a psychiatric genocide. The goal was to eradicate from the population people with certain kinds of minds. For instance, the regime sterilized or killed between 220,000 and 269,500 individuals labeled with schizophrenia—at least three-fourths of all people in the Reich carrying the diagnosis.[36]

Asperger supported the Reich's sterilization law. After he had publicly endorsed it in his 1938 article, "The Mentally Abnormal Child," numerous party reports in his district party file affirmed that "he is amenable to National Socialist ideas of racial care and sterilization legislation." Asperger's loyalty was not just in principle, but also in practice. Another report certified: "He complies with National Socialist ideas in questions of racial and sterilization legislation."[37]

In his writing, Asperger did not hold that biology was destiny, as many Nazi racial hygienists did, but, like Hamburger, maintained that children were products of both genetics and milieu. Asperger wrote an article on twin research to this effect in the January/February 1939 edition of *Der Erbarzt* (*The Genetic Doctor*), an authoritative journal created in 1934 to disseminate Nazi racial hygiene policies and to advise doctors on implementing the sterilization law.[38] Twin research was a staple of Nazi medicine, typically deployed to show how biology determined one's social value. Asperger and Heribert Goll observed identical twin sisters who they said simultaneously developed a virus of hemichorea. One sister, Asperger claimed, was "more intelligent, more mature, with a richer mental life," and it was she who developed more severe symptoms of hemichorea—because, Asperger believed, her "more finely organized brain" made her more susceptible to the condition. The men concluded, individuals' "essential differences and gifts are affected by environment."[39]

Over time, Asperger became somewhat harsher in his eugenicist rhetoric. In an interview with the *Small People's Journal* on September 11, 1940, Asperger likened children he considered to be disabled children to waste. Boasting that he could remediate youths believed to be irremediable, Asperger explained: "With a coarse sieve, many useful things fall in the muck bucket; take a fine sieve and economize—with human souls, too!" Then "slowly, slowly," he said, "some will become useful people."[40]

In 1941 and 1942, Asperger agreed with the premise that some people were "a burden on the community" and that "the proliferation of many of these types is undesirable for the *Volk*, i.e., the task is to exclude certain people from reproduction." Asperger did state that some individuals who might be remediated could find "their place in the greater organism of the *Volk*" and that, for them, sterilization would not "come into question."[41] Yet while Asperger cautioned against the overuse of sterilization, he affirmed it in principle.

For Public Health Offices, administering forced sterilization and other measures of hereditary and racial care was a gargantuan project. It meant gathering and collating information on millions of individuals, tracking multiple facets of their lives and classifying them in a diagnosis regime. The Nazi state had been obsessed with collecting data on its citizens from the outset. Everyone was to possess an Ancestor Passport [*Ahnenpass*], a forty-eight-page booklet that outlined four generations of one's family tree to confirm Aryan ancestry. This was in addition to the Aryan Certificate [*Ariernachweis*] that likewise verified one's Aryan bloodline. The Nazi state systematized demographic information in two censuses in 1933 and 1939. Employing state-of-the-art technology, including the IBM Hollerith punch card machine, the regime then used census designations of Jews and "Gypsies" to later locate individuals for persecution and deportation.

The Reich recorded numerous other aspects of its citizens' lives. Labor Books tracked one's employment history, Health Record Books tracked one's physical condition, the Registry of the Populace [*Volkskartei*] itemized one's functional skills and racial status, and Personal Identification Numbers were to render citizens' information immediately accessible.[42] In the Nazi state, everyone's life was to be evaluated and abstracted into booklets, index cards, and numbers.

Public Health Offices, with their broad reach into the lives of Reich citizens, were primary sites of data collection. Personnel could gather individuals' medical records, family histories, school reports, welfare visits, criminal records, and social and economic status, and funnel the information into a Hereditary Index [*Erbbiologische Kartei*], distilling lives into standardized forms and files.[43] While certain Public Health Offices in the Reich had already begun these compilations, the regime's "Guidelines for the Implementation of the Hereditary Inventory" [*Erbbestandsaufnahme*] on March 23, 1938, was to systematize these efforts. In Austria, a meeting in 1939 disseminated directives for the Hereditary Inventory and involved 250 participants.[44]

University clinics such as Asperger's were instructed to cooperate with the Hereditary Inventory in full, handing over patients' medical files to the Public Health Office. In return, the Public Health Office would grant university clinics access to other types of information about their patients.[45] Despite efforts at systemization, though, officials were operating with unclear records and unclear diagnoses. Medical personnel like Asperger were told to "put a bracketed question mark behind the diagnosis label if it is probable, and a double question mark if it is to be regarded as doubtful."[46] Officials built subjectivity into the Hereditary Inventory, and even presumed it.

Vienna's Hereditary Inventory catalogued subjective pronouncements from a variety of agencies. As the *Vienna Archive for Internal Medicine* explained to physicians in 1940, "One of the main tasks of the Hereditary Inventory is thus to compile and evaluate important information from patient histories, school records, police records, etc., which are now scattered across many locations." While the journal held that "the Hereditary Inventory is limited primarily to persons with negative characteristics"—and that was, indeed, the intent of many in the Public Health Office—there was also rhetoric about it as a potential tool of positive eugenics.[47] Some argued that the Hereditary Inventory "must be seen as less for the eradication of the unfit than for the systematic promotion of the highly valuable—for the benefit of the German people." But positive eugenics would likewise require exhaustive categorization, gathering records from universities and other institutions of higher education.[48]

Staff at Vienna's Public Health Office blended bodily, psychological, social, economic, and racial concerns, registering people believed to have cognitive and biological impairments as well as "asocials," alcoholics, prostitutes, people with sexually transmitted diseases, Jews, half-Jews, "Gypsies," and "wayward youths"—and often combined designations into compound classifications. Social and racial labels came to dominate biological labels; in fact, a majority of people who were classified were physically healthy.[49]

Vienna's Hereditary Inventory was a monumental undertaking. Personnel at the Public Health Office indexed 767,000 people by the spring of 1944—a quarter of the city's population—in what became one of the largest databases in the Reich. Over seventy people worked on the register, combing through birth records, Youth Office records, medical records, police records, Steinhof records, Nazi Party records, and city registries of prostitutes and alcoholics. Vienna's register included at least twelve thousand youths designated with disabilities and at least forty thousand "difficult and psychopathic children from asocial families," many of whom would have fallen under Asperger's purview.[50]

Public Health Offices elsewhere in the Reich likewise compiled massive Hereditary Inventories. The Rheinland indexed at least one and a quarter million people, 16 percent of the population; Thuringia indexed 1.7 million people, a fifth of the population. Hamburg's inventory was the most comprehensive, encompassing 65 percent of the population, 1.1 million inhabitants. It was also the most ambitious, going beyond conventional files into entities such as accident insurance companies and sports clubs.[51] By 1942, Leonardo Conti, head of the regime's Department of Health, estimated that ten million Reich citizens were already indexed—12 percent of the total population.[52]

Hereditary Inventories, in the minds of their architects, ultimately had a "practical" purpose: they were to be "the basis for the implementation of hereditary and racial care measures."[53] In other words, the individualized records prescribed one's treatment or elimination. Regime authorities decided the fates of Reich citizens based on the files, scrutinizing the records to determine marriage loans, marriage permissions, forced sterilizations, arrests, internments in work camps, deportations to concentration camps, and euthanasia killings. Each citizen was quantified in a record that assessed his or her social, economic, biological, and mental attributes, resulting in an overall judgment of one's life, a diagnosis of the entire person.

The Hereditary Inventories exemplified the Nazi diagnosis regime in material form, an effort at mass customization on paper. Yet the files were only a preparatory effort. Indexing lives undergirded the Reich's broader mission to reshape people for collective life—a mission promoted and propelled by Asperger's colleagues in Nazi psychiatry.

5

Fatal Theories

GERHARD KRETSCHMAR WAS born on February 20, 1939, to farmhands Richard and Lina Kretschmar. He was blind, with only one full leg and arm, and had seizures. His parents called their son a "monster." They wrote to Hitler asking for permission to kill him. Hitler sent his personal physician, Karl Brandt, to Leipzig to examine the infant. Brandt declared five-month-old Gerhard an "idiot." The baby was likely given a barbiturate and he died three to five days later, on July 25, 1939. His church records attributed his death to "heart failure."

Gerhard's death was the first recorded of the Nazi child "euthanasia" program. As his case showed, the term *euthanasia* was a misnomer, as most of the children who were killed were not terminally ill, and could have led full lives. But doctors in the program condemned children who they said would become a drain on the state and/ or endanger the gene pool of the German *Volk*. No longer satisfied with the forced sterilization of the genetically "tainted," the Reich radicalized its approach, killing children deemed to be unfit.

Days after Gerhard Kretschmar's death, in

July 1939, Hitler called fifteen psychiatrists to the Reich Chancellery to discuss a program of systematic child killing. The Reich Ministry of the Interior issued a decree on August 18, 1939, that required physicians, nurses, and midwives to report infants and children under three years old whom they deemed to have mental and physical disabilities, including loosely defined diagnoses such as "idiocy" and "malformations of all kinds." The children would enter one of the Reich's thirty-seven "special children's wards" for observation and, regularly, medical murder. To provide incentives for cooperation, doctors and nurses were paid for each child they reported and, at euthanasia centers, received what some called "dirty money"—salary bonuses and perks for children they killed.[1]

Initially limited to babies and toddlers, child killing would be a scientific and deliberative project, based on careful examinations and integrated into the Reich's health care system. After medical personnel reported a child to be disabled, the child's file would be reviewed by the Reich Committee for the Scientific Registration of Serious Hereditary and Congenital Illnesses in Berlin, a front organization of the Reich Chancellery. The committee's three medical "experts" would then send authorization for killing the child to one of the Reich's "special children's wards." In 1939, Hans Heinze, Paul

Schröder's star student, established the regime's first killing center at his State Institute Görden in Brandenburg, where child killing was to be based on personal and purportedly scientific observations.[2] Estimates vary, but between five thousand and ten thousand youths perished in the euthanasia program between 1939 and 1945.

Heinze also authorized adult euthanasia murders as an "expert" in the T4 program, code-named T4 for the address of its Berlin headquarters on Tiergartenstrasse 4. The haphazard adult euthanasia program differed greatly from the individualized and systematic child euthanasia program. Launched in October 1939, adult killings soon moved to mass selections and wholesale deportations from asylums and hospitals to six major killing centers in the Reich, in addition to using drugs and starvation as methods for killing. As the T4 program expanded, it devised the Reich's first gas chambers.

In Vienna, the efficiency of adult killing cleared the way, literally, for child killing. The Steinhof Psychiatric Institute, with its thirty-four ivy-clad pavilions spread across the gentle slopes of one of Europe's grandest Art Nouveau complexes, carried out adult euthanasia in the city. Steinhof had opened in 1907 as a modern, progressive asylum, the largest in Europe. It was also well located—on the outskirts of Vienna yet still a convenient stop from streetcar #47. Steinhof's

Aerial view of Steinhof. The nine Spiegelgrund pavilions are on the left side of the photograph, in the first, second, and third rows up from the bottom. Death Pavilions 15 and 17 are in the third row, farthest to the left.

elegant architecture and gorgeous, leafy 356-acre grounds, providing a desirable place of repose, attracted the well-to-do. Under the Third Reich, however, it became its patients' worst nightmare.

Steinhof was responsible for more than 7,500 deaths between 1940 and 1945—through starvation, deliberate neglect, or mass transfers of patients to the gas chambers at Hartheim Castle near Linz.[3] As Steinhof personnel began to deport 3,200 patients to the gas chambers in the summer of 1940, they emptied enough room to house hundreds of children. The city founded the Vienna Municipal Youth Welfare Institution at

Spiegelgrund on July 24, 1940, on the western side of Steinhof's pavilions, sequestered behind the brick walls and two-tiered windows of buildings 1, 3, 5, 7, 9, 11, 13, 15 and 17, with a capacity of 640 beds. Children were killed in Pavilion 15, while children under observation in Pavilion 17 might be easily marked for death.[4]

Killings at Spiegelgrund began on August 25, 1940. At least 789 children died there during the Third Reich, with the official cause of death for almost three-quarters of them listed as pneumonia.[5] This was supposed to appear a natural cause of death, but it was actually the result of staff issuing barbiturates with the intent to kill. The youths would then suffer weight loss, fever, and susceptibility to infections that then typically resulted in pneumonia. A host of other maladies might lead to death, too, given children's untreated sicknesses and malnourishment. As Ernst Illing, the second director of Spiegelgrund, explained in his postwar trial testimony, "The matter was disguised, no one from the outside was to know about the acceleration of these deaths. There was to be a gradual deterioration of disease which then led to death."[6]

Yet children reacted differently to the drugs, and some died quite quickly. Spiegelgrund doctors presented the killings as a scientific process of trial and error. In postwar interrogations, they related how it took time to perfect killing methods. Spiegelgrund's first medical director, Erwin Jekelius, volunteered that children did not always die from standard doses of Luminal: "Early on, I was personally present several times at these killings in order to see if this process was painful in any way. In our practice, there were two cases in which the poisoning of the sick children did not cause the death of the child, as the dosage of Luminal was not sufficient." So, Jekelius revealed, the doctors resorted to a combined injection of morphine, diallylbarbituric acid, and scopolamine.[7]

Forty-one-year-old Ernst Illing, who succeeded Jekelius as director in 1942, confirmed that "death occurred quite differently depending on the age of the child and whether we first had to calm the child. Death occurred sometimes within hours or only after days." Under his watch, Illing observed, children usually received Luminal or Veronal tablets that were powdered and mixed with "sugar or syrup or other tasty food, so they did not sense the bad taste of the tablets." But, Illing continued, once a child was "in the process of dying, one can no longer rely on swallowing but has to inject."[8]

Franz Hamburger, Asperger's mentor, transferred one of the earliest victims to Spiegelgrund from his University of Vienna Children's Hospital on August 15, 1940. Twelve-month-old Viktor Stelzer suffered from convulsions and muscle cramps, and was thought to be blind. A Spiegelgrund photograph showed Viktor with plump cheeks and closed eyes, his baby hair little more than peach fuzz. Spiegelgrund director Ernst Jekelius, Asperger's former colleague in the Curative Education Clinic, recommended to the Reich Committee in Berlin on November 14, 1940, that the baby be killed. Viktor died two-and-a-half months later, ostensibly of pneumonia.[9]

Another early victim of Spiegelgrund was two-year-old Helmuth Gratzl. The toddler's parents reported that Helmuth began to have seizures at two months of age; the attacks had subsided but, they believed, left the boy with mental and physical impairments, as well as bowel and bladder disturbances. On August 31, 1940, the Health Office of Spittal-Drau authorized Helmuth's transfer to Spiegelgrund. There, Helmuth was restless and cried a great deal. He also developed a fever and passed "thin pulpy stool." Staff administered him Luminal three to four times a day, setting him on the path toward death. Still, his mother sent Spiegelgrund staff detailed instructions on how best to care for the boy—to keep him warm and to give him apples to ease his bowel movements. Helmuth died on October 20, with pneumonia listed the cause of death. Two days later Jekelius met with Helmuth's father, telling him that his son had been born with "severe idiocy and general organ degeneration."

Helmuth's father, according to the case file, approved of the death, saying that it "meant only a release for him and the family." Whether or not this was true, and whether or not the father meant it, this is how the child killers portrayed their work: as emancipation.[10]

Indeed, Spiegelgrund staff appealed to parents' desire to be rid of their children, explicitly touting the benefits of death. On August 8, 1940, upon the direction of the Health Office of Gmunden, the mother of thirteen-month-old Paula Schier brought her daughter to Spiegelgrund. Records contain an image of the baby sitting straight up, small belly button in view, mouthing a tube and looking right at the camera. Paula died one month later, on September 7. Jekelius wrote to her parents that he had done them a service: "you and the child will be spared much suffering." Because Paula had "Mongolian idiocy" (Down syndrome), she "would never have walked or learned to speak, and would have been a constant burden for you."[11]

However, the true intent of the child euthanasia program was not to make life easier for parents, but to purge the Reich of undesirable citizens. And child killers were holding very different conversations among themselves.

TWO DAYS BEFORE baby Paula Schier died at Spiegelgrund, on September 5, 1940, the German

Society for Child Psychiatry and Curative Education held its first conference in Vienna, establishing the grandiose experiment of Nazi child psychiatry as a distinct field. The efforts of Nazi child psychiatrists to transform children were of a piece with Nazi attempts to transform humanity. Their shaping and extermination of supposedly inferior children reflected the regime's shaping and extermination of supposedly inferior nations.

The conference drew over five hundred people to the large lecture hall of the University of Vienna's Clinic of Psychiatry and Neurology— one of the stately stone Palladian buildings in Vienna's ninth district, not far from where Sigmund Freud had lived until just two years before. The institute had been built in 1853 as a lunatic asylum. Now it held the Third Reich's leaders of child development, the "majority in uniform."[12]

The meeting was organized by the sixty-eight-year-old Paul Schröder, who had so deeply influenced Asperger during Asperger's internship with him in Leipzig in 1934. By now widely regarded as the Reich's "father" of child psychiatry, Schröder headed the new German Society for Child Psychiatry and Curative Education, an organization that was founded in the wake of the Paris and Geneva conferences to merge the disciplines of child psychiatry and curative education and align them with the Reich's collectivist and eugenicist principles.[13] The goal of crystallizing Nazi child psychiatry was finally coming to fruition in the Vienna meeting.

Nazi child psychiatrists hoped their discipline would gain greater recognition and power, coordinating and scientifically legitimating Reich children's programs on multiple fronts: clinics, schools, welfare, courts, sterilization, and euthanasia killings. Nazi child psychiatrists were also happy to treat youths who did not appear to have severe mental illness, raising the respectability of their field. Child psychiatrists could demonstrate their potential usefulness to the Nazi state by forging productive workers, soldiers, and citizens.

Schröder delivered the first lecture of the day, declaring in his pronounced Berlin accent, "Child psychiatry is not the care of psychopaths. The few who are truly sick belong with a doctor. Our goal is much larger. We want to understand and recognize, properly assess and guide, purposefully teach and integrate children who are difficult and out of the ordinary."[14]

The Nazi state, Schröder explained, cared about children's deviations from group behavior. As he told the Vienna attendees, "There is demand everywhere today for characterological educational assessment," from schools to juvenile courts. Schröder proposed that Nazi child psychiatry could be of great service to the regime in socializing children, and had specific applications in mind. "The interest of the Hitler Youth and League of German Girls is particularly well known to me," he explained, because of the " 'difficult' children who get into their ranks."[15]

Schröder emphasized that Nazi child psychiatry, like other areas of medicine, was predicated on eugenicist selection. Genetics was decisive; of children who deviated from the norm, some were hereditarily hopeless and some might still be reshaped with a different milieu and proper instruction. Schröder stated that it was critical to differentiate between the two groups of youths— to place them in different kinds of institutions with different kinds of resources. He warned that positive remediation "is not to happen randomly and in the same manner to all 'difficult children,' but with constant expert selection of the valuable and teachable, with equally strict, targeted, and deliberate rejection of those recognized as mostly worthless and ineducable."[16]

Asperger, at age thirty-four, was not a principal player at the Vienna conference; he was neither an invited speaker nor well known among the participants. But he attended the talks and listened carefully, at least carefully enough to report on the assembly for *The Neurologist* [*Der Nervenarzt*], a prominent journal of psychiatry and neurology that was more substantive and less co-opted by Nazi racial hygiene than other journals in the Third Reich.[17] Yet Asperger endorsed the doctrines articulated at the conference. His concept of autistic psychopathy is so saturated with the ideas presented there that it is impossible to decode it without them.

In his conference report, Asperger reiterated Schröder's harsh sentiments about the "worthless and ineducable," and even gave them more force. "After the expulsion of the predominantly worthless and ineducable through early diagnosis of character," Asperger wrote, "this work can significantly help incorporate children who are damaged or not quite of full value into the community of the working *Volk*."[18]

Beyond eugenics and utility, Asperger called attention to the metaphysical dimension of Schröder's approach. He emphasized that Nazi child psychiatry meant no less than the "care for the spirit of difficult children, the care of children's souls."[19] This mandate gave the psychiatrist extraordinary power over the child. To treat a soul, after all, meant judging a child's existence and deciding his or her fate.

HANS REITER, THE top public health official in the Third Reich, affirmed the principle of state control over children in his conference greetings.[20] At age fifty-nine, Reiter had been president of the

Reich Health Office since 1933 and advanced a fascist directive of child development. Children did not just belong to their parents, but to the state, "to the entire *Volk*," he declared, and the task of shaping the body politic was "decisive for the future of the German people." Reiter certainly became adept at excising the unwanted. He was involved in forced sterilizations, mass killings, and human medical experiments during the Third Reich; 250 prisoners at Buchenwald died from one of his typhus tests.[21]

Reiter was only one of an ignominious, even murderous, cast of characters in the Vienna assembly. Most of the fourteen conference speakers had, or would, perpetrate crimes against children. Only three—two of them Swiss—are not known to have supported measures involving child internment, forced sterilization, human medical experimentation, and extermination. Most of these figures have been forgotten to history, but Asperger wrote that he was inspired and influenced by the speakers, praising their "collective sentiment" of "earnest commitment, substantive work."[22] This was his intellectual world. He would base his 1944 diagnosis of autistic psychopathy upon its tenets.

The Child Psychiatry and Curative Education Conference was part of a triumphalist show-case of Vienna's Pediatric Science Week, sand-wiched between the forty-seventh annual meeting of the German Society for Pediatrics and the third meeting of the German General Medical Society for Psychotherapy.[23] Pediatric Science Week was a major undertaking. Organizers even managed to convince the Wehrmacht to grant doctors leave from military service in order to attend. Franz Hamburger oversaw the on-site logistics and delayed the start of the semester at the University of Vienna to procure rooms. Hamburger was dedicated to the cause. In the opening greeting of the week, he proclaimed that the mission was to forge "eugenically valuable families" for the "biological state of Adolf Hitler."[24]

Indeed, the launch of Pediatric Science Week was, perversely, announced side by side in the *Munich Medical Weekly* with the announcement of the opening of the first killing center in the child euthanasia program in the Reich, the Youth Psychiatry Department at the State Institute Görden overseen by Hans Heinze.[25]

Pediatric Science Week was also taking place at a pivotal moment in the history of the Third Reich. In September 1940, the regime was heady with success, reshaping Europe on all fronts. Having invaded Poland and launched World War Two, the Nazi state was carving up the eastern half of the continent and crowding Jews into ghettos. It controlled western Europe from Norway to France and was poised to unleash the

Blitz in the Battle of Britain. In the Reich in 1940, almost anything seemed possible.

Much was happening in Vienna during the week of the conference. At Belvedere Palace, Reich and Italian foreign ministers Joachim von Ribbentrop and Galeazzo Ciano signed the Second Vienna Award, transferring northern Transylvania from Romania to Hungary. Even more dignitaries came for Vienna's Autumn Fair to see country pavilions display national wares from technology to skis to embroidery.[26] The Nazi state promoted Vienna as its style capital, where "Viennese fashion" supposedly "springs straight from the depths of the *Volk*." That season, models with powerful shoulders and pencil-thin eyebrows showed off coats of possum and wolf.[27]

The Reich was refashioning children, too. In another prominent assembly in Vienna that week, Baldur von Schirach handed over the Hitler Youth to new leadership. If Asperger had looked at the newspaper the morning of his conference, he would have seen Schirach admonishing boys in the Reich to feel social spirit, to be "united for all time by inseparable bonds" with "selfless loyalty to this community."[28] Under Nazism it was not enough to conform to the collective; one had to *feel* part of the collective.

But what of children who did not feel community bonds? The German Society for Child Psychiatry and Curative Education was meeting to solve just that. Its published mission was installing sociability, the "alignment of difficult children and adolescents" into the "national community."[29] This meant deciding which youths had the capacity to participate in the *Volk* and how to cultivate them, how to turn youths deemed asocial, social. The Third Reich was about fitting in and fitting together, in external and internal conformity.[30]

The Vienna meeting boasted "unexpectedly strong attendance." Officials came from the Reich Ministry of the Interior, the Reich Health Office, the Reich Ministry for Public Enlightenment and Propaganda, and numerous other regime and party organizations.[31] They were joined by doctors, psychologists, special educators, teachers, welfare workers, and day care providers, as well as by a handful of international guests from Switzerland, Hungary, China, and Chile.

Luminaries from Vienna's academic establishment were there, including the rector of the University of Vienna and the dean of the medical school. Two of Vienna's most renowned psychiatrists backed the conference. Otto Pötzl was the host, and Nobel Laureate Julius Wagner-Jauregg was the official sponsor; the audience gave the eighty-three-year-old "doyen" an "especially rapturous welcome."[32] Still, it was clear the conference was held under the thumb of the regime. People may have known, or guessed, that legendary psychoanalyst August Aichhorn—one of the few followers of Freud who remained in Vienna—refused an invitation to attend and to give a lecture. No supporter of the Nazi state, Aichhorn could not have been pleased when as part of the invitation M. H. Göring, head of the General Medical Society for Psychotherapy, said he would "proofread" Aichhorn's lecture "from a political standpoint."[33] Yet there were plenty of other eminent participants to make up for Aichhorn's absence.

In establishing the field of Nazi psychiatry, the society aimed to shape a new kind of person who would be bound, in body and in spirit, to a new kind of community. It called for a sweeping approach, for "the collaboration (academic and practical) of doctors, educators, and government officials" that would encompass traditional psychiatry, curative education, special education, internal medicine, and state discipline.[34] So while conference participants came from different fields, they operated on four common precepts: prioritizing the *Volk,* eugenicist selection, totalizing treatment, and cultivating community spirit.

Despite broad agreement on the principles, what such a practice looked like in reality was up in the air. Where was the line between children who were remediable and those who were not? What should the state do with children seen to be worthless? Different practitioners supported different solutions, from remediation to incarceration to, even, elimination.

Not all Vienna participants shared the same enthusiasm for the Third Reich. Some were simply pleased to be participating in a scientific conference—gaining recognition and respectability for their fledgling fields. Yet the assembly was a creature of the Third Reich and was shaped by it. The papers of the motley group of scientists and murderers were infused with Nazi principles, bombastic and incoherent. But one must take them seriously, as Asperger did.[35]

KURT ISEMANN, PERHAPS more than anyone else at the meeting, articulated ideas of children's "community feeling" [*Gemeinschaftsgefühl*] that most resembled Asperger's later definition of autistic psychopathy. Isemann informed the Vienna audience that the goal of child development was "first and foremost, converting the character and awakening the will for community."[36]

At fifty-three, Isemann was open and approachable. One colleague described him as "lumbering, with clumsy motor skills," who did not "need the uniform of the senior staff physician for gravitas." He would be seen outside the house in casual clothes, even in a sports cap.[37] In the 1920s and 1930s, Isemann had a positive outlook about children's capacity to overcome their challenges, and thought these challenges should be normalized. He wrote in 1930 that when a child became upset with him- or herself, the doctor should console, telling the child, "Sure there is something amiss [. . .] but you don't need to lapse into fatalism. Besides, you're not so abnormal as you think."[38]

Isemann drew on the concept of *Gemüt*, the metaphysical term for social spirit in his psychiatric circles. At his youth sanatorium in Nordhausen, Isemann's staff held evening pow-wows for "*Gemüt* development" [*Gemütsbildung*] where youths, sitting by candlelight, shared fairytales, religious discussions, and adventure stories. To help the child who "fails socially," Isemann urged, "We must protect him from himself, so that he can again believe in himself and again feel the joy of community life."[39]

At the Vienna conference—ten years later and six years into National Socialism—Isemann's words took on a harsher cast. He now told the audience that only some children could be remediated: the "incorporation of social values" was possible just in "a portion of cases." Isemann listed cases that proved irredeemable: children who displayed "lack of *Gemüt*" [*Gemütlosigkeit*], who "lack the sophistication to forge emotionally significant relationships," and those whose "emotional side is completely hidden behind a curtain," for whom "the prognosis is particularly bleak." As Isemann put it to the assembly, "One never has the feeling of being opposite a solid core, one thinks rather that such a thing does not exist at all in them."[40] Asperger would have also heard Isemann give a similar talk at the First International Congress for Curative Education in Geneva the year before. Isemann had spoken about children who did not have "a normal mental constitution for a social way of life." They would "renounce or reject contact with the community"—with "autism [*Autismus*], community-averse and weak."[41] While "autism" was a well-known descriptor for pronounced symptoms of withdrawal, typically associated with schizophrenia, Isemann's application of the term to milder forms was unusual.

Although Asperger drew on many of these same concepts—and words—as Isemann in his work, Asperger did not mention Isemann's ideas of social attachment in his conference summary. He relayed Isemann's message as simply, "Waywardness must meet certain characterological or psychopathic traits, certain moments of disturbance in character; sometimes remaining states of brain diseases can play a role in these disorders."[42]

Another speaker in Vienna, Anna Leiter, likewise presented ideas that Asperger would use three years later in his treatise on autistic psychopathy. She even introduced a formal diagnosis around the idea of children's insufficient social spirit: "lacking *Gemüt*" [*gemütsarm*].[43] Leiter had worked with Paul Schröder for twelve years in Leipzig, where Asperger would have overlapped with her during his internship in 1934. The only woman speaking at the conference, Leiter does not appear to have been a major figure at the time, but Schröder endorsed her work on *Gemüt* and social spirit. And Leiter was higher profile than Asperger. Several prominent personalities in the field, such as euthanasia leader Hans Heinze, cited her work and linked her research with Schröder's. Reviewers credited her for the diagnosis she created, "lacking *Gemüt*," and drew connections between her ideas and to those of Kurt Isemann (but not to Asperger).[44]

In her talk, Leiter emphasized the extensiveness of her research, based on over a decade of studying 465 children. She described her subjects in terms that Asperger would later use. To Leiter, the children she studied did "not feel joy and sorrow, enthusiasm or warmth," while their "intellect is hyper-vigilant, cunning, and resourceful in the service to their interests that lack *Gemüt*." She diagnosed children as "lacking *Gemüt*" when they showed "lack of empathy, of compassion, ability to love, with respect and devotion as a central defect." Like Asperger, Leiter focused on youths who were "intellectually normal" or "even gifted," but showed "no signs of the capacity for joint actions and experience."[45]

Leiter put her diagnosis of "lacking *Gemüt*" to use for the Reich in the League of German Girls (BDM), the girls' counterpart to the Hitler Youth. Holding that "A person's possession of *Gemüt* is of decisive importance to the community," Leiter assisted "the detection and evaluation of difficult, asocial, and antisocial children and adolescents." As a group leader in the BDM, Leiter stressed the qualities of "attachment" and "love of one's neighbor" to build "comradely spirit." Along with Schröder and his staff in Leipzig and Dresden, Leiter gave classes and "long colloquia" to train other BDM leaders in characterology and the identification of children who did not fit into the group.[46]

However, Leiter differed from Asperger and Isemann in what to do with children lacking *Gemüt*. Whereas Asperger and Isemann stressed that some children could be helped and taught *Gemüt*, Leiter stressed the dangers of those who could not. She provided chains of statistics on the criminal prognoses and heritability of "lacking comradely feelings," quantifying the emotions of the youths' parents and siblings. (In one of her subsets, 36 percent of parents of children lacking *Gemüt* supposedly themselves lacked *Gemüt*).[47] Cautioning the audience that youths lacking *Gemüt* were at risk for criminal behavior, Leiter promoted "efforts to eradicate the antisocial as early as possible." She recommended the children's internment: the "earliest possible preventative detention of these children for the nation as a whole, as they pose an unbearable burden and risk."[48]

Asperger described Leiter's research in his conference report but sidestepped her call for imprisonment. He wrote simply that Leiter "painted a picture of Schröder's categories of children and youths 'lacking *Gemüt*' and 'having *Gemüt*,' the genetic biology, general behavior, and the consistent inability to influence this type educationally, and discussed the necessary conclusions from these findings."[49]

But Leiter was far from alone in advocating the preemptive incarceration of children deemed to lack social feeling. Werner Villinger, a top child psychiatrist in the Reich, talked about isolating the youths in what he called labor colonies. At fifty-two, Villinger was an influential professor of psychiatry and neurology in Breslau, having founded one of Germany's first child psychiatric observation wards at a university hospital in 1920 at Tübingen.[50] Although Villinger had an ambivalent relationship with the Nazi regime and its brutality, he, like other leading and internationally respected physicians, slid passively into Nazi racial hygiene policies, forced sterilizations, human medical experiments, and murder.

On the extreme right of the political spectrum, Villinger supported many ideas of National Socialism—yet had joined the party rather late, in 1937, and reportedly kept an elitist distance from what he considered a lower-class mass movement. Villinger had joined the paramilitary organization of the *Stahlhelm*— yet he left when it was taken over by the SA, the Nazi Stormtroopers. His son said Villinger seemed to think it was "dumb."[51]

Villinger also hedged his involvement with racial hygiene measures. As the psychiatric director at the institution of Bethel from 1934–1940, Villinger was responsible for the sterilization of the "hereditarily ill." But he disliked the hastiness with which doctors and courts decided to force sterilization upon patients, in mere minutes, as well as sterilizations based on ambiguous diagnoses and "borderline cases." So while Villinger lawfully reported patients eligible for sterilization, he supposedly downplayed their alleged defects so that that the Hereditary Health Courts would have to spare them. Villinger supported the sterilization program in principle, though; he served on Hereditary Health Courts in Hamm and Breslau. Villinger also encouraged his patients—youths—to themselves apply for sterilization as "a sacrifice to the *Volk*." Voluntary sterilization was possible after the age of ten in the Reich, and forced sterilization after age fourteen. Villinger said that by April 1935, around

60 percent of Bethel's 512 sterilization requests were submitted "voluntarily." There was such demand, Villinger claimed, that "Our hospital cannot completely fulfill all sterilizations. We have sterilization day only once a week, where only a limited number can be completed. Then it becomes a fierce competition."[52]

At the conference, Villinger outlined a grandiose vision of child development based on community feeling. "Waywardness can arise," Villinger asserted, if children lacked "what one could call cultivation of *Gemüt* [*Gemütspflege*]— to contain egocentricity and awaken and promote the ideal of community."[53] He contended that Nazi collectivism was good for mental health. The Reich offered a single, forceful model for how to be. Before, Villinger explained, there was "an overload in the concepts of freedom and individualism, and a lack of common ideals in child rearing." As a result, "the loss of authority in the 1920s led to a particularly large number of difficult children" who were then "often confused with psychopaths." Thankfully, Villinger boasted, National Socialism cleared up these mental disturbances. Under Nazism, "Authoritarian government and youth leadership has made pseudo-psychopathy rarer among difficult children and adolescents."[54] Still, he warned that for some children it would be "impossible to prevent them from spiritually—often also physically—

infecting healthy, valuable national comrades."[55]

Thus, Villinger argued, the most difficult children should be put into protective custody. They might become asocials or criminals and, to punish their pre-crime, the Reich needed "a preventive detention law [*Bewahrungsgesetz*] that would, in a timely manner, accommodate the practically ineducable." While many people at the time supported some type of preventative detention law, Villinger went so far as to say the law should put asocial children in "labor colonies permanently, or until they prove suitable for a free life."[56]

Asperger left out Villinger's forceful call for child internment in his conference report, as he had with Leiter. Instead, Asperger singled out one of Villinger's most compassionate points about "individualizing the assessment of cases."[57] This reflected Asperger's milder inclinations but was also a testament to the ambiguity of Villinger's position in the Nazi regime.

Over the course of the Third Reich, Villinger would even equivocate when it came to Nazi murder. In March 1941, Villinger was listed as an official "medical expert" for adult euthanasia killings in the T4 program—one of around forty such experts in the Reich. Officially, he evaluated the files of adults who would be killed; yet it appears that he chose to play a small role in the program and avoided making conclusive decisions about deaths. Villinger likewise went along with the actions of others when it came to human medical experiments. He did not conduct his own, but he offered up six psychiatric patients at Breslau for his colleagues' hepatitis research. After the war, Villinger went on to become one of Germany's most prominent child psychiatrists, and he was invited to a conference at the U.S. White House in 1950. Yet it all ended when his ties to the T4 euthanasia program became public in 1961, and he plunged off the Hafelekar's jagged mountaintop in Innsbruck in what some suspect was a suicide. Asperger and another colleague identified the body.[58]

Villinger was very much a man of his era. Like many respected scientists, including Asperger, he wound up following, if tepidly, the strictures of the Third Reich. Villinger was personally, professionally, and politically ambivalent, yet still participated in a program of systematic killing. It is perhaps fitting, then, that Villinger cautioned in his Vienna talk about the dangers of equivocation, of the "lack of inner relationship to moral values, of purposefulness, of earnestness, of depth of *Gemüt* [*gemütstiefe*]."[59]

The two conference speakers who were *not* from the Reich advanced contrasting attitudes toward child development. Josef Spieler and Andre Repond, both Swiss, were gentler and less normative in their approaches. They also had different profiles. Spieler and Repond, along with Kurt Isemann, were the only three out of fourteen conference speakers not known to endorse children's preventative detention, forced sterilization, medical experiments, or killing. That said, Spieler had secretly joined the Nazi Party seven months before the Vienna assembly and was suspected by the Swiss government of being a Nazi spy.[60] And Repond would grow close to Italian dictator Benito Mussolini's eldest and favorite daughter, Edda, after she fled to Switzerland in 1944 in the wake of her husband's assassination by her father and stayed in his Malévoz psychiatric hospital. Although Edda Mussolini had been a close advisor to Il Duce, and was seen as fascism's ideal of a strong, active, and sophisticated "new woman," Repond saw her as enfeebled from parental abuse, trauma, and father issues.[61]

Spieler's message at the Vienna conference was simple: children's differences should be seen as just that, as differences. While the ostensible subject of Spieler's talk was narrow—selective mutism—he began and ended it by exhorting the audience not to make black-and-white judgments about children. And in treatment, Spieler held, "All forms of coercion and compulsion are to be omitted. More important is understanding, encouraging, building bridges of trust." Spieler admonished psychiatrists and educators to guide children toward "a fluid transition into what is normal."[62]

Andre Repond's talk was even more unusual for the conference. He talked about modeling his own practice in Switzerland on American mental hygiene practices, which sought to prevent mental illness by fostering the mental wellness of children through early intervention and care.[63] Repond was also a proponent of psychotherapy. Reich doctors tended to see psychotherapy's inward-looking approach as uncomfortably close to psychoanalysis, which was widely disdained. Though psychotherapy in the Reich was considered less speculative and less radical than psychoanalysis, Asperger wrote in 1942 that there was a "danger" that psychotherapy, though potentially useful, could slide into psychoanalysis, which he scorned as too "rational." He had coauthored in 1939 a scathing review of Charlotte Bühler's "all too impersonal, purely mathematical view" of children, believing that her "superficial" approach missed the "essence of spiritual life." Asperger also seethed in 1942 that Sigmund Freud saw only the "severely abnormal hysterical, obsessive neurotic, or psychotic," and overlooked "everything divine and human."[64] While psychotherapy gained greater respectability in the Third Reich under the direction of M. H. Göring, even Göring admitted at the meeting of the German General Medical Society for Psychotherapy, a conference he headed the next day for Pediatric Science Week, that people still saw the unconscious as a "Jewish construction."[65]

The gulf in tone between Spieler and Repond's normalizing approaches and those of the Reich speakers underscored just how much child psychiatry in the Third Reich had already crystallized around Nazi ideals.

SPECIAL EDUCATION PROFESSIONALS did not have the same prestige as the child psychiatrists at the Vienna meeting, but the four representatives who spoke stressed the same themes in their talks: integrating children into the collective of the *Volk* and separating out children they believed to be a drain on the state.

Over the 1920s, practitioners of special education had become increasingly involved in eugenics—some out of scientific or political belief, and some strategically, because they recognized the fashionable science lent their young profession greater social significance and legitimacy. By the early 1930s, however, special education seemed to be under threat. The depression led to the closing of special schools in 1932 and, in September 1933, the Nazi regime dissolved the German Association of Special Schools and placed special education under the purview of the National Socialist Teachers' League.[66]

The Third Reich increasingly marginalized

children deemed to be disabled, and begrudged resources spent on their care. Feeling under threat, special educators took great pains to claim their work was crucial to the health of *Volk*. They portrayed themselves as gatekeepers for the national community, as arbiters of which children belonged in it or not, eventually endorsing forced sterilization and euthanasia. Like professionals in so many other fields, they participated in Nazi policies less because the regime imposed its ideas wholesale, but because it preyed on job uncertainties and preexisting beliefs. Assisting the Third Reich's eugenicist ambitions became a way for individuals and the field as a whole to find a secure role in the state. And for ardent supporters of racial hygiene measures, Nazism provided the opportunity to realize their most radical and exterminationist wishes.[67]

Like child psychiatrists, special education professionals did not want to be associated solely with only children whom they believed were severely impaired. They sought to raise the respectability of their vocations in the Reich by spotlighting the other side of the eugenicist coin. They called attention to their work with children who they believed had milder disabilities, who they said might—with the high quality special education they provided—be brought into the national community. Special education teachers tried to cultivate children for the *Volk* in various ways. There were, for example, Hitler Youth initiatives of Bann-G for the hearing impaired (*Gehörgeschädigte*) and Bann-K for the physically disabled (*Körperbehinderte*). Eduard Bechthold, who created Bann-B for the blind in 1934, boasted that the boys, wearing distinct yellow armbands with three black circles in an upside-down triangle, would be "flag bearers of the new spirit."[68]

With the Reich's military build-up and war effort, youths deemed to have minor disabilities were deployed more and more for the state, conscripted into the Reich Labor Service and military as warm bodies. Fritz Zwanziger, the head special education representative in the Reich, sent a wartime "summons" to special education teachers to "compile a special portfolio" of their former students' involvement in the war effort, with newspaper clippings, documents from superiors, and military death reports.[69]

Yet Zwanziger denounced children he said could not be helped, who were a burden to the national community. As he explained in Vienna, the Reich Compulsory School Law had conducted a "negative screening" in 1938, requiring all children in standard schools who were "not sufficiently capable of education" to attend special schools—so that "the German special school is now a collection basin for negatively selected children." Another cut in the selection process was necessary: removing "the ineducable student population" from schooling entirely.[70] Erwin Lesch, a special schoolteacher from Munich, felt that children should be slotted into standard or special education as early as possible. He maintained that interdisciplinary teams of teachers and psychiatrists could sort children by age seven.[71]

Eduard Bechthold, a party devotee, stressed the role of Nazi eugenics in special education, declaring that "Our entire educational work is directed toward racial biology." He insisted that special educators push youths to volunteer for sterilization, suggesting that sterilized children could forge even *stronger* social bonds than typical children, gaining *"Gemüt,* and moral power." Because the "sacrifice" of sterilization "did not always come easily," he said, particularly for girls who had to give up futures as wives and mothers—the youths would thrive in social environments, in "a school home that offers regular community, camaraderie, and work."[72]

Karl Tornow shared Bechthold's emphasis on the eugenics of collective feeling. At thirty-nine, he was the most powerful figure in special education in the Reich and a leader in the regime's Office of Racial Politics. As the state spurned disabled children and, potentially, the professionals who cared for them, Tornow had moved to merge the fractured fields. He helped unify caretakers of blind, deaf, and physically or mentally disabled children under one umbrella field of special education. He also urged the Vienna audience to use his term "special education" [*Sonderpädagogik*] for the name of the new society for Child Psychiatry and Curative Education since curative education [*Heilpädagogik*] was "historically loaded and not appropriate to the times. It is individualistic, liberal, and humanitarian." Using the term "special education" instead would give his field equal billing to child psychiatry. Tornow even argued the society should be renamed because the prefix *Heil* in *Heilpädagogik* connoted "reaching salvation," and using " '*Heil*' in this sense" should be reserved "for greeting the *Führer*" with "*Heil* Hitler."[73]

Certainly, Tornow was doctrinaire. He coauthored a slender volume called *Heredity and Destiny* [*Erbe und Schicksal*], which styled itself as a modern textbook for special education students and teachers. Rather than support disabled children, though, the book was propaganda for their sterilization. It was written in simple language on thick, high-quality paper, and contained dozens of photographs that contrasted grotesque images of people allegedly not useful to the *Volk* with glowing images of those who were, including two of Tornow's own children. The book warned that if students with supposedly genetic disabilities did not volunteer for sterilization, the state could come to them: "The authorities may already know of hereditary disease in a particular family and will approach those with hereditary defects." The book also offered 175 discussion questions with an answer key at the back, such as "Why does support for the mentally defective, in money or other benefits, often serve no purpose?" and "Why is it good that this child died at a young age?"[74]

In his Vienna talk, Tornow hoped the new society would lead a "truly Copernican revolution" in which the state would no longer revolve around the needs of the disabled child, but the fate of the disabled child would revolve around the needs of the state. The health of the *Volk* came first.[75] Of course, prioritizing the well-being of society over the individual was nothing new. Child development professionals in Germany and elsewhere had long emphasized children's social utility—producing valuable workers and citizens, as well as protecting society from children's potential dereliction, psychopathy, criminality, and genetic inferiority. But the Nazi approach added a deeper dimension. It required that the populace feel the proper emotions, fostering the regime goal of community connectedness.

To Tornow, special education was spiritual as well as utilitarian. He allowed that "the aim of any special education is attaining as much *völkisch* usefulness from the pupil as possible"; yet it was also vital that children possess collective spirit, "a uniting, animating, and connective attitude, in contrast to the purely isolated way of thinking in previous times."[76] This was fundamental to Nazism, a feeling of "the whole, of belonging together as an organism and unity, bringing together the agonizing and atomizing minds of people who have been fragmented and isolated."[77]

Asperger did not give the talks of the special educators much consideration in his conference report.[78] Asperger was writing for a medical journal, *The Neurologist*, and not for a special education audience. And Asperger likely would not have identified with the crude rhetoric of the speeches given by the special educators. He would have felt greater affinity with the more cerebral eugenics of the child psychiatrists. But the child psychiatrists and special educators were voicing the same priorities: the health of the *Volk*, eugenicist selection, totalizing treatment, and social spirit. The message behind the academic papers was the same as that behind the bombastic propaganda. Nazi child psychiatry, as defined by the Vienna meeting, incorporated people like Paul Schröder as well as people like Karl Tornow. The one type was intertwined with the other.

THE VIENNA CONFERENCE also included Reich officials. While some may have thought their presence odd at a scholarly meeting, it made sense for the new society to feature them—Nazi child psychiatry would require law enforcement. Children deemed asocial, or potentially criminal, would be handed over to the state for punitive measures.

German psychiatrists had long supported the field of criminology, which drew on late nineteenth-century ideas of born criminals. After the turn of the twentieth century, welfare and juvenile justice systems increasingly incorporated psychiatry into their everyday practices. This linkage to science gave psychiatrists' diagnoses greater authority and legitimacy, and offered intrinsic and biological diagnoses for behaviors previously chalked up to poor morality or milieu. Psychiatrists would predict which children would grow up to be unproductive, criminal, or harmful to society.[79] Forecasts could provide a scientific rationale for preemptive action, regardless of the offenses children did or did not commit. Diagnoses were life prognoses.

Under the Nazi regime, the state had the power to act on these hunches as never before. Conference speaker Herbert Francke, a presiding judge of Berlin's regional court, boasted about the Reich's expanded jurisdiction. He held that because "modern criminal law gives the judge much greater discretion than law founded on nineteenth-century liberalism," Nazi judges should "penetrate the personality of the offender" and "distinguish juvenile delinquents who have the makings of future dangerous habitual criminals with scientific certainty." Crimes would be "prevented, either by appropriate educational treatment or by early preventative detention [*Bewahrung*]."[80] Psychiatrists would sniff out and punish pre-crime.

Many child psychiatrists, of course, agreed with preventative detention; conference speakers Anna Leiter, Werner Villinger, and Alois Schmitz had advocated it in their talks too. The idea of preventative detention had entered political debate after World War One, and almost every party from right to left had a stake, as well as prominent figures in the women's movement.[81] In fact, the first draft of a preventative detention law in 1921 was aimed at curbing prostitution. While there was broad support for child internment in principle during the Weimar period, political disagreements and economic crisis by the end of the 1920s hindered passage of a comprehensive law.[82] Preventative detention had been about class and crime, as middle- and upper-class supporters sought to contain an underprivileged set of children who might grow up to be "asocial."

The Nazi regime, however, offered new opportunities for interning problem children. The state had the power to remove them from their parents as never before—and vastly expanded the definition of difficult youths. One of the toughest child welfare administrators in the Reich was conference speaker Walther Hecker, district councilor of Düsseldorf and head of Correctional Education and Youth Welfare in the Rheinland since 1930. He had established the Reich's first youth preventative detention center in the Rheinland in the summer of 1934.[83] A number of Reich regional administrators followed suit, establishing centers in Hannover, Hamburg, Thuringia, Baden, and Berlin.[84] Eventually, in 1939, high-ranking Nazi leader Reinhard Heydrich called for the construction of Juvenile Protection Camps. These were to be as tough as adult concentration camps—even run by the SS— and to contain youths who showed purportedly oppositional, asocial, or criminal behavior. The first camp was for boys aged thirteen to twenty-two, and opened in Moringen in Lower Saxony in 1940, a month before the Vienna conference met; a camp at Uckermark in Brandenburg opened for girls in 1942. The camps held approximately 2,500 youths over the years, and Austria was the top source of referrals.[85]

The Reich's preventative internment initiatives developed ad hoc. Due to bureaucratic infighting and confusion, the regime would not actually codify a uniform child internment law until the spring of 1944.[86] Some officials thought it self-evident that centers should exist within current laws; others regarded them as stopgap measures until the Reich created a coherent policy.

At the Vienna conference, Hecker drew on the latest psychiatric studies to make his case for internment. Although he was a government official, Hecker cited seven different psychiatrists in his talk. "If I am not mistaken, as a layman," he proffered, "The current state of research is almost unanimous that a negative prognosis depends not just on family tree and personality structure, but also the effects of asocial behavior, what Villinger calls the 'overall character.' " Hecker highlighted Villinger's idea of children with "cold *Gemüt*" [the *Gemütskalt*].[87]

Based on these "latest studies" of community spirit, Hecker divided children into four groups of deficiency. He informed the Vienna attendees that the last group was to be locked up: "the asocial who require preventative detention, expecting that born vagabonds will be among them, and those who through their race (Gypsies) or other systemic failings have uncontrollable impulses." Hecker was dead serious; in 1943, he would go out of his way to ensure the deportation from his region of "Gypsies" and even "mixed-blooded Gypsy children" to Auschwitz.[88]

Asperger conveyed Hecker's message. His summary of the meeting highlighted Hecker's "experience as an administrator for the 'restructuring of public alternative education by hereditary predisposition and educational achievement,' " outlining how "the educable, that is those who have a positive worth of performance, must be separated from the ineducable preventative detention cases."[89] Asperger saw how the Vienna meeting enshrined the radical treatment options of Nazi child psychiatry.

IN A BIT of a surprise, the conference concluded with Asperger's work. When Franz Hamburger wrapped up the last talk of the day, he singled out his student by name as an exemplar of what the Third Reich's new methods should look like. Hamburger's final sentences urged the esteemed guests to follow Asperger's model— "Well-run children's centers are able to provide so much good. Other clinics should emulate the kind of care Asperger has established at the Curative Education Department of Vienna Children's Hospital."[90] That was the end of the Vienna meeting: Asperger embodied the Third Reich's new discipline of Nazi child psychiatry.

Paul Schröder bade a warm farewell to the audience, thanking the participants for their "sustained interest throughout the long sessions."[91] He proclaimed the first assembly of the German Society for Child Psychiatry and Curative Education in 1940—with its auspicious turnout of high-ranking personages from child psychiatry, special education, and the Nazi government—a great triumph.

The conference's success outlived the Third Reich. Hermann Stutte, a leading youth psychiatrist after the war, credited his career to the meeting. The talks "were at a remarkably high scholarly level and for me, a novice in the field, the impression it made on me was decisive choosing this profession."[92] Even participants who were critical of the Nazi regime still, decades later, said they valued what one called the "empirical" content of the meeting. A prominent psychiatrist from a later generation, Manfred Müller-Küppers, wrote upon reading the proceedings in 2001 that "the majority of the contributions were irreproachable, and embarrassing ideological tendencies are observable only in some of them."[93]

The German Society for Child Psychiatry and Curative Education would never meet again. While a second conference was scheduled for October 8, 1941, in Würzburg, Schröder died unexpectedly on June 7, 1941.[94] The principal figures in the Reich's T4 adult euthanasia program were to determine Schröder's successor. They had already amassed institutional power for killing adults by directing and funding the organization for adult psychiatry—the Association of German Neurologists and Psychiatrists, headed by Ernst Rüdin. The men now envisaged the German

Society for Child Psychiatry and Curative Education as a vehicle for child euthanasia.

The T4 leaders favored Hans Heinze, the ardent leader in child and adult euthanasia, as Schröder's successor, although Schröder himself had designated Werner Villinger, the cautious T4 euthanasia evaluator, as next in line. The "top experts" in the T4 program corresponded at length about the decision: Werner Heyde, Paul Nitsche, and Herbert Linden (Nitsche and Heyde consecutively headed the T4 program), Viktor Brack, the architect of the euthanasia program, as well as Ernst Rüdin and Hans Reiter.[95] Yet the men never named Schröder's successor and the society dissolved.

Perhaps in the minds of these euthanasia leaders, the direction of Nazi child psychiatry was clear enough. Youths would either be merged or purged. There was no need for another meeting, as there was nothing more to discuss.

6

Asperger and the Killing System

IN LATE 1941, Asperger launched the Vienna Society for Curative Education—which was conceived as a successor organization to the disbanded German Society for Child Psychiatry and Curative Education—along with three of his most murderous colleagues. His cofounders were Max Gundel, head of Vienna's Public Health Office and municipal director of Spiegelgrund, Erwin Jekelius, the medical director of Spiegelgrund, and Franz Hamburger, the director of the University of Vienna Children's Hospital. Jekelius was president of the society, and Asperger was its second vice president.[1]

Together, the four men aimed to synchronize the treatment of children in Vienna, channeling child development efforts under Reich auspices. The new association would coordinate people from different fields—school teachers, special education teachers, child psychiatrists, welfare workers, directors of special institutions, nurses, and medical personnel—through issuing special courses, lectures, and tours of facilities. As Jekelius insisted, child development practitioners "who are directly or indirectly involved with these minors would be unified."[2]

The society may have served a darker mission, too. Given that two founders of the Vienna Society for Curative Education ran Spiegelgrund—Jekelius and Gundel—scholars suspect that the organization may have disseminated the child euthanasia directive behind the scenes, or at least bound the city's children's institutions more closely to Spiegelgrund.[3]

Certainly, Jekelius's inaugural presidential lecture at the society's meeting on December 10, 1941, set a tone that bordered on deadly. He began jovially, emphasizing the importance of curative education and his personal closeness to the society's cofounders, Hamburger and Asperger:

> It is no coincidence that the University Children's Hospital was chosen as the meeting venue for our society. After all, our landlord Professor Hamburger has been practicing curative education vigorously and systematically for decades, quite often as a voice in the wilderness. Although we, his students, have since gone our different ways, this clinic and in particular the Curative Education department remains our spiritual parental home.
>
> On this occasion, I would like to recall the powerful lecture on cura-

education that our Dr. Asperger gave in this very place: —he explained forcefully and convincingly that right now in the Third Reich, with the abundance of new tasks and shortage of labor forces, we should not ignore those "who have been marginalized."[4]

In the same breath as Jekelius praised Hamburger and Asperger, the only men he mentioned by name, Jekelius voiced the idea of life unworthy of life. When talking of the severely disabled, he advised:

> The child does not belong in an educational institution or hospital, but in protection—which, for me personally, means the protection of the national community from these unfortunate creatures.
> False sentimentality is out of place here. We only endanger the work of curative education, which is so important and still so often misunderstood, if we drag along this ballast in our special institutions. It hinders the entire operation without giving even the slightest benefit to the unteachable child.[5]

ASPERGER HAD KNOWN Jekelius a long time. Nearly the same age, they were fellow postdoctoral students under Hamburger, and had worked together for five years at the Curative Education Clinic in the early 1930s, the latter two of which Asperger was Jekelius's boss. Beginning in 1940, they intersected as medical specialists at Vienna's Public Health Office. Jekelius was the Director of Welfare for Mentally Ill, Addicts, and Psychopaths, where he referred people to Hereditary Health Courts for sterilization and advised the committal of patients to sanatoria, including Steinhof, where they might be killed.[6]

By the time Asperger cofounded the Vienna Society with Jekelius, in late 1941, Jekelius was well known in Vienna for his murderous activities. As the director of two euthanasia facilities, he had overseen the deaths of around four thousand adults at Steinhof and one hundred children at Spiegelgrund. At Steinhof, Jekelius was the local "representative of the Chancellery of the Führer" and coordinated the selection and deportation of thousands of adults to the gas chambers of Hartheim Castle in Linz.[7]

The killings had drawn public awareness and outrage from the outset. In October 1940, a crowd gathered in front of Steinhof (which included the Spiegelgrund pavilions) to demonstrate against the euthanasia program, which was dispersed only with the intervention of the police and SS. In another protest, around two hundred relatives of patients who had been killed met at a hotel near

Steinhof to organize a letter writing campaign to Berlin to stop the killings, again broken up by the police. The Communist Party of Graz distributed illicit fliers against euthanasia murders in the fall of 1940.

Viennese widely called Jekelius the "mass murderer of Steinhof."[8] Vienna's state-run newspapers were quick to respond. To improve Steinhof's image, a lengthy, glowing article in the Austrian *People's Newspaper* (*Volkszeitung*) on October 20, 1940, depicted idyllic conditions in its Spiegelgrund pavilions: "The children's bright jubilation emerges from the gardens of the individual wards. Boys and girls romp around cheerfully in the autumn sunshine under the supervision of educators." An interview with the "chief physician" (presumably Jekelius) portrayed the staff as accepting and kindhearted. " 'Our children are children like everyone else,' smiled the director. [. . .] 'With our help, they will soon find their way back into the community!' "[9]

The puff piece was not enough to end the rumors about killings, however. Vienna's main newspaper, the *People's Observer* (*Völkischer Beobachter*), resorted to publishing a direct denial of the murders. According to the article, reports of "*mass executions* in *gas chambers*," as well as of doctors and nurses conducting lethal operations and injections, were simply "silly rumors." Born of "criminality, stupidity, and

197

boastfulness," they were supposedly "invented by criminals and repeated by idiots who sabotage the social structure of the state." The author of the article assured that he had personally toured Steinhof with Max Gundel, where they held "many trembling old hands, whose lasting calluses testify to the consequences of tireless work."[10]

Yet the articles could not suppress public knowledge of the killings. And Jekelius's infamy reached beyond the Reich, as the British Broadcasting Service (BBC) reported on events at Steinhof in the summer of 1941. In September that year, the British Royal Air Force dropped leaflets on Vienna that dubbed Jekelius "the overlord with the syringe." The text warned: "Jekelius haunts the corridors of Steinhof, Vienna's lunatic asylum, in a white doctor's coat with his syringe. He does not bring new life to the ill, but death."[11]

Jekelius was committed to implementing euthanasia as permanent public policy, and he took on roles at the Reich level of the killing system. He helped draft a Reich Euthanasia Law that would specify and legalize conditions for child killing, though it never came to fruition.[12] Jekelius was one of two Reich T4 "experts" in Vienna who reviewed and authorized adult deaths, out of around forty T4 experts in the Nazi state. Jekelius was apparently flexible in his judgments, and welcomed bribes. According to one colleague, "It was an open secret that he took high fees for 'fudged reports' that would save individual patients from deadly deportation."[13]

He freelanced when it came to condemning victims, too. Jekelius scouted for disabled children to bring to Spiegelgrund from other children's institutions, bragging to his colleagues that he had conducted "a whole series of such investigations." But Jekelius's zeal could lead to frictions. His colleagues complained that his scouting expeditions were costly, since Jekelius racked up car costs for 1,107 kilometers of travel.[14]

As Alfred Mauczka, the former head of Steinhof, characterized him, "Dr. Jekelius is a very capable, extremely ambitious man who, however, wants to tackle too much at once, which occasionally puts him at risk for a certain dissipation and volatility." Famed neurologist, psychiatrist, and Holocaust survivor Viktor Frankl described Jekelius in stronger terms: "He was the only man I ever encountered in my whole life whom I would dare to call a Mephistophelean being, a satanic figure."[15]

So active was Jekelius in the Nazi regime that he became engaged to Hitler's sister Paula. She had written to Jekelius to plead for the life of her second cousin, Aloisia Veit, who was a long-term patient at Steinhof. Veit, diagnosed with schizophrenia, faced death in the T4 program.

Jekelius was evidently unpersuaded by Paula Hitler's petition and still sent Veit to the gas chambers at Hartheim. Yet, as Jekelius told Soviet interrogators in July 1948, Paula invited Jekelius to her apartment. "A friendly relationship developed between us," Jekelius recalled, "which in time turned into an intimate relationship." Paula reportedly asked Hitler for permission to marry Jekelius in November 1941, but Hitler was opposed. Jekelius became a high-level concern, as top officials Heinrich Himmler and Reinhard Heydrich discussed arresting Jekelius in their phone conversation November 30, 1941. Jekelius stated that in December 1941, the Gestapo apprehended him during his trip to Berlin and officials pressured him into signing a statement that he was breaking off relations with Paula.[16]

It is unclear why Hitler was against the match; perhaps Hitler did not want his beloved sister to marry a professional murderer. Whatever the case, arrest was an effective way for Hitler to rid himself of an undesirable potential brother-in-law. Jekelius was then to go to Poland on a "special assignment," presumably using his T4 expertise to help establish the first extermination camps in the Final Solution. (The early extermination camps of Belzec, Sobibor, and Treblinka relied heavily on T4 personnel). But Jekelius rejected the assignment, and was put instead into military service in the east.[17]

• • •

THE SECOND MAN with whom Asperger cofounded the Vienna Society for Curative Education was his long-time mentor, Franz Hamburger. If Jekelius was the public face of euthanasia in Vienna, the man who ran the institutions of killing, Hamburger worked behind the scenes to build Vienna's infrastructure of murder. He was Asperger's primary professional associate for fourteen years; virtually everything Asperger published during this time had a byline for Hamburger.[18] Although Asperger cited few scholars in his articles, he routinely extolled and elaborated upon Hamburger's work. It was in Asperger's professional interest to praise his mentor, yet Asperger's deference and reverence appear to have been genuine. Even in the postwar period, decades after Hamburger's death, Asperger credited his philosophy of life to Hamburger. As Asperger reminisced about the Third Reich in 1977:

> Hamburger and I had long and roving conversations about God and the world, particularly issues of guiding and treating people, rambling just as Greek philosophers led their students, knowing that this was precisely the right procedure to release and arrange thoughts, to achieve a rhythm. It all came to clarification and

fruition with investing in youth—in a beautiful community of the German Youth Movement, in the experience of nature, the world, and the spirit.[19]

The stimulating conversations between Asperger and Hamburger during the Nazi period contrasted with the grisly reality of many of the children they treated.

Hamburger, with his clout as director of the University Children's Hospital, became one of the most influential doctors in Vienna during the Third Reich. He moved easily within the polycracy of the regime, connecting its web of medical institutions, governmental bureaucracies, party offices, and pediatric associations. Working at the juncture of traditional medicine and the radical initiatives of National Socialism, Hamburger made himself a power broker in multiple realms. He also had extensive connections to power brokers—including even Reich Department of Health leader Leonardo Conti.

Unlike careerist and hotheaded Jekelius, Hamburger was deliberative, using his influence through shaping institutions, rather than acting as an individual agent. History does not tend to recognize the kind of authority Hamburger wielded. Today few people have heard of him, either as a perpetrator of euthanasia or as a physician. But Hamburger's deeds had lasting effect. Their magnitude only became visible over time. He propagated a radical Nazi racial hygiene agenda through myriad strategies. Hamburger altered existing professional organizations and founded new ones; he published countless articles, gave countless lectures, and organized countless conferences; he launched new programs of biological selection at the Children's Hospital; and he trained a generation of students and staff in Nazi medicine, at least two of whom became prominent in the euthanasia program.[20] Hamburger's story reveals the importance of invisible institutional roles alongside visible perpetrators such as Jekelius.

Espousing both halves of Nazi eugenics, Hamburger advocated helping children who could be rehabilitated for the national community, and eliminating those who could not. He published numerous articles detailing prescriptions for breastfeeding and child rearing, advocating plenty of fresh air, sunlight, and exercise.[21] At the same time, Hamburger wrote about letting children with "poor constitutions" die. He held that "Excessive care of the inferior allows inferior genetic material to circulate" in the *Volk*, and that doctors spent too much time on childhood illnesses. "It would be better to have a birth rate of 30 to 40 percent and a death rate of 10, even 15 percent," he declared, "than a birth rate of 18 to 20 percent and a death rate of only 3 percent." Hamburger even believed in withholding nourishment from premature babies.[22]

Hamburger advocated this double-pronged mission of Nazi racial hygiene long before the Third Reich, and then found in National Socialism a means to promote it. Hamburger's Children's Hospital transferred numerous youths to Spiegelgrund. A sample of 592 medical files of children who perished there showed that the hospital had dispatched forty-four children, or 8 percent of them—many of whom were transferred by Hamburger personally.[23] The real number is likely much higher, as other case files are incomplete, and he would also issue children damning diagnoses who were transferred elsewhere first.

While Asperger effectively worked down the hall, Hamburger also supervised numerous medical experiments on children at the Children's Hospital. One medical student exposed children and infants to extreme temperature changes and measured the effects. Elmar Türk, one of Asperger's associates as a postdoctoral student under Hamburger, used premature infants to study the effect of vitamin D on rickets; knowing that premature babies were particularly susceptible to the condition, Türk withheld prophylaxis, allowing thirteen of the fifteen infants in his control group to develop rickets.[24]

Hamburger took special interest in Türk's lethal

tuberculosis experiments on children. In 1941, Türk selected babies as his test subjects who he considered to be "severely damaged from birth trauma, unviable, and idiotic." He administered a tuberculosis vaccine, Calmette-Guérin (BCG), to two of them, and then infected all three babies with "virulent tuberculosis bacillus." He sent them to Spiegelgrund for observation and, eventually, autopsies. The two vaccinated babies died within a month—not of tuberculosis, but reportedly of pneumonia, the main official cause of death at Spiegelgrund. The unvaccinated child overcame the tuberculosis after a painful four-month ordeal but still died.[25]

Türk repeated his tuberculosis experiment one year later on an "idiotic, syphilitic" three-and-a-half-year-old whom he vaccinated, and a "hydrocephalic-idiotic" one-and-a-half-year-old, Adolf Guttmann, whom he did not. As he transferred little Adolf to Spiegelgrund for observation, Türk sent a macabre so-called "wish list" to the director for the boy's death and postmortem study: "I would request that you inform me in the event of the child's death so that I may be present at the autopsy, as I intend to conduct various histological examinations." While the child still lived, Spiegelgrund staff were to take specialized notes on Adolf's condition and conduct x-rays at regular intervals. Türk added, "I hope you will not be very burdened by this." After Adolf arrived at Spiegelgrund, staff reported that the boy was "quiet and peaceful, laughs occasionally when one strokes him on the cheek."[26] Adolf was killed two and a half months after his arrival.[27]

Hamburger was personally invested in Türk's lethal experiments on children, as Hamburger had devoted much of his own early career to tuberculosis research. He and Türk did not hide their methods but, to the contrary, promoted their work in publications and medical forums. Hamburger even boasted that their use of children was pathbreaking. "The protective effect of BCG, long known for guinea pigs, is only now proven for humans," he proclaimed.[28] And Hamburger was recognized for the success of the human BCG experiments—"the first in the Reich"—even after the war.[29]

Hamburger's postdoctoral student Heribert Goll, with whom Asperger had copublished in 1939, also conducted experiments on babies at the Children's Hospital. Overseen by Hamburger, Goll explained that he selected "only infants unfit to live."[30] For his 1941 publication in the *Munich Medical Weekly*, Goll deprived babies of vitamin A in order to measure the vitamin's effects on the development of keratomalacia, a common source of blindness. The condition dried the cornea and membrane that covers the white of the eye, resulting potentially, over time, in frothy patches called Bitot spots, ulceration, infection, and rupture of the eye. After Goll withheld vitamin A from the infants for months, a number of them did, indeed, develop preliminary keratomalacia. Then, in a second experiment, Goll sought to infect babies with keratomalacia by placing secretions from the eye of one girl with the disease onto the eyes of four healthy children. When the method failed, he tried again by localizing the bacteria, which again failed.

Goll raised the stakes of his research in his 1942 publication for the *Munich Medical Weekly*, depriving twenty babies of fats and vitamin A in periods of up to three hundred days. After the infants died—perhaps forcibly killed, perhaps perishing from their maltreatment— Goll examined their livers from autopsies. Six-month-old Anna Mick was selected for the study; her health had been "robust" despite her hydrocephalus and bed sores on her head. She wasted away on Goll's diet, lying in the Children's Hospital while staff prodded her eyes and body for fluid and tissue samples. In less than four months, Anna died from "increasing feebleness."[31]

Asperger worked in the midst of his colleagues' human experiments at the Children's Hospital and would have known about their deadly methods, which they touted in prominent journals. He walked past babies in his daily life who were injected, infected, and starved.

Indeed, being a Hamburger protégé in Nazi Vienna was no small matter. The Children's Hospital had close institutional and personal ties to Spiegelgrund, and many of Hamburger's advisees besides Jekelius, Türk, and Goll followed Hamburger's lead in lethal work. Due to their complicity in the regime, all of Hamburger's postdoctoral students after 1945 lost their Venia legendi, or authorization to teach at a university (but not Asperger). And nine of eleven Hamburger students lost their positions after 1945 (again, not Asperger). The "Hamburger school" was so decimated and discredited with the end of the Third Reich that it had scant intellectual influence on postwar pediatrics and psychiatry, and it is little known today.[32]

Asperger's decision not to join the Nazi Party exempted him from this discredit, and he was the only Hamburger student to make a name for himself in the postwar period. But Asperger was just as close to Hamburger as the other students, if not closer. Hamburger's son even suggested that Asperger had a favored status with Hamburger, asserting that Asperger was "the student who was closest to my father, and personally the most similar to him."[33]

Asperger—in cofounding the Vienna Society for Curative Education with Franz Hamburger, Erwin Jekelius, and Max Gundel in 1941—was collaborating with three top perpetrators of child killing in Vienna. In order to operate in these spheres, Asperger had to demonstrate initiative and extraordinary reliability. Asperger knew this since, as he admitted later in life, he was fully aware of the euthanasia program.[34] His affiliation with child euthanasia leaders was an active, not a passive, choice.

AT ONE MEETING of the Vienna Society for Curative Education, Asperger publicly urged his colleagues to transfer what he called "difficult cases" of children to Spiegelgrund. He declared before the audience that while promising youths should receive "ambulatory observation" in a ward that recreated a real-life "free situation,"

> For all difficult cases only a prolonged and stationary observation is proper, like those carried out in [my] Curative Education Department of the Children's Hospital or in the reformatory Spiegelgrund.[35]

The recommendation to send "difficult cases" to Spiegelgrund could have been benevolent, suggesting that children would receive good care at his colleague Jekelius's institution. But because Jekelius's activities were widely known, and Asperger, too, knew of the euthanasia program, Asperger's remarks had a specific context and subtext. His audience might well have heard a far different message.

Moreover, Asperger was employing the language of the killing system. At Spiegelgrund, "prolonged and stationary observation" did not suggest active care—treatment, therapy, education, or intervention—but static evaluation. The phrase may sound benign, but it was also a code term in the killing process. "Stationary observation" of a child's educability and value to the *Volk* was a step in the selection process to determine life or death.[36]

Asperger then brought up "eugenic issues" before the Vienna Society, pointing out that "proper assessment" of children was "already a good portion of their 'treatment.' "[37] Again, one could take these words at face value, as advocating careful care of children. But "treatment," or *Behandlung*, was a euphemism that euthanasia personnel used for killing a child.[38] It is curious that Asperger used quotation marks around the word, which suggests he might, indeed, be signaling a veiled meaning for " 'treatment' "—especially on the heels of recommending "prolonged and stationary observation" at Spiegelgrund. After all, the Vienna Society was run by notorious Spiegelgrund leaders, and Jekelius's inaugural address had already set the stage with his reference to children unworthy of care. Given widespread knowledge of the euthanasia program in Vienna, it is likely that many in the audience were aware of the potential consequences of sending "difficult cases" to Spiegelgrund, as well as the regime's desire to eliminate children deemed to be defective.

Whether or not he intended it, Asperger was invoking the specific site, vocabulary, and processes of child euthanasia protocol. And whether or not Asperger intended it, his colleagues at the curative education conference could have deduced that meaning from his words.

THE VIENNA SOCIETY for Curative Education that Asperger had cofounded ceased meeting in March 1942—three months after the Gestapo had apprehended Jekelius—but Asperger's field of curative education continued to be associated with Spiegelgrund. That same month, city administrators designated the Vienna Municipal Youth Welfare Institution at Spiegelgrund an official institution of curative education, renaming it the Vienna Municipal Curative Education Clinic at Spiegelgrund. One 1942 edition of the *People's Observer* [*Völkischer Beobachter*] specifically touted the number of "curative education professionals" working there.[39]

The *People's Observer* also linked curative education to the selection and expulsion of severely disabled children. The newspaper relayed that curative education professionals

211

gave a "convincing impression of responsible scientific work for the *Volk*," as they secured the "prevention of genetically diseased offspring, protection from asocial people." The newspaper hinted at the elimination of children. Spiegelgrund "spared the productive nation of burdens, who—with the rapid rise of the greater Reich—are simply seen as against nature."[40]

The prominence of curative education in Nazi euthanasia was notable, since it had been previously so peripheral to mainstream Viennese psychiatry and psychoanalysis. But it came to the fore in the Third Reich as its emphasis on remediation expanded into selection and elimination. Death became a potential "treatment" option in the toolkit of Nazi eugenics.

Curative education practitioners were relatively small in numbers yet had a disproportionate role in child euthanasia positions. According to one tabulation, five of its seven prominent physicians in Vienna were major perpetrators: Hamburger and Jekelius, as well as Spiegelgrund doctors Marianne Türk, Helene Jockl, and Heinrich Gross. This ratio was far higher than in any of the other, much larger schools of Viennese psychiatry.[41]

Heinrich Gross, one of the most notorious figures, came to work at Spiegelgrund in mid-November 1940 as child killings were gaining momentum. He was barely twenty-six, having graduated from the University of Vienna Medical

School just the year before and worked for a short time at the psychiatric institution Ybbs an der Donau. At Spiegelgrund, Gross served under medical director Jekelius, ten years his senior. Like Jekelius, Gross had been a Nazi enthusiast when the party was still a fringe terrorist organization in Austria; he joined the Hitler Youth in 1932 and the SA in 1933, gaining successive promotions to SA senior squad leader by 1938.

Seven months after Gross came to work at Spiegelgrund, in June 1941, he went to Germany to train for six weeks under curative education proponent Hans Heinze, who taught killing methods to aspiring euthanasia doctors, one of the top three figures in child euthanasia in the entire Reich.

When Gross returned to Vienna after his training with Heinze, the death rate at Spiegelgrund more than tripled, from twenty-two in the first half of 1941 to seventy-two in the second half of the year.[42] Heinze's instruction was apparently so valuable that, six months later, in January 1942, Gross returned to Görden for more. Gross also emulated Heinze in harvesting and preserving victims' brains. Heinze was distributing many hundreds of adult and child brains to German physicians for research as Gross began his collection of children's brains at Spiegelgrund for his own work. Children at Spiegelgrund called Gross, who practiced medicine in military uniform, "the Scythe" or the "Grim Reaper."[43]

The second director of Spiegelgrund, Ernst Illing, also trained with Heinze. Like Heinze, Illing had spent his early career at the University of Leipzig, and Illing then followed Heinze to Görden in 1935. Illing worked under Heinze for seven years, conducting some of the Reich's first child killings. Illing was highly trained, then, when Heinze and Vienna's Public Health Office tapped him, at age thirty-eight, to succeed Jekelius as medical director of Spiegelgrund, where he served from July 1, 1942, until April 1945.[44]

As director of the Curative Education Clinic at the University of Vienna Children's Hospital and cofounder of the Viennese Society for Curative Education, Asperger held important positions in the field and was an advocate of its agenda. He was not, himself, on the list of curative education practitioners who were prominent in euthanasia, but he was trusted in the highest echelons of the killing system, associating with its leaders such as Jekelius, Hamburger, and Gundel. Asperger was not as active in the child euthanasia program as his colleagues in Nazi child psychiatry, but he was in the club.

And child euthanasia came to pervade Vienna's medical community at large, reaching far beyond just curative education, as many doctors acquiesced and even welcomed the measures. Illing described in his October 1945 deposition how Viennese physicians readily ridded their wards of children they deemed disabled. He singled out Hamburger and Asperger's Children's Hospital by name:

> My clinic was always overcrowded since other clinics, the Welfare Clinic, the Children's Hospital Glanzing, and the University Children's Hospital handed over, or wanted to hand over, these hopeless cases—obviously in the belief that euthanasia was legally possible at my clinic due to the aforementioned directive [euthanasia order], while they themselves were not allowed to conduct euthanasia. I am completely confident that the leaders of these institutions were in the know about euthanasia and the aforementioned directives.[45]

ASPERGER HAD PUBLICLY encouraged his colleagues to transfer "difficult cases" of children to Spiegelgrund—and he followed his own recommendation.[46] It is exceedingly difficult to estimate exactly how many children Asperger transferred to Spiegelgrund, or how many of them may have died. Medical histories are available for only 562 of the 789 children killed at Spiegelgrund, and many of those are incomplete. Case files are often thin and fragmentary, with cramped notes written in shorthand or on scraps of paper. Not all physicians or clinic names appear in the transfer records. Extant documents, however, suggest that Asperger had a hand in the transfer of dozens of children to their deaths at Spiegelgrund.

In 1942, Asperger was the "curative education consultant" on a seven-member commission for the city of Vienna that assessed the "educability" of children at Gugging care facility. Austrian scholar Herwig Czech has uncovered that Asperger's panel reviewed the files of 210 children in a single day, slotting them into special schools supposedly appropriate to their level of disability. The commission deemed 35 of the 210 children, 9 girls and 26 boys, "incapable of educational and developmental engagement." These youths were sent to Spiegelgrund, as the written committee instructions required, to be "dispatched for Jekelius Action."

"Jekelius Action" was an instruction to kill. All of the 35 youths transferred by Asperger's commission died. Gugging was a major feeder for Spiegelgrund; of the 136 Gugging children removed to Spiegelgrund during the war, 98 perished, ranging in age from two-and-a-half to sixteen years old. This was a mortality rate of 72 percent, and meant that one in eight children of the 789 known to have died at Spiegelgrund came from Gugging.[47]

Besides working on this city selection commission, Asperger recommended transfers to Spiegelgrund as a medical consultant for the Nazi administration. As he worked for Vienna's Public Health Office, juvenile justice system, youth offices, and the National Socialist People's Welfare Organization (NSV) that ran Vienna's system of children's homes, he had multiple points of contact with Spiegelgrund.[48] If schools, courts, the Hitler Youth, and the NSV required an expert opinion on a child, Asperger conducted an assessment. It appears that Asperger recommended Spiegelgrund on numerous occasions. Again, the exact number of children Asperger slotted for Spiegelgrund is difficult to assess from fragmentary records. But his recommendations are scattered through case histories.[49] And his opinions mattered. When Asperger deemed two boys, Friedrich K. and Karl Sp., "incapable of education," their reform school ordered them to Spiegelgrund on the "earliest possible transfer."[50]

ASIDE FROM RECOMMENDING the transfer of children to Spiegelgrund, Asperger launched children into Vienna's children's institutions with highly unfavorable diagnoses—sending them on potential paths toward Spiegelgrund. As parents and schools came to Asperger for diagnostic evaluations, he had the power to remove children from their families and to shape their medical records. The hazards of entering the system with a negative diagnosis were widely known. Abuse, hunger, and violence were common in Vienna's children's homes, not just in Spiegelgrund, though transfer there was the ultimate threat. Of a sample of 312 cases, about two-thirds of the children who died at Spiegelgrund had been transferred from other institutions.[51] Asperger, for example, diagnosed "inferiority of almost all organs" in one child who wound up at Spiegelgrund.[52] In the Nazi state, such language could be interpreted as a license to kill.

It also mattered where doctors first sent children. Asperger transferred a number of youths to St. Josef's Children's Home in Frischau and Pressbaum Special Children's Home in the Vienna Woods. After Gugging, these were two children's homes that sent the greatest number of children to Spiegelgrund. Pressbaum and St. Josef's housed up to 120 and 70 youths, respectively, and both institutions were for the "feeble-minded and children who are not educable, as well as idiots and the mentally ill."[53]

Several children who Asperger sent to St. Josef's and Pressbaum were eventually transferred to Spiegelgrund and killed. For example, Asperger ordered the institutionalization of Hildegard Landauf, who suffered from epilepsy, at Saint Josef's. From there she was sent to Spiegelgrund's death pavilion number 15 in January 1943, at age sixteen-and-a-half. Hildegard underwent the painful procedure of encephalography on May 4—as one of Spiegelgrund's test subjects—and twelve days later, Spiegelgrund director Ernst Illing recommended to Berlin that she be killed. Hildegard, he told the Reich committee, was "expected to require continuous institutionalization and care, no longer educable, no employment expected." She died the following month. Her mother was able to visit her at Spiegelgrund, but her father, reportedly devoted to Hildegard, was fighting in the war in Latvia.[54]

Another victim was three-year-old Richard Draskovic, who had Down syndrome and a history of diphtheria, whooping cough, bronchitis, and frequent colds. Asperger institutionalized Richard at Pressbaum and he was sent to Spiegelgrund, where his photograph showed a gentle face, a stray lock of blonde hair, and a frame that looked painfully thin. Eight days after his arrival at Spiegelgrund, Jekelius requested permission from Berlin to kill Richard as "incurable."[55] Pneumonia was the boy's ostensible cause of death.

Parents' ability and willingness to care for their children may have been a factor in Asperger's decisions to remove a child from his or her family. When the mother of Berta Foucek went to see Asperger, it was clear she did not want the girl from the start, having attempted several abortions. She found her daughter difficult to care for; Berta was paralyzed on the right side and had epilepsy. When Berta's father died of tuberculosis and Berta's mother found herself a single parent, she brought Berta to Asperger, who authorized her institutionalization at St. Josef's. From there Berta was sent to Spiegelgrund and she died in 1943, reportedly of gastroenteritis and pneumonia.[56]

The case of three-year-old Ulrike Mayerhofer likewise suggests that Asperger may have considered the parents' wishes. Ulrike's mother had taken the girl to several doctors in Vienna who, presumably, did not authorize institutionalization. Upon examination, Asperger noted that Ulrike was "severely autistic, very inaccessible from the outside." It is notable that Asperger used the term "severely autistic," since he would later claim that he had never seen full-fledged autistic psychopathy in girls or women. He was perhaps using "autistic" as an adjective or believed that Ulrike's condition was not due to organic causes. In either case, Asperger determined that "since the child is a heavy burden at home, especially with regard to the healthy siblings, institutional placement is advised." Asperger sent Ulrike to St. Josef's, which transferred her to Spiegelgrund in April 1944. Upon admission, doctor Marianne Türk wrote in Ulrike's file that "the child is extraordinarily thin and weak, does not respond when one addresses her, does not show any reaction to sound stimuli, but it is not certain whether this is due to a lack of hearing or to low mental functioning." Director Illing wrote to Berlin for permission to kill Ulrike a month later, in May. He reported that the girl would not stay in bed, but "constantly stood in the corner," and that "improvement or cure is impossible." Ulrike died a month and a half after Illing's report, with pneumonia the purported cause of death.[57]

ASPERGER'S WARD ALSO sent children directly to Spiegelgrund. Staff recommended at least seven children to Spiegelgrund who did not perish, and at least two who did. Hamburger's Children's Hospital, and Asperger's clinic, were known as a source of referrals.[58]

Of the children who did not die at Spiegelgrund, it is possible that Asperger's clinic still marked some of them for death. Staff transferred youths directly into the hands of Spiegelgrund directors—directly to Erwin Jekelius as he visited Asperger's ward, and directly to Ernst Illing's killing pavilions.[59]

Of the children Asperger recommended for Spiegelgrund, available evidence suggests that at least two died. Both of the girls were severely disabled. Two-and-a-half-year-old Herta Schreiber, the youngest of nine children, had suffered meningitis and diphtheria. Asperger evaluated the toddler and concluded that Herta's "permanent placement at Spiegelgrund is absolutely necessary." His clinic transferred Herta on July 1, 1941, to Pavilion 15, the killing pavilion.

At Spiegelgrund, Herta's photograph showed her crying, her dark hair shaved, and staring straight into the camera. Herta's mother reportedly beseeched doctor Margarethe Hübsch, in tears: "If the child could not be helped, perhaps it would be better if she should die, as she would have nothing in this world anyway, she would be a laughing stock of the others." Hübsch explained that, "as a mother of so many other children, she would not wish that on her, so it would be better if she died."[60] Herta's mother conveyed at least some of her sentiments to Asperger, too, as he noted in his Spiegelgrund transfer order that "when at home, this child must present an unbearable burden to the mother."[61] On August 8, Jekelius sent Herta's records to the Reich Committee in Berlin for authorization to kill the girl. Herta died soon thereafter, two months after Asperger's transfer. Pneumonia was Herta's official cause of death.[62]

Five-year-old Elisabeth Schreiber also died after Asperger recommended her transfer to Spiegelgrund. Elisabeth's mother said that a head cold in the girl's second year of life had left Elisabeth unable to talk and with "motor unrest." The family lived in a small apartment with five children and was purportedly unable to care for her anymore. Asperger and the District

Youth Office advised that Elisabeth be sent to Spiegelgrund.[63] The girl went temporarily to St. Josef's Children's Home, where Spiegelgrund doctor Heinrich Gross picked her file on one of his "selection trips." Elisabeth arrived by group transport at Spiegelgrund on March 23, 1942. She looked calm in her photograph, with close-cropped hair and bangs matted in a crooked line on her forehead.[64]

At Spiegelgrund, Elisabeth was eager for connection. One nurse wrote in a daily report that the girl could only speak a single word, "mama," but tried to communicate with other vocalizations and sign language. Elisabeth had "a friendly nature, very affectionate and flattering with caregivers." She was "very sensitive and moved easily to tears and, if treated strictly, cries and hugs the nurse." Yet the girl was embracing her killers. Her caregivers gave hugs, it seems, alongside lethal doses of barbiturates. Gross had reported Elisabeth to the Reich Committee in Berlin for killing, diagnosing her with "congenital feeble-mindedness of the highest order." Elisabeth was subjected to multiple lumbar punctures, likely a subject of Spiegelgrund's medical experiments. She then died quickly. Her physical restlessness abated and, on September 13, her chart stated she "slept the entire day, waking only for meals." She was diagnosed with pneumonia on September 29 and died the next day. Her brain was harvested, jarred, and kept in Dr. Gross's collection of over four hundred children's brains in Spiegelgrund's cellar.[65]

In all, Asperger appears to have been involved in the transfer of at least forty-four children to Spiegelgrund—at least nine youths from his clinic, two of whom died, and thirty-five youths that his city commission marked for "Jekelius Action" and died. Given that he served as a consultant to numerous city offices, and that the records are incomplete, the total number of children Asperger recommended for Spiegelgrund is likely higher.

These youths were not simply statistics, however, nor an abstract set of symptoms. Asperger personally examined many of them, touching their bodies and talking to them face-to-face. How he and his staff judged the children—and decided their fates—was a formidable and perilous process.

7

Girls and Boys

CHRISTINE BERKA WAS referred to Asperger's clinic for purportedly antisocial behavior. Almost fourteen, with chin-length straight brown hair and brown eyes, she was from Vienna but, like many other children in the Third Reich, had been evacuated out of the city to a camp to escape the Allied bombing. She was also escaping a terrible relationship with her stepmother, who was all too happy to be rid of the girl.[1]

The director of the camp in Lower Austria, Karoline Reichart, had expelled Christine in May 1942. She described Christine as an outcast. Christine was "constantly a loner and pensive," failing to form social relationships. Reichart said that "no one wanted to befriend her" or to share a room, and that Christine was "vindictive to her comrades!"[2] Another problem, the director stated, was that Christine stole from the other girls. She "always washed with others' soaps without asking, and also put on others' clothes even if her comrades refused." Christine pilfered, among other things, a spool of green thread from Gretl Eder (discovered in Christine's laundry), a spool of white thread from Hilde Capek (discovered under Christine's sofa), and a pencil sharpener from Lilli Pichler (discovered in Christine's bedding). Poignantly, Christine had stolen the nicest items—soap, lace, and a book—to send to her stepmother who rejected her.[3]

Reichert made Christine itemize her crimes in front of the other girls, which "cost half a day!" Christine's stepmother had to come to the camp for interrogation. In front of twenty-nine people, the stepmother denounced Christine's "entire behavior." With the family disgraced, Reichart gloated, "It is now unpleasant for the parents."[4] She reported Christine to the District Welfare Office, which then referred her to Asperger's Curative Education Clinic for evaluation.

Asperger's department judged Christine even more harshly. Handwritten notes from one observation called her "reckless, thieving," with "poor moral conduct." The girl did "not comply," and did not "look and listen." With her "closed, inhibited" personality, Christine was "hard to reach" and "never cared for the other children."[5]

Fragments in Christine's file, however, suggest she did feel emotional attachment. She drew an inviting picture for the clinic—of blue cornflowers in different states of bloom growing next to red tulips, with two yellow butterflies tending each. The bright cornflowers grew from the ground, their three stems extended out, while the twin tulips grew in a red polka-dotted pot.[6] Christine also had a warm vision of her future. When writing down her future employment goals, Christine, wistfully earnest, wanted to connect with other people and places:

> First, I want to do the compulsory labor year with farmers. After the compulsory year I want to take a course in stenography and a course in typewriting and go into an office. Most of all I want to be with farmers, in a household or in the field. Or with small children. I like playing with them and to care for them and go walking and lay them down after lunch. In the household I can help with cooking, cleaning, shopping and small things like that. That is my wish. Or a gym teacher. I enjoy sports. Especially equipment and ball sports. I don't like school especially. I like assignments. Also writing and shorthand are my favorite subjects.[7]

These words suggest a girl full of life, with active interests in community, school, work, domesticity, and sports. Considering Christine's bitter relationship with her stepmother, it is perhaps most touching that she wanted to take care of children in a happy household.

In his publications, Asperger advocated

qualitative assessments as part of respecting every child as "a unique, unrepeatable, indivisible entity" and cherishing "the innermost essence of the personality." Caregivers in his clinic, he said, were open-minded and appreciated the nuances of children's play. A newspaper article about Asperger's clinic in the *Small People's Journal* (*Das Kleine Volksblatt*) on September 11, 1940, spotlighted the importance of stimulating children's imaginations, with "large dolls, even matadors for boys, a whole library of fairytales and children's books" overflowing in the ward's "beautiful, giant bright rooms with grand windows."[8]

Given this rhetoric, Christine's drawings and writings should have factored into Asperger's diagnosis of Christine.[9] Yet Asperger decided on July 14, 1942, that Christine had a "far-reaching antisocial character." He said she was "difficult to influence from the outside," and had "little warm feeling in nature." Asperger deemed Christine "hateful in many situations, vulgar and rude."[10] He did not believe she was struggling with emotional or mental challenges: it was her personality. Asperger wrote in his large, rough handwriting (though born left-handed, he was taught to write right-handed) that Christine's official diagnosis was not a psychiatric condition, but a "character variant." She was "egocentric, vulgar, oppositional, and underhanded."[11]

After seven weeks of evaluation, Asperger

called for Christine's transfer to a correctional institution. She posed a "significant criminal threat" and, Asperger noted, Christine's stepmother "refuses her."[12] His clinic transferred the girl to Theresienfeld reformatory. Then, when Theresienfeld sought to send Christine home ten months later, in May 1943, Asperger's clinic rejected the request for release out of hand. Without considering another period of observation, the ward explained that "We know the girl quite well from long observation in the clinic and are not to assume that her character has substantially changed in the short time since she left."[13]

Clinic reports not only fail to represent Christine—the child who drew cheerful flowers and wrote of her hopes for the future—they render her indistinguishable from other children Asperger described. Christine had entered the Curative Education department as an individual, because of individual circumstances and individual interactions with her particular camp director and stepmother. But Christine left Asperger's clinic as a generic type, as "egocentric" and "antisocial," just like any number of children judged by the institutions of Nazi psychiatry. Christine was dehumanized before she was institutionalized.

The notes of Asperger's Curative Education department concluded that Christine lacked emotional or spiritual connections to others. She had "no *Gemüt*."[14]

● ● ●

ASPERGER'S DEFINITION OF autistic psychopathy emerged not just from the theories of Nazi psychiatry, but also from its clinical practices, through his encounters with the children he treated.

The medical histories of two boys, Fritz V. and Harro L., make for a stark contrast with those of two girls, Elfriede Grohmann and Margarete Schaffer. Asperger featured Fritz and Harro in his 1944 postdoctoral thesis as exemplars of autistic psychopathy; the two girls, Elfriede and Margarete, were not granted the diagnosis. Yet since the girls' unpublished files bear striking similarities to Asperger's published descriptions of Fritz and Harro, their medical histories shed light on how Asperger approached the diagnosis through his practice. Furthermore, since Asperger's clinic sent both girls to Spiegelgrund, their cases also exhibit the factors he and his staff used to send children there.

Margarete and Elfriede's archival files are rich in detail but fragmentary. Since handwritten observations and typed notes often lacked signatures, it is difficult to attribute opinions and decisions to specific individuals, or even to Asperger himself—given that he served as a doctor in an infantry division in Croatia in 1944 and 1945, and the clinic was bombed in 1944. Moreover, although the voices of Elfriede,

Margarete, Fritz, and Harro come through in snippets of writings and drawings, most of what we know about them is in the words of psychiatrists and nurses, whose accounts even of basic factual information—the children's physical descriptions, family backgrounds, and quotations—must be read with a critical eye, as they are highly colored by the assumptions and prejudices of the time.

According to her file, Elfriede Grohmann came to Asperger's clinic when she was thirteen, in April 1944. She was from Neunkirchen, a town of twelve thousand in Lower Austria along the Schwarza River, about forty miles from Vienna. Her mother, Katharina Grohmann, was unmarried when she had Elfriede. She allegedly left Elfriede's father, Karl Postl, because he was "a stubborn, domineering, and quarrelsome man" as well as "an avid card player." As Katharina Grohmann struggled to earn a living as a single mother, she gave Elfriede to the care of her grandparents until the girl was eight years old. There, according to her mother, Elfriede became spoiled, "similar in character" to her father.[15] In 1938, Katharina Grohmann married Bruno Tintra, an upstanding Nazi Party member who worked in health insurance. The couple took Elfriede back from her grandparents and had two daughters of their own.[16]

Katharina Grohmann said Elfriede was "a

nervous, easily excitable child." The mother had experienced "mental excitations" during her pregnancy, but Elfriede's birth and developmental milestones were normal. While no hereditary diseases had been reported in the Grohmann family, Elfriede had suffered a number of illnesses: measles, diphtheria, chicken pox, and rheumatoid arthritis.[17]

Elfriede was reportedly very calm when she arrived at Asperger's ward, asking only, "When am I coming home; yes I am only staying here a few days."[18] The ward would keep her for seven weeks, however, under close scrutiny. The photograph of Elfriede in Asperger's clinic file showed her with light brown eyes, soft features, and thick medium blonde hair pulled back with a twist. Handwritten notes described Elfriede as tall for her age, 5′ 6″, with a slightly bent nose, an asymmetrical oval face, and narrow-set eyes, and a large mouth. Department notes depicted her body as well toned and well proportioned, but her skin was a "yellowish color, moist," as she purportedly sweated heavily.[19]

The Office for People's Welfare in Neunkirchen had referred Elfriede to Asperger's clinic in April 1944 for inappropriate behavior at home and in her community. Youth services reported that Elfriede said "entirely confusing things and gives the impression of an abnormal person."[20] She had begun to "run away and escape at every opportunity" without "any discernible external cause." The girl would be "inadequately clothed" and stay out several nights at a time.[21] Although the Youth Office speculated that Elfriede might have been jealous of her two- and four-year-old siblings, Asperger's clinic did not give credence to Elfriede's complaints about her family. Staff said that her answers were "obviously designed," and she gave "quite insufficient reasons" for disliking her position in the family. Rather, the Curative Education department suggested that Elfriede's running away from home might be related to the onset of menstruation.[22]

Thirteen-year-old Margarete Schaffer, like Elfriede, was reportedly raised with a working-class background and in "unfavorable domestic conditions." Her father, Franz Schaffer, was a tinsmith's assistant and known as a "drinker" and ne'er-do-well.[23] He had been repeatedly convicted of theft and was serving a two-year prison sentence. Margarete's mother, Marie Schaffer, was considered "hereditarily tainted," having biological defects of mind or body.[24]

The commissioner of Vienna's twenty-second district sent Margarete for psychiatric evaluation in August 1941 for delinquency, inappropriate behavior, and straying from home. The precipitating event was her abortive apprenticeship with a tailor. On Margarete's first day, she was said to have lollygagged on an errand and bought over

70 reichsmarks of flowers and paper goods on her boss's credit. She did not show up to work her second day. Margarete also allegedly tried to borrow money from others, and traded items she stole from her family, including her father's bicycle.[25]

Moreover, Margarete was said to have "impossible conduct at home." She would be "especially cheeky with her mother, incite her siblings against her, and be very unwilling to help with the household."[26] According to the district commissioner, "If the mother then talks to her, she just jumps out of the window (apartment is at ground level) and runs away, suddenly disappears, and simply stays out for half a day." The report stressed that this behavior occurred at intervals of fourteen days to three weeks, whereupon Margarete would then be "good again for a time." As with Elfriede, Margarete's behavior was attributed to menstruation. Even though Margarete had not yet begun menstruating, the commissioner conjectured, "there may be a connection" with the girl's "apparently intermittent disturbances."[27]

Elfriede and Margarete, like Christine, were referred to Asperger's clinic for aberrant behavior at home and in their communities. They had rocky relationships in their families, particularly with their mothers, and reportedly did not integrate into the society and social norms around them.

While Elfriede and Margarete also apparently had trouble in school, this was hardly of any concern. The Neunkirchen welfare office simply said that Elfriede had been reprimanded for "completely erratic acts" at school, yet did not deem her life there worth further discussion. The district commissioner likewise stated that Margarete had left school at the age of thirteen, without amplification.[28] Those were the only mentions of school in Elfriede and Margarete's files.

By contrast, the two boys Asperger would feature in his 1944 autism treatise, Fritz V. and Harro L., were referred by their schools—although both boys were much younger than Margarete and Elfriede, and it would seem that less was at stake. But in the heavily gendered expectations of boys' and girls' behavior in the Third Reich, what mattered was girls' competence in private life, in domestic duties and personal relationships—and boys' competence in public life, in discipline, achievement, and peer integration.[29]

Asperger wrote that Fritz had a normal birth in 1933, hit normal childhood milestones, and did not suffer any illnesses or health problems. But Fritz was expelled from kindergarten "after only a few days." Teachers reported that he "attacked other children, walked nonchalantly about in class and tried to demolish the coat racks." It was said he could "not align with any children's community." Fritz was "always alone" and "never tolerated nor engaged with other children."[30] So Fritz's school reported the boy for observation, and he came to Asperger's clinic in the fall of 1939.

Fritz's difficult behavior at home was treated as almost incidental. Asperger did relate that Fritz "never did what he was told." He did "just what he wanted to, or the opposite of what he was told." He wouldn't sit still, "always restless and fidgety." Worse, Fritz "tended to grab everything within reach" and "had a pronounced destructive urge, anything that got into his hands was soon torn or broken." Fritz had a brother two years younger who was "also somewhat mischievous and difficult, but not nearly as deviant as Fritz."[31] Despite Fritz's long-standing challenges at home, however, it was school behavior that counted most.

Harro's school, too, reported him for problems with obedience and social integration. The eight-and-a-half year old was an only child with "unremarkable" and "perfectly ordinary" development. Since his father had wanted to provide him the best education, the boy had been doing a twenty-five-kilometer train commute between his village and Vienna by himself every day since he was seven, demonstrating responsible behavior.[32]

But problems were mounting in the classroom.

Harro purportedly "did not do what he was supposed to do," rather "exactly what he wanted to." In lessons he "answered back and with such cheek that the teacher had given up asking him so as not to lose face in front of the class." Harro had failed second grade and, while repeating it, continued to fail all of his subjects. Harro's teachers also said "little things drove him to a senseless fury" and that he had a "savage tendency to fight."[33]

With Fritz and Harro his primary examples of autistic psychopathy, Asperger imputed "sadistic traits" to autistic children. He declared that " 'autistic acts of malice' " were, in fact, characteristic of the disorder, stressing the "primitive spitefulness" and "negativism and seemingly calculated naughtiness of autistic children."[34] He stated that their "delight in malice, which is rarely absent, provides almost the only occasion when the lost glance of these children appears to light up."[35]

Fritz, Asperger insisted, would get "a wicked glimmer" in his eyes and perpetrate "always the worst, most embarrassing, most dangerous thing." The boy "appeared almost to enjoy people being angry with him" as a "pleasurable sensation which he tried to provoke by negativism and disobedience."[36] Asperger admitted that it was "not quite true" that the boy's "relations to people" were "only in a negative sense, in mischief and aggression." Asperger allowed that "on rare occasions," Fritz would "reciprocate" emotions. He "would declare that he loved his teacher on the ward," and "now and then he hugged a nurse." Reports of loving, hugging, and reciprocating would suggest that Fritz had greater depth of feeling than Asperger attributed to him. But Asperger dismissed the boy's expressions of attachment. Fritz's embraces did "not seem like an expression of a genuine feeling of affection, but very abrupt, 'like a seizure.'" Asperger even had distaste for Fritz's hugs, which did "not have a pleasing effect."[37]

Asperger described the "malicious behaviour" of autistic children as targeted against the community at large, with no greater purpose than self-gratification. He said Harro "attacked other children, gnashing his teeth and hitting out blindly."[38] Asperger characterized the two other boys he featured in shorter case studies in his treatise in similar ways. Ernst K., who Asperger thought more impaired than Fritz and Harro, was "quite a spiteful boy," a "trouble-maker" who "acted like a red rag to his class," "hit or verbally abused other children," and would "pinch or tickle" them or "stab them with his pen."[39] Hellmuth L., a boy who Asperger deemed severely disabled, "was always 'in another world'" and did "a lot of malicious things," such as "hiding or destroying objects, especially when he was little." Asperger warned that, with autistic children in general, "Water supplies in the house are particularly popular targets for mischief [. . .] but equally popular is throwing things out of windows." Autistic malice, Asperger concluded, came down to a lack of emotional connectedness: "Their malice and cruelty too clearly arise from a poverty of *Gemüt*" [*Gemütsarmut*].[40]

CLASS SEEMS TO have played a role in how Asperger's clinic treated the children. In the cases of working-class Margarete and Elfriede, their files do not contain records of clinic staff either talking to their parents or gathering detailed information on their backgrounds. The girls' histories were taken primarily from second-hand reports by the officials who referred them to Asperger's clinic. The perspectives of the girls' mothers is represented superficially, while those of the fathers are absent entirely. Perhaps detailed family histories were less important or assumed for poorer families who did not meet two-parent bourgeois norms.[41]

On the other hand, Asperger appears to have talked to Fritz and Harro's parents at great length. He portrayed them as higher class, intelligent, and respectable—as well as dedicated, knowledgeable caregivers. Asperger was impressed that Fritz's mother supposedly came from a family of "mostly intellectuals" at the "upper echelons of society."

Many of her relatives fit "the mad-genius mould" and "wrote poetry 'quite beautifully.' " She even "stemmed from the family of one of the greatest Austrian poets." Fritz's mother said the boy "strongly resembled" his grandfather, who was "an exceptionally difficult child and now rather resembled the caricature of a scholar, preoccupied with his own thoughts and out of touch with the real world." Asperger allowed that Fritz's father came from an "ordinary farming family," but added that he had risen greatly in status to be a "high-ranking civil servant."[42]

References to class and intellectual pedigree infused Asperger's physical description of Fritz. Asperger said Fritz's face "showed fine and aristocratic features, prematurely differentiated," as his "baby features had long since gone." Asperger projected this stature onto children with autistic psychopathy in general: they were of "almost aristocratic appearance," and "early thoughtfulness has formed their faces." He generalized, "Autistic children lose their baby features very quickly" and, like Fritz, were "highly differentiated, finely boned."[43]

Asperger was similarly impressed with Harro's lineage. After conducting a detailed interview with Harro's father, as he had with Fritz's parents, Asperger confirmed that although Harro's father "comes from peasant stock, [he] is a typical intellectual." A painter and sculptor in Siebenburgen, Transylvania, he fled the Romanian army into Austria through Russia during World War One. He had eked out a living the past two decades, now making brooms and brushes. Asperger conjectured that Harro's father must have stood out in his village as "highly eccentric." He told Asperger that he, his wife, and many of their relatives were "very nervous people."[44]

Asperger's definition of autistic psychopathy reflected his admiration of Fritz's and Harro's family backgrounds. He asserted, as in Fritz's case, "Many of the fathers of our autistic children occupy high positions." As in Harro's case, "if one happens to find a manual worker among them, then it is probably someone who has missed his vocation."[45]

To Asperger, autistic psychopathy might, in fact, be a result of higher-class breeding. He held, "In many cases the ancestors of these children have been intellectuals for several generations," and are even from "important artistic and scholarly families." In autistic youths, Asperger claimed, "sometimes it seems as if of [their ancestors'] former grandeur only the eccentricity remains."[46] Given these descriptions, one wonders if what was called "eccentricity" in an upper-class child might be deemed a character failing or mental illness in working-class children such as Elfriede or Margarete.

ASPERGER'S CLINIC CHARACTERIZED Margarete, Elfriede, Fritz, and Harro in almost identical terms. Although Asperger emphasized the importance of respecting each child's uniqueness, writing on the first page of his 1944 thesis that every child was "a unique, unrepeatable, indivisible being ('in-dividuum'), therefore ultimately incomparable with others," clinic staff defined the children with a shared laundry list of problems: blank expressions, avoidance of other children, and impulsive behavior.[47] In their medical histories, Margarete, Elfriede, Fritz, and Harro become mere names attached to generic traits.

According to Asperger's clinic, Margarete did "not participate at all in the community of children." She did not join in conversations, did "not laugh," and did not "swing" with the group.[48] Elfriede also misread social cues, maintained Asperger's staff physician Dr. Rohracher. The girl would "assess the situation, the behavior of others, and also her own person completely wrong." Elfriede was unaware of the effect of her behavior on others; she might overreact to trivial matters or "laugh for no apparent reason." The clinic's official report concluded that her "entire behavior is never correctly adjusted." Two different handwritten notes were even more blunt: Elfriede "was always peculiar" and a "very abnormal being."[49]

Asperger described Fritz and Harro in comparable terms as the girls. In Fritz, Asperger said, "Appropriate reactions to people, things and situations were largely absent." The boy did "not have the right emotional relationships with anyone"; Fritz "wandered around alienated" and "it was impossible to get him to play in a group." He "did not appear to take notice of his environment." His eye gaze was "odd," and "mostly, if he didn't have a wicked glimmer in it, it went into space." Fritz simply "fell out of the community."[50]

Harro, too, "never became warm, trusting or cheerful," according to Asperger. He "never" would "join in a game with others." Rather, his "lost gaze was often far away." The boy "remained a stranger," failing to "form any close relationships, either with another child in the ward or with an adult."[51] Asperger likewise described the two other boys in his case studies in sweeping ways. Ernst "always stuck out from the group" and "remained a stranger, walking between the other children without ever properly taking part in their games." Hellmuth "did not have any genuine human relationships," and "did not really fit into this world."[52]

Asperger's clinic reports not only generalized about the children's ways of relating—to the point where their descriptions are interchangeable—they also generalized about the youths' disobedience. Asperger held that Fritz, for example, "did not know the meaning of respect and was utterly indifferent to the authority of adults." Fritz "talked without shyness even to strangers" and used only the informal form of address, *Du*, instead of the formal *Sie*. He "did not care if people were sad or upset about him."[53] As for Harro, Asperger said he "could be shamelessly recalcitrant when disciplinary requests were made." Even if Harro was "temporarily impressed by the teacher's authority," he "would at least grumble to himself." Harro also called undue attention to himself; "said to be an inveterate 'liar,'" he "told long, fantastic stories, his confabulations becoming ever more strange and incoherent."[54]

The staff in Asperger's department described Elfriede and Margarete in the same terms. Elfriede acted without thinking, without "critical consideration." She had "a naughty, erratic way and gives into this urge without regard to the disciplinary situation after." Margarete, too, could "not be influenced from any side." She was "prone to exaggerated reactions of protest" and "often abusively cheeky with the teachers." Asperger's staff said that both girls made up stories. Elfriede would "narrate impossible incidents," and Margarete told "boastful and fantastically elaborated lies."[55]

Clinic personnel depicted the four children as similarly impetuous. Fritz "gave full rein to his own internally generated impulses" which, Asperger believed, were "unrelated to outside stimuli." Fritz would "suddenly start to beat rhythmically on his thighs, bang loudly on the table, hit the wall, hit another person or jump around the room." Harro acted "without considering the consequences." He even "left his desk during lessons and crawled on the floor on all fours."[56] Clinic reports said Elfriede also had "quite unpredictable, impulsive, completely unmotivated actions." She would "create a lot of unrest and commotion," and "jump suddenly up from the table, fetch something, etc."[57] Asperger and his colleague Dr. Luckesi portrayed Margarete as "volatile and erratic. Totally unconcerned, uncritical and unreliable."[58]

Lacking bodily control, the children were reportedly oversexed. Asperger disapproved of how Harro's "wayward, reckless activity" led to "wicked sexual shenanigans with other boys." These supposedly "came to homosexual acts, coitus attempts!" Fritz, at six, was too young for such things. But Asperger said that "in many cases" of autistic psychopathy, masturbation "appears early, is practised intensively and obstinately." The youths "may masturbate in public, exhibitionistically, and they cannot be made to desist"—"since any feelings of shame or guilt are largely absent."[59] The Curative Education Clinic also considered Elfriede and Margarete to be oversexed. According to a handwritten observation, Elfriede demonstrated "arousal in the society of boys," whom she "hunts with flashing eyes, red-faced." Margarete was referred for psychiatric observation because she was allegedly out on the streets at night with "several male acquaintances."[60]

DESPITE THE SIMILARITIES in the clinic's generic descriptions of Elfriede, Margarete, Fritz, and Harro, the children's individuality emerges between the lines of their medical histories. Scraps in Elfriede's file depict a girl who hardly resembles the clinic's summary reports of her as socially disconnected and out of control. Rather, we see a thoughtful child with a number of emotional attachments. For example, one note observed that Elfriede "writes little letters all day long" to people in her life, which suggests that she felt a number of bonds. Elfriede wrote so many letters that another note suggested she had "graphomania."[61]

Elfriede's capacity for affection is palpable in a letter she wrote to her mother: "Dear Mommy! How are you? Are the two pests already in kinder-garten? I hope I can come back to you soon!" Elfriede also wrote to Viktorine Zak, Asperger's head nurse. Elfriede appears to have given Zak a present of food and, addressing her in intimate terms, wrote "Dear head nurse! Many greetings from your girl. And if you do not eat this then I do not speak a word with you and am very angry. It should bring you joy."[62]

However, Elfriede's outreaches were apparently not always welcome on the ward. Another handwritten note, perhaps in Zak's handwriting, disdained Elfriede's attachment, remarking that "her affection for me is a strained, unnatural thing."[63] Beyond the staff's harsh opinions of Elfriede, there are hints of her mistreatment. As she wrote in a plaintive letter to Dr. Aulehner:

> If I do not come home soon then I will die even earlier of sadness. For what Nurse Künk is doing to me is already not nice any more. And I have done nothing to her. I can't sleep a single hour all night long because the Nurse Künk is so ghastly to me.[64]

Most fateful, perhaps, was Elfriede's clash with a clinic nurse the day before the head doctor's examination. Children on the ward wanted to look their very best for the exam, according to a handwritten report. They were right to, given how deadly a doctor's judgment would be. To make a better impression, Elfriede asked a staff nurse to cut off her long braids. The nurse complained that, after her repeated refusal, Elfriede "suddenly came out of the bathroom with her braids cut off" and "ran around excitedly, like a lunatic, hid from me."[65] One wonders how this incident affected the nurse's report, how the evaluating doctor saw Elfriede, and how her hair looked for the appointment that likely decided her fate.

Asperger's clinic did not give Elfriede a psychiatric diagnosis. Elfriede's troublesome traits, as Margarete and Christine's, were attributed to menstruation. Because Elfriede's problems, especially running away, had "become especially conspicuous since menarche," the presiding Dr. Rohracher decided on "a prolonged medical observation right now in the time of puberty." Not only was "complete supervision of the girl absolutely necessary," Elfriede might eventually require "hormone therapy."[66]

Following the terms of Nazi psychiatry, Rohracher also deemed Elfriede ineducable. She warned, "The girl represents a significant burden on educators" and was simply not up to "educational requirements." Though Elfriede's file says nothing of her intelligence, Rohracher felt that schooling would be wasted on her. The doctor did "not consider it advisable to place her in an educational institution."[67] A diagnosis of ineducable suggested she would be a drain on the national community, moving a child from the path of remediation to elimination. And indeed, a mere seven weeks after her arrival, Rohracher would sign Elfriede's transfer from Asperger's clinic to Spiegelgrund—specifying "Dr. Illing's department," the man in charge of the murders.[68]

Elfriede felt foreboding while in Asperger's clinic. She was deeply fearful about where his ward might send her. As Elfriede wrote to her uncle Ferdinand, "I'll tell you only one thing we will not see each other again. And this is the very last letter you will receive from me I'm very sorry." Elfriede also wrote a farewell letter to her mother, warning that this was "perhaps even the very last mail since I not know if we will see each other again. Because I can't know if I won't die in this trip."[69] Given that both letters are still in Elfriede's file, Asperger's clinic likely never sent them to her loved ones before it transferred Elfriede to Spiegelgrund.

Margarete had an even more harrowing ordeal than Elfriede. Authorities took Margarete from her home and institutionalized her three times between 1941 and 1944 for misbehavior—including two stays at Asperger's clinic and two stays at Spiegelgrund. Margarete first came to the Curative Education department on August 23, 1941, and stayed four weeks for observation. As Asperger and his colleague Luckesi put it, "The mother, who also still has three small children, can not supervise the girl enough, despite her best intentions, because she escapes over and over again and gets up to all sorts of mischief." While Margarete's district commissioner had referred her for unruliness, Asperger's clinic wound up labeling her with a more fundamental character failing. A handwritten note summarized that Margarete was "in danger of waywardness (deceit, abnormal embarrassing acts, and staying out for hours)."[70]

Asperger's clinic seems to have positioned Margarete for transfer to Spiegelgrund. Erwin Jekelius, head of Spiegelgrund at the time, visited Asperger's clinic on September 19, 1941, as he scouted Vienna's clinics for youths he could send to Spiegelgrund. According to clinic notes in Asperger's ward, Margarete was "introduced" to Jekelius, suggesting she may have been pre-selected. She was transferred to Spiegelgrund the same day.[71]

Thus began Margarete's bewildering rounds of institutionalizations, transfers, and discharges. At Spiegelgrund, doctors Margarethe Hübsch and Helene Jockl, who were involved in the killing of hundreds of children, diagnosed Margarete with "schizophrenia with manic-depressive phases." They said her "facial expression is remarkably empty, even in seemingly animated conversation." She would "laugh without reason," wearing a "light grimace" that was "stiff and mannered."[72] Hübsch and Jockl decided the girl was "mentally ill and requires permanent stay in a mental institution" due to her "educational difficulties, moral endangerment."[73] In May 1942, Hübsch and Jockl requested Margarete's transfer to Steinhof, Vienna's institution overseeing adult euthanasia. They also suggested that "sterilization is appropriate." Margarete was at Steinhof until October 7, 1942, and then discharged home for unclear reasons.[74] Margarete had survived Vienna's two deadliest institutions: Spiegelgrund and Steinhof.

A month later, in November 1942, police picked Margarete up at 9:30 p.m. "near the East train station, where she was hanging around with soldiers." Although fifteen-year-old Margarete now had a respectable job as an unskilled worker at the firm Kletzer, she reportedly "hung around the streets until the wee hours," and stole from her mother to give a man she knew cigarettes. Margarete was also said to still be "cheeky with her mother and did not obey her at all." Otto Pötzl's famed psychiatric clinic evaluated Margarete on December 10, 1942. It found that Margarete "faces serious moral endangerment and difficulty in the workplace." Pötzl's clinic doubted that Margarete was "capable of work at all," and recommended her "earliest transfer to Pav. 17 (Dr. Illing)" at Spiegelgrund, a lethal prescription.[75]

Margarete went back to Spiegelgrund on January 13, 1943, where director Illing assessed

Margarete positively. While he did find her "very impulsive" and "very restless and distracted," Illing reversed the previous diagnosis of fellow Spiegelgrund doctors Hübsch and Jockl, stating: "There is no evidence of a mental illness (schizophrenia, manic depressive illness, etc.)." He even chided his colleagues that "the medical history entries from then did not prove schizophrenia." Illing felt Margarete could be "returned to her parents on a trial basis." She was "tentatively educable."[76] So Margarete was released home again.

As Margarete would still allegedly "escape her home and wander around," she was sent back to Asperger's clinic for a second time. From April 18, 1944, to May 30, 1944, Margarete would have overlapped almost exactly with Elfriede. A nurse took Margarete to bathe soon after she was admitted. Apparently upset, Margarete confided the horrors of her numerous institutionalizations. As the nurse relayed in a handwritten note, "Immediately upon entering the bathroom she was very talkative." Margarete spoke "a lot about her life" to the nurse. "She was imprisoned and does not like to remember the time in the cell. After her punishment she was in an institution where she had to work hard." The nurse seemed annoyed to hear about Margarete's misfortunes: "In questioning about her crimes, she reports a lot of trivialities in detail, but not the essentials.

It puts the listener's patience to the test. One is happy when she is finished." The nurse also noted Margarete's body "was not particularly dirty, but she had very many pimples."[77] Physical critiques were important to clinic staff, who would note that although Margarete "already had pronounced full feminine body forms," she "lacks youthful tone and turgor," and the overall "appearance of the youth is very unmaidenly." Moreover, Margarete's "movements are rather cumbersome, without any grace."[78]

Margarete appears to have been nervous during her time in Asperger's clinic. She was anxious to know exactly what Asperger's staff was saying about her. One staff member wrote, "When we report to each other about the children in the morning, she is always hanging around near us." Margarete's worry was certainly understandable, given that preceding observations had sent her to two rounds at Spiegelgrund. A nurse mentioned that during a physical examination with Dr. Feldmann, Margarete was purportedly "embarrassed, sensitive, often cheeky."[79]

In the face of constant evaluation, Margarete seemed eager to demonstrate her virtue and value in Asperger's clinic. She wrote a note to nurse Neuenteufel promising, with lofty vocabulary and resolution, "My ambition is only one thing. Never again to falter in life. And I will try to rise up, alone and slowly." Criticizing herself, Margarete beseeched the nurse, "Please forgive my nuisance. I'm still young and stupid."[80] Margarete was nervous about her father's opinion of her, too. Vowing model behavior, she wrote:

> Dear father! I imagine my future back home again with you. From where I want to work diligently again. I would like to work with children, but I know that in wartime you cannot choose your work. I will therefore do what is asked of me. I imagine how nice it would be if we were all together again.[81]

On her second day at Asperger's clinic, Margarete drew a poignant picture that captured both her self-image as an outcast and her hopes for a warmer future. She depicted an idyllic house full of bright, cozy rooms. It featured a dinner table set with a red checkered tablecloth on a red-and-white-patterned rug, with flower pots and a picture of a mountain landscape along the wall. Another room had polka-dotted wallpaper and a kitchen table with a blue flowered tablecloth, yellow legs, orange chairs, and a bowl of apples on top. A large yellow and red rocking horse looked on. The only life was a solitary figure crammed into a bathroom in the lower left corner. The person sat in a big bath—as Margarete had the day before upon her admission to Asperger's clinic—and was tiny, with only the head peaking out. A large jet of water from the shower spout poured over her head, obscuring it, and the figure was cut off by a thick shower curtain from the rest of the happy house.[82]

Asperger's clinic doubted that Margarete's visions and efforts were heartfelt. One note called Margarete superficial and insincere: "Her good, civilized behavior is determined in a primitive way by expediency, not greater insight or ethical motives." Margarete only wanted "to make a good impression." Another report even called Margarete's supplications "suspicious piety." Because of Margarete's purportedly crude motivations, Asperger's department pronounced, "She remains completely unreliable despite the apparent improvement."[83]

The Curative Education ward did agree with Illing's opinion at Spiegelgrund, however, that Margarete did not have a full-fledged mental illness. She merely had a "very poorly differentiated personality on a low intellectual level with some psychopathic traits, but certainly not a psychosis." As with Elfriede and Christine, Margarete's problems might indeed be attributed to her gender, "an unfavorable reaction of the girl to puberty" and "premenstrual moods."[84] Asperger's clinic finally decided that Margarete could be a productive member of the national community, admitting that "Her job performance is actually good." The staff spared her a third institutionalization at Spiegelgrund—"since the girl is very well usable and efficient for work"— and affirmed her stay at a home in Luisenheim.[85]

Within three years, Margarete's diagnoses had run the gamut: from "waywardness" to "manic depressive insanity" to schizophrenia to menstrual problems to being "tentatively educable." Doctors' orders had also run the gamut: from sterilization to Spiegelgrund (twice), and to release home (twice). Deadly in its arbitrariness, Nazi psychiatric diagnosis came down to individuals' decisions and shifting criteria—in which haphazard, hasty words had enormous impact on children's fates.

Thankfully, despite what Margarete and Elfriede endured, it appears that both girls survived Spiegelgrund and Vienna's deadly network of children's institutions. At least there are no records of their deaths in the registers of children who perished in the euthanasia program. Still, their lives would be forever marked. The nurse's note from Margarete's time in the bathtub upon her second intake in Asperger's clinic said that "her desire is to care for children, but she doubts whether she still can after all this."[86]

While Margarete and Elfriede were sentenced to Spiegelgrund, Asperger treated Fritz and Harro with patience and extraordinary care. The boys' behavior seems to have been more problematic for the ward, but the boys were seen as having greater potential. Asperger believed that Fritz had "a genuine chance for remedial education." Although Fritz, "with his considerable problems, could not be taught in a class," Asperger granted Fritz a "personal tutor on the ward," going to the trouble of getting "the consent of the educational authority" in Vienna to do so. With intensive therapy, Asperger boasted, his department got Fritz to pass a state school examination. It then supported him attending the third grade of a primary school as "an external pupil" so he did not lose a year of school.[87]

The elaborate programs of intervention that Asperger developed to support Fritz's unique learning style resembles those in use today. Asperger suggested the child with autistic psychopathy would benefit from an individual classroom aide, and "may need a minder to the end of his school years and often beyond." Asperger also recommended that parents and educators devise clear schedules, "establishing an exact timetable in which, from the moment of rising at a particular time, every single occupation and duty was outlined in detail."[88]

Above all, Asperger said caregivers must develop strong emotional attachments to the child with autistic psychopathy—which, again, stood in sharp contrast to the cold treatment Margarete and Elfriede received in his clinic. Asperger proclaimed that one needed to show "genuine care and kindness if one wants to achieve anything at all." The youth with autistic psychopathy "can be guided and taught," he said, "only by those who give them true understanding and genuine affection."[89]

In short, Asperger felt children with autistic psychopathy should be treated with *Gemüt*. The child should experience "uninterrupted reciprocity with his care-giver, constantly building up his own responses and modifying them according to the positive or negative outcome of his encounters." The connection between adult and youth, then, generated *Gemüt* that would transfer to the youth. The connection was metaphysical: a "living unity that exists between the leader and the child," a "unity of reacting to one another in innumerable conscious and unconscious relations."[90] Whereas Asperger's clinic doubted that Elfriede and Margarete were capable of social connection and required isolation, the *Gemüt* of boys with autistic psychopathy might be stimulated if one invested in it through extraordinary attention and sensitivity.

Asperger interpreted boys' relationship difficulties and impulsivity as autistic psychopathy, while his clinic staff, in keeping with long-standing trends in European and American psychiatry, interpreted girls' relationship difficulties and impulsivity as hysterical and female, related to their menstrual cycles. Whereas Asperger's department dismissed the girls as irremediable and sent them to Spiegelgrund, the boys' apparently worse behavior in the clinic received intensive care. They were on the favorable side of Nazi psychiatry's eugenicist coin, and might be integrated into the *Volk*.

WHAT ACCOUNTS FOR the difference in the boys' and girls' treatment? Asperger claimed in his 1944 autism thesis that out of the "more than 200" autistic children his clinic had identified in ten years, "We have never met a girl with the fully fledged picture of autistic psychopathy."[91] Asperger's vague reference to "more than 200" cases did not sound overly precise. But he was categorical that autistic psychopathy was a male diagnosis. Asperger did allow that some mothers of autistic children had "autistic features," and that some girls had "contact disturbances which were reminiscent of autistic psychopathy." But Asperger surmised these symptoms were due to hormones, not an underlying condition: "It could be that autistic traits in the female become evident only after puberty."[92]

The distinction between boys and girls, as Asperger saw it, came down to intelligence. Expanding upon the gender stereotypes of his time, Asperger based his idea of autistic psychopathy on the differences he saw in their cognitive capabilities. For Asperger, autistic psychopathy was abstract thinking par excellence. "Abstraction is so highly developed that the relationship to the concrete, to objects and to people has largely been lost."[93] It was boys who had the capability of higher-order thinking. Boys, Asperger contended, had "a gift for logical ability, abstraction, precise thinking and formulating, and for independent scientific investigation," while girls were suited "for the concrete and the practical, and for tidy, methodical work."

Put simply, "abstraction is congenial to male thought processes, while female thought processes draw more strongly on feelings and instincts." These were what Asperger called fundamental "sex differences in intelligence." Thus, Asperger concluded, "the autistic personality is an extreme variant of male intelligence," and even "of the male character."[94]

Certainly, Asperger was not alone in his ideas of boys' special cognitive abilities. Within Nazi psychiatry, he would likely have been familiar with the work of Wilhelm Weygandt, who was trained by Werner Villinger, prominent in Asperger's circles. Weygandt published on "talented imbeciles," building off earlier research by Moritz Tramer and Max Kirmsse on people who had unusual talents in math, music, art, memory, and factual knowledge despite other cognitive disabilities—individuals who Asperger might diagnose as autistic. Weygandt proclaimed that only 10 percent of people with such special abilities were women. Weygandt emphasized, in words similar to Asperger's, that women were "instinctive, emotional, unproductive, [and] subjective," citing the " 'physiological idiocy of the female.' "[95]

Asperger devoted a large portion of his autism treatise to intelligence testing and speculating about autistic abilities. There were no tests from Elfriede, Christine, or Margarete in their files—only drawings and scraps of personal writings.[96] But while the girls displayed similar behaviors as Fritz and Harro, Asperger's clinic interpreted only the boys' idiosyncrasies as signs of superior intelligence.

Atypical speech, for example, signaled exceptional capabilities in what Asperger called "favorable cases" of autistic psychopathy.[97] Autistic children had "a special creative attitude towards language," Asperger wrote. They could "express their own original experience in a linguistically original form." Though "often quite abstruse," Asperger held that autistic children's "newly formed or partially restructured expressions" showed unique insight.[98]

When Asperger asked Fritz on his intelligence test the difference between a fly and a butterfly, he was delighted to hear Fritz say: "The butterfly is snowed, snowed with snow," and "He is red and blue, and the fly is brown and black," as these seemed refreshingly creative answers.[99] Asperger also praised how Harro "coined each word to fit the moment." When asked the difference between a stove and an oven, Harro said that "the stove is what one has in the room as a firebringer."[100] Such use of "unusual words," Asperger declared, was an "example of autistic introspection."[101]

However, Asperger's clinic found Margarete's neologisms neither terribly charming nor clever. One handwritten note said that Margarete had "no imagination," and was "neither humorous nor intelligent, just unpleasant." At Spiegelgrund, Margarete's "creation of words" was simply a "mannered and awkward way of expressing herself." Her "tendency to rhymes, stringing together of words," would "suggest manic depressive insanity."[102]

Even Margarete's mature conversations indicated her inferiority. "Her speech is precocious, too wise," staff reported, and her use of "stilted idioms, hackneyed phrases" stemmed not from superior intelligence, but from a "certain primitive refinement." While Margarete's "unchildlike" way of talking was primitive, Asperger deemed the boys' refinement genuine.[103] He celebrated how six-year-old Fritz talked 'like an adult,' " and how one could talk to eight-year-old Harro "as to an adult." Even Ernst, who Asperger believed was more disabled, spoke "like an adult."[104]

The boys also demonstrated autistic intelligence by talking at length about subjects of their own interest, without much regard for the conversational partner. Asperger wrote of Fritz that "Only rarely was what he said in answer to a question," and that Harro "did not respond to questions but let his talk run single-mindedly along his own tracks." Ernst, too, talked "regardless of the questions he was being asked," but his " 'asides' were quite remarkable."[105] The Curative Education Clinic judged Margarete's digressive speaking, however, an inadequacy: "She gives roundabout, lengthy accounts" and "never comes to the end." Rather than a sign of intelligence, this showed "her uncritical, uncontrolled way of thinking."[106] Margarete was flighty—while the boys showed acuity.

That Asperger paid so much attention to the boys' intelligence is all the more notable given how difficult it was to measure. Despite resistance from the boys, Asperger invested a great deal of effort into proving their capabilities. "Testing was extremely difficult to carry out" with Fritz, for example. He "constantly jumped up or smacked the experimenter on the hand," and "would repeatedly drop himself from chair to floor and then enjoy being firmly placed back in his chair again." When presented with the Lazar system of testing that was traditional at the clinic, Fritz refused to imitate rhythms beaten out; he balked at math calculation problems. When asked about the difference between a tree and a bush, he answered only "there is a difference." When asked the difference between a cow and calf, he returned, "lammerlammerlammer. . . ."[107]

Yet Asperger was willing to impute skills to Fritz that he did not demonstrate in the testing. When Fritz repeated up to six digits from memory, Asperger remarked, "One was left with a strong impression that he could go further, except that he just did not feel like it." Asperger based his claim that Fritz had "extraordinary calculating ability" on discussions with the boy's parents and, later, individualized instruction in the ward.[108] Fritz's skills would not have been revealed without the intensive efforts of Asperger and his colleagues to uncover it.

Testing Harro was just as difficult as testing Fritz, Asperger held. "A lot of energy went into simply making him do the tasks," since Harro would "shut off completely when a question did not interest him." But Asperger, as with Fritz, gave the boy the benefit of the doubt. He deemed Harro's unusual answers evidence of unusual intelligence. On the difference between a lake and a river, Harro explained: "Well, the lake, it doesn't move from its spot, and it can never be as long and never have that many branches, and it always has an end somewhere."[109]

Would Asperger have gone to the trouble of

soliciting responses from Elfriede and Margarete if testing the girls had proved as challenging? It is hard to imagine that Asperger and his colleagues would have found such unclear responses from them as captivating. More likely, they would have been judged similarly to Christine, whom Asperger determined—without any recorded tests—to have slightly below average intelligence, with "very little interest in intellectual demands."[110]

Asperger also proclaimed that autistic boys had unique powers of perception: a "special clear-sightedness" that was "seen only in them," with special capabilities to "engage in a particular kind of introspection and to be a judge of character." He maintained that their "psychopathic clarity of vision" was uncanny, almost miraculous.[111]

One "distinctive trait" that Asperger highlighted was autistic boys' "rare maturity of taste in art." Whereas "normal children" gravitate toward the "pretty picture, with kitschy rose pink and sky blue," he claimed, autistic children "may have a special understanding of works of art which are difficult even for many adults." In Asperger's opinion, they were especially good at "Romanesque sculpture or paintings by Rembrandt."[112] Asperger gave no evidence for his claims of "special clear-sightedness" in autistic psychopathy. The right or wrongness of his claims notwithstanding, it is doubtful his clinic gave either Elfriede or Margarete an opportunity to judge either Rembrandt paintings or Romanesque sculptures.

ASIDE FROM CONJECTURES about male autistic intelligence, Asperger was unclear about many aspects of the diagnosis. To Asperger, conditions of autistic psychopathy could manifest in any variety of ways. As he wrote of autistic children, "Not every one of them has every trait," and "Individual differences within the type are great." The youths differed "by the degree of contact failure, by the level of intellectual and personal ability, but also by numerous individual characteristics, special modes of reaction, special interests."[113]

In speech, for example, Asperger did not have set standards for what counted as autistic. There were "many possibilities." The voice might be "soft and far away," or "refined and nasal," or "shrill and ear-splitting," or "over-modulated," or "sing-song." While Asperger acknowledged that his criteria were diffuse, there was unity in their disunity: "They all have one thing in common: the language feels unnatural." Apparently, one of the ways Asperger determined what was "unnatural" was the humorousness of the children's mistakes. Their speech is "often like a caricature," he said, "which provokes ridicule in the native listener."[114]

Asperger likewise claimed that while autistic

children had a range of different body types and physical abilities, they all fell short of contemporary masculine physical ideals in some way. Harro was shorter than average, and "his arms and legs looked as if they were too short for his body." His "posture too was odd," as he "stood broadly, arms held away from the body, as a portly gentleman or a boxer might do." Fritz was of "delicate build" and his veins were visible beneath his skin, which was "of yellowish-grey pallor." The boy's "musculature was weakly developed," Asperger related, and his "posture was slouched, his shoulders slumped, with the shoulder blades protruding."[115] In his short description of Hellmuth, Asperger wrote that the boy's "appearance was grotesque." He reportedly "had noticeably increased salivation, and when he talked one could hear the saliva bubbling in his mouth." He was also "grotesquely fat." Since age eleven, Hellmuth had "distinctly formed 'breasts and hips' " as well as "knock knees and flat feet," and "when one shook his hand, it seemed as if it had no bones and were made of rubber."[116]

Asperger wrote that some children's deviations from the norm could appear farcical. Their "conduct, manner of speech and, not least, often grotesque demeanour cries out to be ridiculed," he said. Harro was supposedly "an object of ridicule" and "directly provoked teasing" from other children for his "strange, slightly funny dignity" and "strange and comical behaviour."[117] Asperger noted "motor clumsiness" in "almost all autistic individuals."[118] Fritz and Harro, as well as Ernst and Hellmuth, were all "very clumsy" and poor athletes, unable to integrate with group sports. Harro's "movements would be ugly and angular" and he was certainly "not a skilled fighter."[119] Asperger asserted that "autistic children also do not have a proper attitude towards their own bodies." Itemizing the boys' failures of grooming, he generalized that autistic children lacked "cleanliness and physical care. Even as adults they may be seen to walk about unkempt and unwashed."[120]

Asperger's idea of autistic intelligence, which was central to the diagnosis, arrived at another nondefinition. He admitted it was hard to generalize about autistic children since "the findings can be contradictory and different testers can come to different intelligence estimates." Asperger's core idea of autistic psychopathy— finding social interactions difficult to navigate— was also nebulous. It meant, basically, not fitting in: "In early childhood there are the difficulties in learning simple practical skills and in social adaptation. These difficulties arise out of the same disturbance which at school age cause learning and conduct problems, in adolescence job and performance problems, and in adulthood social and marital conflicts."[121]

In other words, Asperger's idea of autistic psychopathy was a totalizing, yet totally amorphous diagnosis. Asperger used it for some children to suggest their humanity; but he used it for others to deny their humanity. It was revealed in children's "physical appearance, expressive functions and, indeed, their whole behaviour," and meant judging the child's very existence.[122] No detail was irrelevant, no realm of a child's life was independent from the diagnosis. Autistic psychopathy encompassed every corner of the psychic universe, from unthinking habit to extreme emotion to intellect. It encompassed multiple milieux—from mind to physiology, from the school to the family to the community. It got to the heart of what it meant to be human in the Third Reich.

IN THE CONCLUSION to his treatise, Asperger argued that children with autistic psychopathy could be valuable to society. "Autistic people have their place in the organism of the social community," he declared, and "they fulfill their role well, perhaps better than anyone else could."[123] He also defended children with developmental differences in general, contending that "Abnormal personalities can be capable of development and adjustment," and that "Possibilities of social integration which one would never have dreamt of arise in the course of development." In an oft-cited quote, Asperger reiterated his 1938 pronouncement that doctors had "the right and the duty to speak out for these children with the whole force of our personality. We believe that only the absolutely dedicated and loving educator can achieve success with difficult individuals."[124]

While many have interpreted Asperger's benevolent words as standing up to the cruelties of the Third Reich, the charitable remarks appear only at the end of the thesis, marking an abrupt shift in tone, and seem almost tacked on. The bulk of the treatise—in tone and details—was disparaging of autistic children. Aside from Asperger's speculation about autistic intelligence, his descriptions of the youths were harsh.

Moreover, Asperger's generous rhetoric was in line with that of his colleagues in Nazi psychiatry—even those directly involved in child euthanasia killings—who made big-hearted proclamations about disabled children. Asperger's murderous mentor, Franz Hamburger, stressed the importance of championing disabled youths "even if we believe optimism is not warranted." Hamburger cautioned against diagnosing children too hastily, as well as prematurely informing government authorities of a child's diagnosis. With "assiduous, optimistic treatment," Hamburger held, the physician "can achieve so much good." One must invest intensively in the child: "Feelings of joy, of confidence, that the teacher awakens are of the greatest importance for such children."[125] Even Ernst Jekelius, as head of Spiegelgrund, defended the worth of disabled youths. The goal of curative education, he declared, was to "integrate as many children and youths as possible into the processes of German work and life," and he boasted that careful teaching had helped "many formerly 'difficult children'" who otherwise "probably would have gone to the dogs." With proper care, Jekelius hoped, such children might "now receive the Iron Cross for bravery."[126]

While Asperger, like his colleagues in the euthanasia system, argued for the capabilities of some children, he likewise saw a sharp eugenicist hierarchy. For autistic children, Asperger delineated a "range" in "levels of ability" and social worth. Asperger outlined this in the bluntest terms, charging that people with autistic psychopathy spanned "from the highly original genius, through the weird eccentric who lives in a world of his own and achieves very little, down to the most severe contact-disturbed, automaton-like mentally retarded individual."[127]

Essentially, autistic psychopathy had both positive and negative traits, and one could add up a ledger to determine a child's value. Asperger held that youths on the "most favorable" end of his "range" might be superior to "normal

271

children." As adults, they would "perform with such outstanding success that one may even conclude that only such people are capable of certain achievements." This was "usually in highly specialised academic professions, often in very high positions" such as "mathematicians, technologists, industrial chemists and high-ranking civil servants."[128] Asperger was stressing traits that were valuable to the Nazi state, and this may have been a strategic attempt to defend these children from persecution. But he also attributed some traits to autistic children—such as artistic taste in Rembrandt paintings and Romanesque sculpture—which were rather unusual to spot-light if he did not believe in them. In this regard, Asperger's treatise might be read less as a defense of children with disability per se than as an aggressive claim for the "special abilities" of some children with his diagnosis.[129]

At the same time, Asperger's overall judgment of children with autistic psychopathy was derogatory. "In the majority of cases," Asperger argued, "the positive aspects of autistic traits do not outweigh the negative ones." He main-tained that autistic children had the potential for achievement only "as long as they are intellectually intact," and he devoted the majority of his case descriptions to such "able autistic individuals."[130] Since Asperger did not dwell upon those at the "less favorable" end of his "range," his emphasis on one type of child gave a misleading impression of what he meant by autistic psychopathy in general. Paradoxically, it was Asperger's eugenicist focus on the "favorable cases" in his thesis that obscured the extent to which he was eugenicist.

Asperger drew a sharp line between children with positive versus negative worth. Fritz and Harro, to whom Asperger devoted the vast majority of his treatise, were on the "most favorable" end of the autistic spectrum. Ernst was what Asperger called a "middle case"; it was unclear "whether Ernst was particularly able or mentally retarded." Asperger wound up concluding that in this "middle" area of the spectrum, "the negative aspects outweigh the positive ones."[131]

He was unequivocal about children he deemed more disabled: they would be of little social value. "From this middle group there is a smooth transition further along the range to those mentally retarded people who show highly stereotyped automaton-like behaviour." These individuals, Asperger continued, might "have crackpot interests which are of no practical use," such as with "rote memory" for things like calendar dates or tram routes.[132]

Asperger was brutal about these "less favourable cases." Drawing on images of "asocial" and "dissocial" individuals in Nazi psychiatry, Asperger prophesied that these children would grow up to "roam the streets as 'originals,' grotesque and dilapidated, talking loudly to themselves or unconcernedly to passers-by."[133]

Moreover, Asperger denied the humanity of autistic children he saw as more impaired. Throughout his thesis, Asperger referred to them as "intelligent automata," and spoke of "the automaton-like nature of the whole personality." He called Hellmuth "an autistic automaton."[134] Asperger's idea of automata referred not only to the children's lack of productive value to society, but also to their incapacity for social feeling. Those at the "unfavorable" end of Asperger's range of autistic psychopathy would remain outside the national community.

Asperger went so far as to say that these children, who he believed could not "be an integral part of the world," would be *unable to learn,*" (emphasis in original). This term was consonant with Nazi psychiatry's idea of "ineducable," a key criterion for killing in the euthanasia program.[135] In effacing a child's individuality, such labels of Nazi psychiatry rendered children unrecognizable as human, let alone as individuals. They were sentence of psychiatric death, and given to children who found themselves led to killing centers, facing actual death.

8

The Daily Life of Death

FRIEDRICH ZAWREL WATCHED Spiegelgrund killings unfold day by day. The teenager had a view of the death pavilion, number 15, through the scratched milk-glass window of his cell in Pavilion 17. "I often saw it from my window, that children's corpses were taken away," he later recalled. The first time, "I told the nurse about it, and then she threatened me with the [corpse] handcart if I didn't behave."[1] Zawrel also tracked the death toll from inside the dormitory. As he walked past the beds on his way to empty his chamber pot, he explained, "I knew exactly when someone was designated for killing from Pavilion 17 [. . .] and I could even count them. In the corner, in the bed, I know, was a small child, whether it was a boy or a girl, you couldn't determine, but with blond hair, and two days later, there was one with black hair there. And there was no additional bed, they were all empty. Right, and they were always taken away at 2 p.m. to Pavilion 15."[2]

Staff registered the deaths in the "Book of the Dead," an unassuming black-and-white marbled notebook with victims' intake dates, birth dates, and death dates. Spiegelgrund was the second-largest killing center in the Reich; it boasted the highest death rate and trained killing staff for other "special children's wards." As ninety personnel worked there at any given time, including four to five doctors first led by director Erwin Jekelius and then director Ernst Illing, it was a major undertaking.[3]

THE CHILD EUTHANASIA program was designed to kill youths with purportedly biological disabilities, yet Spiegelgrund was concerned with social belonging, too. Doctors assessed youths according to their perceived ability to join the *Volk*—with physical disability only one criterion for killing. Being "alien to the community," or *Gemeinschaftsfremd*, was another criterion.[4] Based on children's behavior and family standing, doctors prophesied children's future ability to work and assimilate into the national community. This was likewise true at other Reich killing facilities, where transgressions like bedwetting, incorrect answers on test puzzles, and juvenile delinquency might lead to death. But at Spiegelgrund, up to 70 percent of the children who were killed did not have quantifiable physiological impairments. Rather, staff issued subjective judgments of lower cognitive functioning or no specific diagnosis at all. Most of the youths who perished at Spiegelgrund—three in five—had amorphous diagnoses of "imbecility" and "idiocy." Ten percent did not have specific diagnoses.[5]

Socializing children was a stated mission of Spiegelgrund. Hans Krenek, its "educational and psychological director," boasted of the institution's methods. He described how Spiegelgrund divided children who were "particularly difficult" but "still not hopeless" into three groups, where they would learn how "to integrate into the social community." Staff accomplished this through "cultivation, strict discipline, continuous occupational therapy, and very special care for the sense of community [*Gemeinschaftssinn*]."[6] Children's fates, then, hinged on their ability to assimilate. "Hopeless" children could not be integrated into the community.

Strictly speaking, Spiegelgrund was an arm of social services, not a medical facility. It belonged to Vienna's sprawling welfare system, and was dubbed, in different pavilions and at different times during the Third Reich, an educational institution, a reformatory, and a "curative education clinic," one node in a much larger labyrinth of brutal children's homes and correctional facilities.

Indeed, numerous children came to Spiegelgrund through Vienna's nightmarish network of children's homes, frequently enduring years of abuse in them. Spiegelgrund survivor Alfred

Grasel, whose homeless single mother put him in the welfare system when he was two weeks old, described how his childhood is "only memories of homes, of all the homes. Among them are homes I didn't even know about anymore, like Dreherstraße, the Central Children's Home on Bastiengasse, the Mödling Orphanage, the Hyrtl Orphanage, Spiegelgrund, then the Foster Care Service, then Dreherstraße, then Juchgasse, the home for apprentices, and then the concentration camp."[7]

The welfare institution that funneled the most children into Spiegelgrund was Vienna's Foster Care Service (*Kinderübernahmestelle*, or KÜST), the intake center for the city's orphaned, abused, and purportedly troublesome youths. In one sample of 312 children who were killed at Spiegelgrund, the Foster Care Service had referred almost a third.[8] It was a grim irony that the Foster Care Service became a hub in the Nazi killing system, as it had been a model institution of Socialist Vienna in the 1920s. The same progressive institution that had sought to care for children who had fallen through the cracks of society was now condemning them for having fallen through the cracks.

The focus on social factors reflected the preoccupation of Asperger and his colleagues with group assimilation and *Gemüt*—branding children who did not conform as "alien to the community." Social status mattered. The Foster Care Service often transferred to Spiegelgrund children from poor families who were struggling on the margins of society. Nazi authorities did not hesitate to remove youths from disadvantaged parents who officials might label "asocial" or "hereditarily inferior." In a study of 207 children who were killed at Spiegelgrund, at least 40 percent were deemed to have come from families with "serious problems."[9]

Parents might voluntarily place their children in the welfare system if they could not care for them. Many saw this as a temporary measure, hoping that institutions or foster parents could look after their children until they were able to secure better housing or employment. Ferdinand Schimatzek's mother, for example, had placed her son in foster care as a baby but, as he approached four years old, she felt she was able to take him back. As she contended with long hours at a metal grinding plant, though, she soon returned the boy back to the Foster Care Service. There, staff reported that Schimatzek had "behavioral problems" and "burnings on upper and lower arm," perhaps from his previous time in foster care, and he was transferred to Spiegelgrund.[10]

A number of children at Spiegelgrund came from single-parent households. In the sample of 207 youths who were killed, 60 percent were cared for by one parent; around 30 percent had fathers away at war, 10 percent had a parent who had died, and 20 percent were born out of wedlock, which carried a heavy stigma at that time. Alois Kaufmann explained that when he was born, "it was a disaster" for his single mother and she was "in total despair." His grandfather purportedly told her, "Take your child and jump with him right away into the Mur river, that would be best." Kaufmann's mother gave him up to a monastery instead and then, after a series of foster parents, Kaufmann found himself at the Foster Care Service—which then transferred him, at age nine, directly to Spiegelgrund's Pavilion 15. Kaufmann remarked, "I had no clue that this was the death pavilion." After two to three weeks of observation, doctors decided Kaufmann would be allowed to live and moved him to another ward at Spiegelgrund.[11]

Sometimes parents placed children in the welfare system who *were* able to care for their children—but did not wish to. Franz Pulkert's father and stepmother took him to Vienna's Foster Care Service when they bore their own biological son. Pulkert remembers how his stepmother used to hit him with a carpet beater. "That was common, these methods, but actually that didn't [bother me] that much, for me, this was the mother, and that's it." The Foster Care Service transferred Pulkert to Spiegelgrund at age three, where he stayed in Pavilion 15, the death ward.

Pulkert was eventually deemed worthy of life and released from Spiegelgrund after two years. Yet Pulkert's stepmother still did not want him at home, and returned him to Spiegelgrund within less than a year.[12]

Children were also brought to the Foster Care Service for supposed delinquency. This encompassed a range of behaviors. Eight-year-old Ernst Pacher found himself at the foster center and then Spiegelgrund after waving to an enemy airplane. Karl Uher, who had lived with a series of foster parents since he was a baby, was taken at age eight for allegedly setting fire to a barn; it was proven three months later that Uher was innocent, but by then it was too late. He was at Spiegelgrund. Friedrich Zawrel, branded "hereditarily defective" because of his father's alcoholism and bullied by classmates, said he skipped school and "walked around Vienna all day long."[13] Karl Hamedler ran away from home; he recounted how, at his father's, "I was being beaten all the time, I couldn't stand it anymore." But the military police picked up Hamedler at the Northern railway station and sent him to the municipal Foster Care Service, where he was transferred to Spiegelgrund and spent time in Pavilions 15 and 17.

Many youths, certainly, were transferred to Pavilions 15 and 17 because of their biology—30 percent of children who perished at Spiegelgrund were diagnosed with physical disabilities. One in ten had Down syndrome, with smaller numbers labeled with cerebral palsy, hydrocephalus, epilepsy, and brain injuries or disorders.[14] Yet even a straightforward physical diagnosis could be overlaid with social and subjective pronouncements. Karl Jakubec was sent to Spiegelgrund's Pavilion 15 with a club foot; but authorities did not leave his reported defects at that. Doctors declared that Jakubec, though just a baby, was "feeble-minded to a mild degree." He was also reported to come from a "hereditarily inferior family," as his mother had been diagnosed with "psychopathy with epilepsy" after a suicide attempt, and his father was "nervous and quick-tempered."[15] Three-month-old Walter Steyneck had Down syndrome—which at Spiegelgrund was grounds enough to kill a child—yet Ernst Illing further justified his death request to the Reich committee in Berlin by claiming that Walter's father was a former alcoholic, "sexually impulsive," with fourteen children, and that his mother had a "speech impediment." The baby died two weeks later, ostensibly of pneumonia, as his parents were visiting.[16]

SPIEGELGRUND'S EMPHASIS ON social assimilation and its integration into Vienna's welfare system was evident not only in its intake practices, but also in the experiences of children who were kept there. Survivors stressed how the measures they suffered at Spiegelgrund differed little from other children's homes in Vienna, both before and after the Third Reich. Spiegelgrund, like many institutions at the time, meant brutal regimentation, appalling conditions, and violent discipline. Franz Pulkert, who had spent his childhood in multiple children's homes, said "there were dozens of institutions where the exact same things happened." Karl Uher agreed: "I emphasize, not only at Spiegelgrund, even though this is the only institution they recognize. But the facilities where I was, like Mödling, which are believed to be mere orphanages, weren't different [. . .] it was no different. My punishments were harsher than in a prison." The difference between Spiegelgrund and other children's homes, of course, was that Spiegelgrund was a center of Nazi extermination.

The interviews and memoirs of Spiegelgrund survivors give some voice to the victims, sketching the lives, deaths, and traumas of children who suffered.[17] As recollections, shaped by the time and audience for which they were expressed, they are tricky sources. The recent survivor interviews held at the Documentation Center of the Austrian Resistance, especially, are records produced by two sides, in a dialogue whose one-half is not heard. Moreover, the remembrances do not represent all of the experiences of children victimized at Spiegelgrund. None of the interviewees, except Karl Jakubec with a club foot, were labeled with physical defects. They were at Spiegelgrund for reasons of social standing and/or social behavior. These survivor sources are also entirely male, save one, even as the gender ratio of children killed appears to have been roughly even.[18] And lastly, of course, while five of the twelve interviewees did have brushes with death during their stays at Pavilions 15 and 17, and bore witness to the horrors that transpired there, they cannot render the ordeals of the 789 children who were forever silenced.

ARRIVAL AT SPIEGELGRUND was seared in the memory of many survivors. Rudolf Karger remembered it was on "a beautiful autumn day" in September 1941. He saw "a nice hallway, everything clean, shipshape, and there was a nice day room and a dormitory with about 20 to 25 beds, a little room—charge office, a bathroom, well, and then there was a little hallway." He noted there were also "such small cells, the size of a regular cell, with a lock and a peeping hole, and I thought well, is this where they lock up the fools, I don't know. Yes, it caught my eye, but in the beginning I thought it looked pretty nice." Karger was optimistic. "The nurses greeted me and so on, and I thought, well, this cannot be too bad, at my uncle's I was beaten, and here I will have at least my quiet. But it turned out to be the opposite, and already the next day I knew that this was no good at all."[19]

Franz Pulkert, with more foreboding upon his arrival at Spiegelgrund, recalled that "everything was dark somehow." Johann Gross noticed that the "pavilions looked pretty much the same. On the facades a lot of red bricks, and all were surrounded by a fence." He was struck that "all windows were barred, most with glass one couldn't see through."[20]

Ernst Pacher said he was led to a bathroom with a large iron door; staff told him to undress and put him into an ice cold bath. Inside the pavilions, as Ferdinand Schimatzek described, there were "huge dormitory rooms lit by steely blue light that was shining into every nook and cranny."[21] Leopoldine Maier recollected: "The dormitory was like a hall, and right and left there were beds of steel, that is, metal beds with metal inserts, with extremely coarse mattresses on them. [. . .] Our heads were at the window, our feet towards the middle, we were lined up there one after another with a 'Kotze'—that's how we called these blankets, rough, milled blankets."

Survivors said the daily routine ran like clockwork. After waking at six in the morning, Maier recited, "We had to jump out of our beds and we had to stand next to it and then we had to go to the washroom. There were tubs with faucets with cold water only and we had to wash ourselves." Children brushed their teeth with a hard block of toothpaste. Once, Maier confessed, "I was so hungry I ate the whole piece." She was punished, "of course."[22]

Bed-making was onerous. Sheets had to be "straight as a ruler, that precise, otherwise it was torn apart, and you had to do it again," said Ferdinand Pauer. He explained that children could be punished for any little misstep. "Fingernails, for instance, she'd come, you had to show your fingers. Splat, another slap. The next day, your food was cancelled." Pauer described the uniform of short pants and a jacket, either striped or green with long stockings, as well as the lack of clothing. "We had no winter coats, I didn't know there was such a thing. Or no long pants, not at all." Without heating in the rooms, Leopoldine Maier added, "we were freezing right down to the bones. Your entire inside was cold."[23]

Then came breakfast, which was meager. In Alois Kaufmann's account, children joked that their bread slices were so thin "we could see through it as far as Paris." They also called one of the liquids they regularly received "the Danube" because it was blue. This was better, though, than later in the war, when "circumstances got much, much worse," and the thin cabbage soup had worms swimming on top.[24] Children were inventive looking elsewhere for sustenance.

Ferdinand Pauer depicted how youths would go to the fence and pick woodbine: "We rolled up the leaves, squeezed them and ate them, or else the lime leaves, we gathered the nuts, opened them, and when we had about ten, we'd put them in the mouth. Or this, what is it called, bear's garlic. We ate just about everything that was possible."[25]

Even as Spiegelgrund survivors spoke of constant hunger, children were lucky if they could keep the food down. Leopoldine Maier related how if "you vomited it, you were forced to eat it, spoon by spoon, until it was down again. Of course, I vomited again, and the vomit had to be eaten again and this was a nightmare. I still dream of it sometimes." Rudolf Karger recalled another child who could not stomach the semolina with skim milk that staff served on Tuesdays. Every week, "Two orderlies held him, forced fed him, and whatever he vomited was shuffled back until the plate was empty."[26]

Staff might issue children "vomit shots" as punishment. These injections of apomorphine induced hours of stomach pain, vomiting, and dry heaving.[27] Johann Gross portrayed the onset of the drug like a "hard blow to the stomach, everything cramped so that I could barely breathe. And then the nausea began right away, I was already at the toilet bowl and my breakfast was gone. I had to gag again and again."[28] Spiegelgrund staff likewise gave youths the "sulphur cure," injections of sulfur and related compounds that caused extreme pain and paralysis. Johann Gross received these shots, too. He maintained that they felt "first like ice in the thighs, and more and more like needle pricks." After mere minutes, Gross could no longer sit and "finally fell to the ground."[29] Friedrich Zawrel claimed he received the "sulphur cure" eight times and the muscle pain would last up to two weeks.[30] Spiegelgrund staff would also keep children heavily sedated. Struggling to find words, Alfred Grasel explained, "I was—not unconscious, I wouldn't say that, I don't know anything from that time. I was in the cell and apathetic, slept, but didn't sleep, I don't know."[31] Karl Hamedler voiced the same confusion, "I constantly got shots, over and over again, so I was in a permanent state of delirium."[32]

The daily life of children at Spiegelgrund varied a great deal depending on the pavilion. Some children were allowed to go to a school of sorts, though survivors admitted they learned little. To Franz Pulkert, "They kept bringing up the history of the German Reich and such things. But I cannot remember any proper lessons." Children might receive limited free time outside on the grounds, or inside a spartan recreation room with a handful of games. Required sports could be torturous, however, held Ferdinand Pauer. "We were all emaciated, we had no strength."[33]

Life was harder for Rudolf Karger, who found

himself in Pavilion 11, the correctional ward. He was among adolescents he called "unsettled and disturbed" due to life circumstances, as well as some "outright hysterical, ill-tempered and all of these things, who could not be brought under control." The youths underwent exercises in absurdity, such as hours-long marches around the courtyard. Or, Karger contended, "For hours or the whole day they forced us to tear apart our beds and remake them again properly, tearing and remaking." The children faced "punishments, always punishments, punishments, punishments," Karger repeated. "Bestial punishments they were, sadistic punishments."[34]

Nighttime routines in all the pavilions were strict. A major fear was having to go to the bathroom. Leopoldine Maier recounted harsh repercussions for leaving the bed, such as beatings, cold showers, and possibly no food the next day. Yet wetting the bed meant other penalties, such as "kneeling, standing for hours on one leg, and the punishment got harsher if you cried [. . .] Running in circles, up and down, push-ups, and all of this in a thin shirt." And, Maier went on, "The one who had wetted his bed was called upon in front of the whole class—no, in front of the whole dormitory—and was attacked, cursed and so on." Humiliation was the standard corrective to urine and excrement accidents. Ferdinand Pauer loathed the weekly underwear checks. "You'd stand there naked, handed over your underpants, but in a way that everybody could see whether there was a brown stain." Pauer thought back, "Thirty boys would watch," and then "everybody would laugh."[35]

Survivors hated how Spiegelgrund pitted children against each other. "That's the worst in such situations, that you turn into an inhuman being yourself," said Leopoldine Maier. "You were not supposed to speak with other kids, that's the way it was. One was really on one's own, and totally alone with one's fears. For any child, this is horrible." Rudolf Karger agreed, "They took care that nobody made friends with anybody, and whenever they punished us they used to say: "For this, you can thank this guy!" Frictions could quickly turn violent. "The law of the jungle ruled," lamented Karl Uher.[36] In the words of Alois Kaufmann:

> It was horrible. We beat each other, the stronger ones beat the weaker ones, the supervisors wanted it, yes, and they liked that. We took the beds apart so the other guy would fall through, we beat each other, we [plunged] them in the water. Yes, we did all the things to each other that the Nazis liked us to do. There was no solidarity. [. . .] Fights were fought for two tenths of a ladle of soup, for the

smallest leftovers. Someone said "If you give me a bread now,"—and I shouldn't say this aloud—"If you give me bread, I'll do with you . . . in the bed," and so on; well, such were the circumstances. [. . .] We were real sad[ists]. We were trained to turn sadistic even against each other.[37]

Ferdinand Pauer deplored how staff dehumanized the children. "You were a number, period." Karl Jakubec concurred, "they destroyed our dignity. One couldn't achieve any dignity." Then, "when you thought you could do a bit, right away they'd push you back down, unbelievable."[38]

Some children became inured to the violence. Karl Uher held that he even preferred to be beaten than to conform to Spiegelgrund methods: "I know I was disobedient and naughty, I admit it. [. . .] the rules they set were no rules, not for me. Don't ask me why. I preferred to receive beatings or being in the punishment group." Alois Kaufmann laid out the stages of adaptation: "At first, we cried when we were slapped or beaten. But soon, we didn't cry anymore. This kind of behavior disappears very soon and is replaced by a phase of laughing. Later, we only laughed. We really laughed at our supervisors. Which in turn . . . , but we enjoyed this. The [angrier] they were, the more we were grinning, although the beatings did hurt."[39]

At age fourteen, Friedrich Zawrel received ever more extreme punishments for his recalcitrance. After Zawrel refused to take the pills he was given at night and approached an orderly about escaping, staff subjected him to an asylum method known as the "wrapping treatment."

Two days, dry sheets, wet sheets, stark naked, and the sheets were wrapped around like a mummy, all over you were. . . , only the head was left out, and you were tied down with belts all over, and then you were lying in the cell, they put me on the floor, and I only looked up to the sky, that is, to the ceiling. I was unable to turn left, I was unable to turn right, unable to stretch my legs, to draw in my legs. And one should try this once, how long you can endure in a bed without turning, right. And I said already often, I again . . . , for a time I had stopped praying because I thought nobody helps me anyway, but then I again started, and I even asked for forgiveness for not having done it for so long because I thought I will be helped, but I wasn't helped. And when they let you out, the sheets were never dry because you were lying in your own urine. And especially atrocious it was when because of that it started itching, and you couldn't scratch, and you had to endure until it faded by itself, this was brutish what they did.

Later, orderlies fetched Zawrel to take him to Pavilion 15, which he knew was the killing pavilion. Trying to verbalize his panic, Zawrel explained, "One thing I know, there are experiences you cannot relate. It is so horrible, and one cannot find [words]." As the orderly told him to strip, Zawrel was convinced he was about to be killed. Fatalistic, he thought: "My life was kind of in a shambles, I wouldn't have lost much at all."

Spiegelgrund director Ernst Illing came to take Zawrel from his cell, naked, and led the boy to a podium before a room of young nursing students. Zawrel relived the incident: "Illing explained with a baton what it was about my physical appearance that indicated I was genetically and sociologically inferior. The ears were too large for him, arm distance too large, and he pointed out everything, right. And I was so ashamed." At the end, Zawrel remembered, "With the baton he hit me on my ass." Compounding the degradation, "almost 30 girls were laughing. For them it was like a circus performance."[40] Zawrel then became a frequent specimen for the students. "I was so scared, shocked and so terribly embarrassed that I only realized what was happening to me the sixth or seventh time. [. . .] it took a very long time for me to deal with the humiliation."[41]

Things became even worse for Zawrel. When he insulted a Spiegelgrund doctor, he said he endured rounds of severe beatings and "vomit shots" as punishment. A nurse, Rosa, feared what else might be in store for Zawrel and helped him escape, alerting him when the guards were chatting with the nurses in the office and the pavilion door was open. Zawrel fled into central Vienna and lived a hidden, tenuous existence. He met his mother secretly, at night at the Rochus market, "always after onset of the wartime blackout." His mother would give him some food and spare change, but Zawrel did not want to continue putting her at risk, and decided to no longer meet with her. Then, driven by hunger one night, Zawrel pilfered a package at the Northern railway station and was picked up by police. He was sentenced to Kaiserebersdorf prison, which he said was "really, one could almost say, a concentration camp."

Other children managed to escape Spiegelgrund, too—for a time. At age fifteen, Alfred Grasel was tasked with delivering food to Spiegelgrund pavilions on the small electric train that traversed the grounds. While en route one day, Grasel hopped into the tuberculosis sanatorium and over the fence, "and for several days I was free." But Grasel's foster mother returned him to

Spiegelgrund. Again Grasel managed to escape, and this time he hid out in Vienna's famed central Prater park. The Order Police soon caught Grasel, though, sleeping inside a boat. When Karl Hamedler escaped from Spiegelgrund, he likewise headed for the Prater, which drew him "like a magnet." Hamedler had been walking with a Spiegelgrund nurse in the Ottakring district past the final stop for Tram #46, when he impulsively turned toward a tramcar and "jumped right on." Hamedler was caught after two days, though he managed to escape again—this time through the orchard in the back yard of the firefighter's station. After three days, he was caught once again.[42]

Once caught, children who escaped Spiegelgrund confronted horrendous consequences. Rudolf Karger had escaped while riding the tram with two Spiegelgrund nurses through Vienna. "Feeling homesick," Karger simply stepped off the moving car. He went to his grandmother's apartment, but the nurses showed up there two hours later to take him back to Spiegelgrund. Upon Karger's return, he recounted, "They pushed me down to a chair and shaved my head, well, they pulled my hair out rather than shaving it, until I was bald." Staff repeatedly dunked Karger in ice water. This was the "immersion cure," an asylum method that Friedrich Zawrel depicted as "water, down, up, down, up, down, up that you think you'll suffocate." Karger was also submitted, naked, to what was called the Salzergasse, after a street in Vienna. As he described, "Left and right the boys are standing, and you have to walk the path between them, and they can beat you, that was the Salzergasse."

Karger sustained weeks of observation in Pavilions 15 and 17, ostensibly being evaluated for death. He wound up in Pavilion 11, the correctional group. Karger's grandmother was granted regular visits, along with the family members of other children. But Karger did not mention his abuse to her. He remembered, "They put up benches in the hallway, where our relatives sat with us, and the orderlies walked back and forth telling the visitors how nice they are to us." But when visitors left the staff confiscated their food and gifts, and the violence resumed. Karger remarked, "I never told my grandmother what they did to us, for she certainly would have come [. . .] and she would have probably ended up in a camp herself. So I didn't tell her this. Well, I just told her that we were fine and such. Subconsciously, I had already gotten the message."43

Visits could prove important, though, if relatives did learn the truth. Leopoldine Maier spoke of a nurse who advised her mother to visit every Sunday, who warned that "the children who are not visited will disappear and perish somewhere." So Maier's mother made the journey to Spiegelgrund every week from Mödling, outside Vienna, an hours-long "nightmare" journey by public transportation. Maier was not always allowed to see her mother, though—if she had vomited up her food that week, not eaten it all, or lost weight. But her mother kept coming all the same. Maier was in anguish. "I knew she was there, in the visitors' room and I cannot go to her. This is a feeling, this is awful despair and anger and fear." But Maier's mother was able to get her out of Spiegelgrund at the end of 1944. She was saved.[44]

Desperate relatives, though, were not always able to get to Spiegelgrund to see their child's condition, provide comfort, and press for release. From afar, family members could only send heartbreaking letters of love, preserved in the children's case files, like the one from nine-year-old Anna Luise Lübcke's mother at Christmas in 1943. Anna Luise had been transferred to Vienna all the way from a children's institution in Hamburg; her mother wrote, "My dear Anneliese, my thoughts are always with you, mommy is coming to you soon, which will be a great joy [. . .] Now my dear Anneliese, continue to do well and be very good until we can see each other again; wishes from all my heart." Spiegelgrund doctors condemned the girl, however, due to spastic paralysis in all four limbs. While doctor Marianne

Türk noted that "the child's mental abilities are astoundingly good," and that Anna Luise was "extremely inquisitive and asks everything possible of any person who is around," doctor Ernst Illing sent Anna Luise's file to Berlin for permission to kill the girl. Her physical condition, Illing said, made her "incapable of education or practical training, and excludes even the slightest possibility she might be able to work in the future." Anna Luise died at Spiegelgrund in the early morning of January 13, 1944, with pneumonia listed as the cause of death. Her mother made it to see her only the day before.[45]

In another tragedy, Ernst Ossenkamp was separated from his family who lived in Mönchengladbach, Germany. After playing a prank on a streetcar with six friends from school, Ernst had been institutionalized for "dangerousness to the public." He was transferred to Spiegelgrund from Germany at age twelve, where Ernst Illing petitioned Berlin for his killing as "ineducable and likely to be in permanent need of institutionalization." Ernst's family tried desperately to stay in touch, sending him letters and parcels. His sister, Marianne, wrote to Ernst on October 28, 1943: "Today, Nanni baked some nice cookies and made a small package of them. I hope you really enjoy it. Do the pears taste good? Soon we will send a fruit parcel. As soon as I have school vacation, I'll be back to you and take you home. As long as you are good, I'll come soon." But Ernst died the following day, purportedly of febrile inflamation of the intestine and pneumonia.[46]

Seventeen-year-old Erika Maria Stanzl wrote to her mother about her fears in Pavilion 15, Spiegelgrund's death ward. Erika had been sent to Spiegelgrund for disobeying her mother and sneaking away from home, but, poignantly, now beseeched her: "In the new ward where I am, many children have no visitors. Please mommy, bring them something too." Erika was scared by the horrific conditions in the death ward, telling mother, "Everything here is haywire. It's one thing after another. One child fell on the bed and knocked out his upper teeth and bled. So far I'm fine. Only I vomited once from a child with ulcerous ears, then I had to lie in bed." But Erika, like the children she feared for in Pavilion 15, died, too—officially designated with pneumonia. Doctor Helene Jockl had written to the Reich committee in Berlin that Erika was "fully developed physically, but nearly incapable of work. Very good retention, but lack of critical thought, inhibitions, and objectivity. Childish judgment." These were sufficient reasons to kill.[47]

BY THE TIME Spiegelgrund's killing program was in full swing, in mid-fall 1942, almost twice as many youths were dying in the killing pavilions as were leaving alive. Within the next two-and-a-half years, approximately 300 children were released or transferred from Pavilions 15 and 17, while 540 perished.[48] The Reich also expanded the pool of children who might fall victim to the killings. While the child euthanasia program initially targeted infants and toddlers under three years old, the age ceiling rose over time to eight, then to twelve and, ultimately, to sixteen.[49]

Staff at Spiegelgrund had a greater hand in selecting children for death than did personnel at most of the Reich's other "special children's wards." Usually, children deemed to have disabilities were first reported by outside doctors or authorities to the supervising Reich Committee in Berlin, which then ordered the children's transfer to a killing center. At Spiegelgrund, however, the process was reversed. Spiegelgrund doctors themselves reported children to Berlin who they believed should be killed. And they might go ahead with killings without waiting for formal authorization from Berlin.

Spiegelgrund's second director, Ernst Illing, inflicted diagnostic practices on children that could be deadly. Pneumatic encephalography, for example, was an excruciating procedure that injected air into children's brains after the removal of spinal fluid in order to conduct X-rays showing the cerebral ventricles.[50] Spiegelgrund doctors also collected children's body parts for research. Most notorious was Dr. Heinrich Gross, who preserved the brains of over four hundred children in jars meticulously stacked and labeled on shelves in the basement, which he used in his research through the 1980s. Indeed, the body parts of children killed at Spiegelgrund were disseminated among a number of research facilities, providing the basis for research long after the war.[51]

Certainly, children kept at Spiegelgrund were haunted by the specter of death. They had different degrees of knowledge of the killings—from hushed hearsay to eyewitness encounters—but many children sensed the peril that faced them. Fright and uncertainty were part of everyday life.

Alois Kaufmann was cowed by the fearful talk among the children. "I didn't dare to say a word, because I had heard that those who complain would be taken away and so on, there were rumors." Also etched in Kaufmann's memory were the selections that happened every two to three weeks, when Spiegelgrund doctor Heinrich Gross "came up and pointed at some of us; he said, 'You, you, you and you.' The children were taken from the group. The first children they selected were the bedwetters or harelips or the slow thinkers." Kaufmann continued, "We did not dare ask where they were taken. We never saw them again."[52] Ernst Pacher did dare to ask where the children were taken. "Sometimes some boys disappeared, and when you asked something like 'Won't he return?' or 'Did he go home?'— 'Don't ask such stupid things, or you'll end up there, too!' Such were the answers we frequently received from our orderlies." Rudolf Karger likewise stressed how nurses and orderlies hinted at dire consequences for disobedience. "They were constantly threatening us and warned that we'll see what will happen to us," said Karger. " 'Yes, you'll see.' "[53]

Survivors talked about the ominous handcarts that carried children's corpses across Spiegelgrund grounds. Rudolf Karger knew that the wagons were used "to transport the dead people" but, he said, "We didn't know who was inside." Ernst Pacher recounted what happened when he walked by workers drawing the cart: "We were, of course, curious, and we stared at them, and once one of them grinned back at us and said: 'Do you also want to be in there?' We got really scared, for the grin alone was something sinister to me." One day, Alois Kaufmann worked up the courage to look inside a cart when it was untended. As he opened the lid, he saw "little Karl W. who was lying in this green cart. He was dead. He had just been sitting at the desk behind me at school."[54] The scene witnessed by Johann Gross was even more macabre. As a worker pulled a handcart past a file of children walking to Spiegelgrund's school, Gross described, "In the small wagon—nothing but little dead children! They lay crisscrossed like dolls who had been thrown away, their limbs twisted unnaturally. Most of the small bodies had a very peculiar color. It was a kind of a red-green-blue." According to Gross, the nurse minding the children worried that the sight would cause unrest among the youths and called, " 'Silence up front! Or maybe one of you wants to ride with them?' "[55]

Amid survivors' accounts of fear and horror, there were some stories of sympathetic Spiegelgrund staff who went out of their way to protect children—such as the nurse who helped Friedrich Zawrel to escape, or the nurse who advised the mother of Leopoldine Maier to visit every week in order to secure the girl's release. Ernst Pacher remembered one nurse who saved him directly from death. When he had a severe abscess under his left arm and was at risk of blood poisoning, the night nurse, Mrs. Windhager, secretly drained his abscess. Pacher recalled, "I did not weigh anything, for we were just skin and bones, and she carried me out and said to me: 'Hush, no word from you and make no fuss, for we must not be noticed." She added, " 'You know there is a doctor who put you on his list, and you are to get an injection, but I am going to prevent that.' "[56]

But such stories of magnanimity are rare. And these same nurses nevertheless worked in an institution of systematic killing. Without compliance such as theirs and other staff, the murder of children would not have been possible. As Karl Jakubec's near-death experience in Pavilion 15 suggested, children's fates were sealed by an unending stream of impassive personnel:

They always gave us an injection, no, or if you were a bit too restless or, like a child is, a bit active some days, or say we're crying more or something, or also from pain or something, then they simply went so with sedative injections, what they injected didn't really matter anyway, the main thing was that they injected something, and the main thing it was quiet for a while. And then it was just terrible for us, and then also some died after. [. . .] It didn't even matter to us, because we had become so phlegmatic that we actually didn't care what they did. So when they came, the first time you were scared, afraid . . . , Jesus they are coming again already, and what is it now, but with time you become so phlegmatic that you say, well, you can't change things, you have to just accept it.[57]

IN THE FACE of these ghastly survivor stories, it is difficult to comprehend the actions and beliefs of those who ran the killing center. With scant documentation, the perspectives of Spiegelgrund perpetrators are largely lost to history. What remains are a handful of trial testimonies given by some Spiegelgrund defendants soon after the war. Pairing these with the victims' interviews is, of course, problematic. Spiegelgrund perpetrators were concerned with self-exoneration in the face of the death penalty. Their interrogations occurred in an adversarial political climate in the immediate aftermath of the crimes, and were not—as the victims' interviews—aimed at understanding events decades hence. Still, the perpetrators' strategies of defense are themselves telling, and part of the story of Spiegelgrund.

Many euthanasia perpetrators said they saw the killing of children at Spiegelgrund as a key part of Nazis' double-pronged mission to help children deemed redeemable, and to purge those who were not. Erwin Jekelius made this explicit in his 1948 interrogation by the Soviet secret police (NKVD) in Moscow: "The entire activity of the clinic was to be carried out in two directions: healing sick children and killing those who were terminally ill."[58] Thirty-one-year-old Spiegelgrund doctor Marianne Türk maintained that selections were grounded in firm principles of Nazi science. In her October 1945 hearing in Vienna, she stated that "this was supposed to be something completely new, basing proper treatment on observations, so that children would be directed correctly."[59] At Spiegelgrund, "observation" meant determining a child's potential usefulness to the *Volk*. Staff would weed out youths deemed to be a burden on the national community, as physically and/or behaviorally incapable of education or future employment.

Spiegelgrund doctors used the language of social utility to substantiate their death requests to the Reich committee in Berlin. The vast majority of applications labeled the youths with blanket terms such as "ineducable," "unable to work," and "in need of continual care." Only rarely did doubt creep into the pronouncements—and if it did, it did not necessarily change the outcome. When Ernst Illing reported two-month-old Hannelore Fuchs, who had Down syndrome, to Berlin in July 1943, he said that her "cure or improvement" was "unlikely, though cannot yet be decided with certainty"; notwithstanding the equivocation, Hannelore died two days later, with the official cause of death "weakness of life." Perhaps the usual doses of barbiturates had acted quickly on the infant, as Spiegelgrund doctors explained happened sometimes.[60]

Illing sent an even more ambivalent petition to Berlin regarding seven-year-old Peter Pörzgen. At the same time Illing graphically detailed the effects of Peter's hip joint tuberculosis, from pus-filled fistulas to disfiguring bone suppuration,

Illing complimented Peter's personal qualities. "The child maintains good contact, language comprehension and vocabulary are adequate," Illing wrote, "he is always quiet, friendly and comfortable."[61] Illing's rare praise was not sufficient to spare Peter, however, who died two weeks later.

Although killing children was to become a permanent part of the Nazi health care system, it was to be conducted in secrecy. As Jekelius portrayed the process, "Before we started killing children, I arranged a secret meeting of the medical staff (10 doctors and nurses), explaining the situation and taking an oath from each of them to preserve strict secrecy about all related measures."[62] Spiegelgrund nurse Anna Katschenka said at her 1946 interrogation in Vienna that she received the message loud and clear; Jekelius reportedly "explained to me that I should never talk about incidents at the institution and also ask no unnecessary questions."[63] Katschenka elaborated, two years later, that Jekelius had told her there was "a secret decree by the Reich Ministry of the Interior that such incurable patients should be euthanized (in relation to children up to 16 years of age). I considered this decree to be binding as public law, and I saw in it my justification." Katschenka concluded, "With euthanasia I was never conscious of acting unlawfully."[64]

Perpetrators were matter of fact in the accounts they gave in their trials, representing the killing of children as a professional clinical practice. Marianne Türk stressed, "I did not proceed carelessly, but considered whether I should report a child scrupulously and at length."[65] The killings were part of scientific protocol. Ernst Illing praised the approach in his postwar interrogation: "I regarded the new doctrines as serious and responsible."[66] He suggested that Spiegelgrund performed a valuable service because "none of the children would, in my opinion, ever be remotely capable of education or work."[67] The killings offered yet another method for perfecting the *Volk*.

Deaths also became part of the daily routine.[68] Marianne Türk and Heinrich Gross even resided on the Spiegelgrund grounds, with Ernst Illing choosing to live with his family in Pavilion 15, the death ward.[69] After the war, Türk reflected on just how habituated she had become to the life of murder, ordering overdoses of Luminal, Veronal, and morphine in injections and in pulverized tablets added to cocoa powder or other foods that children would gladly eat. "With the cases that we had by the dozens in the institution, putting an end to this human wretchedness was an automatic thought." Türk outlined how the implementation of death orders was quotidian, too:

The nurses—who undertook the actual execution since they added the sleeping pills to the food—had access to the medicine cabinet. They would be told by Dr. Illing or me that the decisions about child X or Y had arrived, and the nurses then knew what they had to do.[70]

At the same time Spiegelgrund defendants offered cold explanations, they argued that the killings were acts of compassion. Anna Katschenka, for example, claimed that Jekelius told her that "children who could no longer be helped at all were given a sleeping aid so that they could 'go to sleep' painlessly."[71] Killing was done, she asserted, from a "purely human standpoint," in cases where there was "no prospect of improvement, and the children's unnecessary agony should be shortened."[72] Marianne Türk insisted that the children did not suffer an "agonizing death," but only gently "fell into a slumber," as killing was an "act of mercy."[73]

THE PARENTS OF children who died at Spiegelgrund had varied reactions. Many believed—or chose to believe—the death notices that came in the mail which said their child had perished from pneumonia or other natural causes. Others might have suspected wrongdoing; after all, knowledge of the killing of the disabled was widespread in Vienna.

Some parents who feared that their children might face death tried desperately to rescue them. The mother and father of Günther Karth, for example, had given up all of their five children to Vienna's welfare system; they were poor and deemed to have an "asocial family." When Günther grew sick at age six, he was transferred to Pavilion 15 at Spiegelgrund. Alarmed, his father wrote to get the boy back, invoking supposed Reich principles: "We will not allow it, he is our flesh and blood, he belongs to us. We will not rest until we have the child, since we're now in the Third Reich, where justice should reign." Günther's mother wrote an emotional appeal: "I beg you again to give me the child before it is too late, I plead and beg you, as my heart is aching and broken with anguish and grief." It is unclear what Günther's mother meant by "too late," but it was indeed too late. Günther died in June 1944.[74]

The mother of Felix Janauschek was more explicit about the stakes of life and death at Spiegelgrund. At sixteen, Felix had been diagnosed at Spiegelgrund with the "highest degree of dementia after cerebral palsy," though staff lauded his phenomenal talent and passion for playing piano. Felix's mother likewise invoked Nazi justice, warning that since her husband was a long-standing member of the Nazi Party, she would appeal to her district leader [*Gauleiter*] for her son's release. She also signaled that she knew what fate might befall Felix, demanding, "I want my child. My living child."[75] Felix died in March 1943.

As a nurse in Vienna, Anny Wödl knew in advance that her son, Alfred, would be killed, and negotiated the terms. Wödl had sent Alfred to live at Gugging at age four because he had difficulties walking and talking. She grew afraid once she heard about the killing of the disabled in Vienna, and met with other parents to take action. She brought her concerns directly to Hermann Linden at the Reich Ministry of the Interior in Berlin. When Wödl learned that Alfred himself faced "transport," she went back to Linden to appeal. Linden allegedly told her, "We can fulfill your wish as an exception. We will allow the child to be brought to Spiegelgrund from Gugging, but the child must die."[76] Alfred was transferred to Spiegelgrund in February 1941; in his photograph, he looked askance at the camera in three-quarters profile, with closely cropped brown hair and visible ribcage. Wödl testified after the war, "I begged Dr. Jekelius, that if the death of my child could not be stopped, that it be quick and painless. He promised me this." However, upon seeing Alfred's corpse, Wödl said she "was struck by the look of pain on his face."[77]

The mother of Herta Gschwandtner, Luise,

openly confronted Spiegelgrund staff about the killings. Herta was born "mongoloid," and transferred to Spiegelgrund in 1943 at one-and-a-half years old. She died just eleven days after her transfer, ostensibly of pneumonia. Luise Gschwandtner was incredulous at the speed of her daughter's death. She wrote to Ernst Illing and Spiegelgrund nurses, "I still can't grasp why my dear little Herta had to leave me so fast, to die so quickly. [. . .] We still can not believe that our child Herthi was not curable." Gschwandtner went on, "I am completely heartbroken. I would gladly sacrifice my life for my child. . . . Please excuse me for my bad writing, which I wrote with very tearful eyes." In her letter, Gschwandtner went so far as to suggest that Herta was murdered. "Now I have to bear twice the pain because people are saying straight to my face that she was simply poisoned, so to speak, eliminated."[78] Illing wrote back that nothing was amiss with her daughter's death. He warned Gschwandtner that he would launch police action if the deaths at Spiegelgrund continued to be questioned: "I would also ask you to vigorously oppose rumors of that kind; if necessary, I will lodge a complaint against such rumormongers."[79]

But rumors about the killings were rife in Vienna, and exacerbated families' anguish over the deaths of their children. The parents of two-month-old Hermine Döckl were devastated when their daughter, diagnosed as "mongoloid," perished five weeks after her admission to Spiegelgrund, reportedly of pneumonia. The Döckl's family doctor, Hans Geyer, asked Illing to give him a medical accounting of Hermine's death in order to alleviate the relatives' torment; he said a proper explanation would bring the family "peace and dispel all of the hushed rumors and conjectures." Hermine's mother, Geyer warned, was "expressing suicidal intentions and cannot be left alone." Illing replied simply that the infant had "severe weakness of life" and that the good doctor should surely know that "mongoloid" children had shorter life expectancies.[80]

The majority of parents' letters in the case files of children killed at Spiegelgrund are heart wrenching. They voice sorrow, disbelief, anger— and frequently demand more information about how their children died. There was, nevertheless, a wide range of responses. A number of families expressed acceptance, even approval of their child's untimely death. After all, many in the Reich even sought their child's admission to killing wards in the hopes their child might perish.[81] They might complain about the burden of caring for their child, perhaps while struggling to make ends meet, with other children at home or a husband away at war. Yet discussion of child-killing was not just limited to the strains of the Third Reich. The idea of ending "life unworthy of life" had circulated long before the Nazis came to power. In 1925, Ewald Meltzer, the head of an asylum in Saxony, grew so concerned about the ethics of the issue that he asked the parents of children at his institution: "Would you agree to the painless curtailment of the life of your child if experts had established that it was suffering from incurable idiocy?" To his dismay, 73 percent of the parents who participated in the survey answered "yes."[82]

Spiegelgrund staff said that some parents held explicit conversations about death wishes for their children. The mother of a toddler who Asperger transferred to Spiegelgrund, Herta Schreiber, allegedly told doctor Margarethe Hübsch, "It would be better if she died."[83] Marianne Türk noted that one mother of a child with epilepsy "thought it would be a comfort and a reassurance to her if the child could close her eyes forever."[84] Both children were, indeed, killed.

Parents did not necessarily agree on the best course for their child. Because Ilse Philippovic suffered from epilepsy, the doctor at her boarding house reportedly advised her father that "it would be best for the child to go the way of all flesh." Ilse's father initiated her admission to Spiegelgrund—a week before Ilse's eleventh birthday—"without saying anything to his wife." Ilse died a month later from supposedly "unknown" causes.[85]

Parental attitudes were not to be a factor in selecting children for death, as Spiegelgrund procedures were to follow purportedly scientific principles. Marianne Türk, in her trial testimony, insisted that Spiegelgrund doctors operated independently of parental pressure: "When parents demanded euthanasia, and that happened, they were always denied."[86] Ernst Illing explained that it was important to keep the process in the hands of medical professionals. As Illing put it, "There were also parents who approached me to make use of euthanasia, and I refused because the criteria for it were not met. The dangers of this new method were removed, in my opinion, as only responsible people were entrusted with these things."[87]

While the reports of Spiegelgrund staff may be viewed with skepticism, some parents' own letters suggest approval of their children's deaths. This came in various forms. Most often, parents spoke of early deaths as merciful. When six-year-old Rosa Schörkhuber died a month after her arrival at Spiegelgrund—as Ernst Illing reported to the Reich committee in Berlin that "no possibility of employment is expected"—her mother wrote to Heinrich Gross, "It is best for her, as she has already suffered a great deal with convulsions." Rosa's mother did remark, though, that "I can not believe how quickly she went."[88] Since ten-year-old Marion Eisenach, photographed in a neat plaid top with short bangs and a short haircut framing her face, had Down syndrome, Illing wrote to the Reich committee that "the child is ineducable and, with probability bordering on certainty, will not be capable of work." After Marion died, her mother wrote to Ernst Illing, "The Almighty had done a good deed, now my child is in good hands, many thanks for the loving care you gave my little Marion."[89]

Some relatives went beyond the formal rhetoric of acceptance and sent chilling thank-you letters. Two letters involved teenage boys— fourteen-year-old Max Reichmann, who was deaf and purportedly developmentally impaired, and sixteen-year-old Hubert Imkamp, who was paralyzed and blind in one eye. Jekelius justified Max Reichmann's death to the Reich committee because "no capacity for work was expected" and he was a "Jew"—one of at least four children designated as Jewish who were killed at Spiegelgrund. Max Reichmann's aunt did not mince words, exclaiming "I think my sister will not be unhappy that her unhappy child has been released!" She was unequivocal: "It is better now that he is no longer alive! I thank you again."[90] When Hubert Imkamp died six weeks after his transfer to Spiegelgrund, his father lavished praise on Ernst Illing. "Allow us to express our most profound thanks to you and your institution for the valuable services you have rendered to our son Hubert in a sacrificing manner. Unfortunately we could not go to the burial due to poor transportation. Be assured you will always have our sincere gratitude and esteem."[91] The extent to which these relatives deduced the youths' actual cause of death is not clear—but the satisfied subtext of their letters certainly is.

SURVIVOR LEOPOLDINE MAIER, contemplating her experience at Spiegelgrund, suggested that complicity in the cruelty—and in the Nazi system as a whole—was pervasive and inescapable. She said people's potential for depravity would torment her throughout her life:

> Each person raises the question in me: Are you for me or against me? It was always a question of survival. And that question still lingers with me somehow when I meet somebody: With whom is he siding now and with whom was he siding then. And would he have helped you had he known or would he not have helped you at all. [. . .] I am not angry with anybody for how can you be mad with somebody when the evil has no name, when the evil is just a part of life, like it was the case there. But the evil belonged there, it was everyday life, and nobody questioned it.[92]

9

In Service to the *Volk*

THE MISSION TO eliminate undesirable children mirrored the Reich's ambition to eliminate undesirable populations. While Nazi psychiatrists killed youths at home, sequestered behind the walls of hospitals and sanatoria, the Reich wreaked Armageddon across a continent.

The Second World War was so destructive that historians have difficulty even estimating its death toll. Over sixty million people perished around the globe—fifteen million in battle and forty-five million civilians—around 3 percent of the world's population. The war involved seventy nations that spanned seas, oceans, and four continents. The scale is difficult to grasp. War and occupation hit eastern Europe hardest, claiming, for example, up to twenty-seven million Soviet citizens (14 percent of the population) and up to 5.8 million Poles (over 16 percent of the population). Germany lost between 6.6 and 8.8 million people, at least 8 percent of its population.[1]

The Nazi state aimed to establish a new order in Europe. From 1939 until 1942, its goal appeared to be in sight. The Reich occupied territories, created satellite states, and forged alliances across eastern and western Europe, from Bulgaria to Estonia to Norway to France. Germany even had aspirations in North Africa, too, waging war in Morocco, Algeria, Tunisia, Libya, and Egypt.

In Vienna, most people, including Asperger, supported the Reich. Many were pleased that the Nazi state invested in rebuilding the Austrian economy; as Germany coordinated Austria into its war machine, unemployment dropped, large firms boomed, commerce modernized, and people enjoyed well-paying jobs in industry and greater social mobility. Austrians resented, though, how the Reich dismantled Austrian autonomy and even Austria as an entity. The former nation became seven Reich districts, or *Reichsgaue*, that were collectively called the *Ostmark* and, after 1942, the "Danubian and Alpine Reich Districts." The new boundaries tripled the size of greater Vienna, making it the second-largest city in the Reich—yet the regime reduced Vienna's power from a capital to a provincial city and kept Austria peripheral to the Reich overall.

Vienna's inhabitants accepted the mass persecution and expulsion of Jews, as the extreme anti-Semitic violence that had accompanied the Nazi annexation was followed by more methodical measures. At first, the regime encouraged Austrian Jews to emigrate, an initiative spearheaded by Adolf Eichmann's Central Office for Jewish Emigration in Vienna. Emigration involved daunting paperwork and extortionate fees, but 117,000 out of the 192,000 Jews living in Austria were able to leave between 1938 and 1940, or six in ten. For those who remained, life became progressively more painful. Jews were forced to wear the yellow Star of David and were banned from public transportation, stores, and parks. They lost their jobs, businesses, and homes.

Jewish emigration became more difficult after the start of the war and, by October 1941, the Reich switched to a policy of exterminating Jews. The regime began forcibly transporting Austrian Jews to ghettos and concentration camps in eastern Europe—approximately 47,555 people. Deportations were particularly public affairs in Vienna, more than in Germany, with crowds gathered to watch and jeer Jews' expulsions to the east.

The Reich's greatest ambitions were in eastern Europe, where it sought to create a hierarchical racial paradise for Germans. Under "General Plan East" [*Generalplan Ost*], the war would clear "living space," or *Lebensraum*, for Reich citizens, who would colonize and control indigenous populations. Germany began to implement the plan after it invaded Poland in 1939, having signed a nonaggression pact with the Soviet Union. The Nazi state expelled nearly one million Poles and Jews from western Poland eastward—clearing them from their homes—and moved around six hundred thousand ethnic Germans from elsewhere in eastern Europe into the emptied territory.

The Reich found additional opportunities for remaking eastern Europe with its invasion of the Soviet Union in June 1941. In Operation Barbarossa, the German Wehrmacht came within twelve miles of Moscow and, as it advanced, German forces subjugated Slavs, destroyed populations, and established racial rule over immense territories. German forces also captured 5.7 million Soviet prisoners of war, of whom 3.3 million died in German custody—the second-largest population group killed by the Reich.

Reengineering eastern Europe proved a logistical nightmare, however. The chaos radicalized Nazi population policies and, combined with pernicious anti-Semitism, escalated the Nazis' ghettoization and murder of Jews. The decision to annihilate Europe's Jewry in the Final Solution was finalized at the Wannsee Conference in January 1942. Mobile killing units murdered roughly one million Jews in mass shootings. Around three million Jews perished in concentration camps, eight hundred thousand in ghettos, and hundreds of thousands in gas vans, labor battalions, evacuation marches, and operations in the Balkans. In all, six million Jews died in the Holocaust, two-thirds of European Jewry.

Austrians played a disproportionate role in Nazi killing operations. Although only 8 percent of the population of greater Germany, Austrians represented 14 percent of the SS membership and 40 percent of personnel in extermination programs.[2] Some of this imbalance was because German Nazis took plum jobs in Austria and assigned Austrians to the occupied territories in eastern Europe, but much of it was due to virulent homegrown anti-Semitism. Also, when it came to racial and biological persecution, Viennese physicians and officials came to occupy a unique position in the regime. As the second-largest city in the Reich, close to Eastern Europe and with a large Jewish population, Vienna was at the forefront of lethal policies and initiatives.

Many Austrians came to identify with the Nazi state, increasingly bound to it through the experience of war. People shared widespread enthusiasm for the Reich's initial triumphs from 1939–1942—and disappointment as the tide turned toward defeat with losses in the immense battles of Stalingrad and Kursk in 1943, and the American and British D-Day Invasion in Normandy in June 1944. The existential stakes of the war tied individuals to the regime.

Public opinion in Vienna soured over daily conditions. People grumbled about privations, rations, and food shortages. Different segments of the Austrian population had different complaints. Farmers lost laborers to industry and the military; workers faced increasing controls; Catholics deplored Nazi attacks on the church. Austrian Nazis complained they were sidelined by German Nazis who took leadership roles in government and relegated Austrians to less important positions. After years of underground struggle, Austrian National Socialists felt they deserved more. As elsewhere in the Reich, people liked and disliked different aspects of Nazi rule, based on region, class, and interests. This variation prevented discontent from coalescing into substantial resistance. So despite widespread dissatisfaction, society upheld the regime—as there was no other alternative—and most citizens remained loyal until the end.

For Asperger and his associates in Vienna, quality of life remained relatively high throughout the war. Reich citizens fared well compared to the populations they subjugated, typically better fed, housed, and spared the ravages of the battlefield. Unlike in World War One, when Vienna faced catastrophic food shortages, starvation, and civilian unrest, the Viennese population remained supplied and at peace. Vienna was also spared the worst of Allied bombing. The Allies unleashed explosives on sixty-one Reich cities during the war, destroying one in five homes and killing around six hundred thousand civilians; the fire-bombing of Hamburg and Dresden raised street temperatures over 1,500 degrees Celsius that turned people into ash in seconds. But Vienna, known as the "Reich's air raid shelter," was out of reach until the Allies established bombing flotillas in Italy in the spring of 1944. Missions then aimed for tactical targets in the city, rather than carpet bombing, and killed twenty-four thousand civilians.

As Europe collapsed, Germans and Austrians continued to sustain the Reich. Asperger and his colleagues worked through the destruction, publishing, debating, and delivering lectures to one another. Nazi child psychiatry was only a small pocket of activity within the regime's efforts to remake Europe. But practitioners took their task seriously, and continued to work in earnest even as the continent descended into mass slaughter.

The Third Reich harnessed a curious juxtaposition of efforts, of total war versus erudite debates, of genocide versus journal articles. But the task to mold the mind mattered, as psychiatrists discussed the finer points of Nazi philosophy while carnage raged around them.

DURING THE WAR, Franz Hamburger sought to promote his faculty and the research at the University of Vienna Children's Hospital. As he had purged Jewish and liberal physicians, the number of associate professors dropped from twenty-three in 1930, to seventeen in 1938, to an average of eight during the years of the Third Reich. The number of research papers presented per year fell from thirty-six, to twenty-five, to an average of eight. Hamburger rushed to fill the vacuum. In short order, nine of his advisees, including Asperger, gained promotion between 1940 and 1945. Hamburger's students spent less time on their postdoctoral theses than had their predecessors under Pirquet, averaging ten versus thirteen years, and were younger at their time of completion.[3] Asperger, like his colleagues, appears to have benefited from the expulsion of his Jewish and liberal colleagues, writing his thesis in their wake.

The thirty-seven-year-old Asperger may have worked in haste, without sufficient time amid all of his other activities to conduct thorough research. Hamburger noted to the university administration in December 1942 that, due to Asperger's "exceptional dedication to the children entrusted to him," Asperger was not spending much time on his postdoctoral thesis; he was coming to his research "just now."[4] In the end, Asperger's research appears to have been thin. Though he claimed in the thesis that he had seen "more than 200" cases of autistic psychopathy in ten years of practice, he did not elaborate on this nebulous record base and, besides case studies of four boys, mentioned few other children in his thesis.[5]

Asperger presented his postdoctoral thesis on autistic psychopathy just before he was drafted into military service in a Vienna medical unit, in October 1943. A few months later, he was sent to work as a field doctor for a Wehrmacht infantry division in the Axis puppet state of Croatia, formerly Yugoslavia, which was one of the ghastliest theaters of the Second World War. There until August 1945, Asperger confronted widespread atrocities, guerrilla violence, ferocious Wehrmacht reprisals, and the ethnic cleansing of over 320,000 Serbs.[6] Up to 11 percent of the population of Yugoslavia was killed—among the highest national fatality rates in Europe. Asperger, according to his daughter, wrote of ever-present danger in his diary, and of the injuries and deaths of comrades and enemies alike.[7]

Yet personally, Asperger appears to have had a positive experience in Yugoslavia. His daughter maintained that Asperger's diary is full of descriptions of the mountain wilderness he so loved, as well as of the local people he encountered—their festivals, customs, and traditional garb. He suffered no injuries beyond a bout of dysentery. Asperger also felt strong bonds with his comrades, stressing that war was "where you have to care for others."[8]

Later in life, Asperger emphasized what he had gained from his time in Yugoslavia, highlighting his fortitude and heroism. Echoing long-standing masculine ideals of proving one's mettle in battle, Asperger recalled,

> I was in Croatia, deployed in the partisan war. I wouldn't want to have missed any of these experiences. It is good to know how you behave when facing danger, as the bullets whistle by—it is also a place where you are tested.[9]

Apparently Asperger found fulfillment amid the carnage and the Wehrmacht's notoriously vicious conduct in Yugoslavia. Reich reprisal policy, for example, meant killing one hundred citizens for every German soldier killed. Yet Asperger insisted that he himself was innocent of any violence. It was "a great gift of fate that I never had to shoot anyone," he maintained after the war.[10] Thus although Asperger was surrounded by mass murder, he himself was not a direct perpetrator, and so was not compromised. He actually called himself a bit of a hero. He said he saved the day when his unit got lost retreating westward at the end of the war:

> I must say that I got my whole unit over the border to Austria with my *Wandervogel* [youth group] methods, with a lot of luck, of course, but I guided because I could

orient myself with my Busole [compass] and the stars and the others could not. Finally, we were saved.[11]

During his time in Yugoslavia, Asperger was able to maintain ties to his clinic, exchanging letters with department staff and keeping up with work, news, and patients. Three of Asperger's articles were published while he was away, one in mid-1944 on postencephalitic personality disorder and two in early 1944 that were from his postdoctoral work, including his seminal treatise on autistic psychopathy.[12]

ASPERGER'S POSTDOCTORAL THESIS, "The 'Autistic Psychopaths' in Childhood," can be read as a culmination of his experiences during the Third Reich. As the regime radicalized, so, too, did Asperger's writings. Asperger's definition of autistic psychopathy sharpened year by year, as he described it in ever more judgmental, social, and eugenicist terms, and incorporated ever more elements of Nazi child psychiatry. He wrote at different points in time:

> 1937—"There are as many approaches [to child development] as there are different personalities. It is impossible to establish a rigid set of criteria for a diagnosis."

1938—"This well-characterized group of children who we name 'autistic psycho-paths'—because the confinement of the self (*autos*) has led to a narrowing of relations to their environment."

1941—"A group of abnormal children, who we refer to as 'autistic psycho-paths' [. . .] they live their own lives without an emotional relationship with the environment."

1944—"The autist is only himself (*autos*) and is not an active member of the greater organism which he is influenced by and which he influences constantly."[13]

In 1937, Asperger had cautioned against creating diagnoses; in 1938, only months after the Nazi annexation of Austria, he had described autism as a "well-characterized group of children." In 1941, this became "a group of abnormal children." By 1944, Asperger was employing fascist rhetoric of the *Volk*, pronouncing autistic children to be outside of "the greater organism."

Asperger also raised the ante on social con-nectedness. What he had called autistic children's "narrowing of relations to their environment" in 1938 hardened, in 1941, into living "without an emotional relationship with the environment."

Which then hardened, in 1944, into a state of total solipsism: "The autist is only himself."

He grew more critical of autistic children. In another publication from 1944, "The Curative Education Care Center" in the *Viennese Clinical Weekly,* Asperger disdained "those who go their own way, the autistic, who can not integrate, and therefore constantly rub against the community." He stated that his clinic was to teach children "passable assimilation," to "grow up correctly within the community."[14] Parents could jeopardize children's socialization, Asperger warned. In line with the views of the Nazi state, Asperger stressed the importance of replacing family bonds with group bonds—as well as the centrality to that process of the Hitler Youth, the League of German Girls, and state-run schools and care centers.[15] In cases where Asperger suspected parents posed a "danger" to children's integration, his clinic ordered "regular monitoring" and even "home visits."[16]

In his 1944 thesis, Asperger emphasized Nazi psychiatry's concept of *Gemüt* and social connectedness. Since Asperger's introduction to the treatise was not included in the published English translation, it is not known to an English-speaking audience.[17] So while Asperger cited eminent figures such as Ernst Kretschmer, Ludwig Klages, and Carl Jung in the body of his thesis—and his work has been interpreted in terms of those more mainstream figures—Asperger framed his work with the ideas of Nazi child psychiatrists and *Gemüt* in the introduction. And it is these Reich concepts that provided the basis for Asperger's ultimate definition of autistic psychopathy.[18]

Asperger introduced *Gemüt* as the "most important side" of the character. In adopting this terminology, Asperger was breaking with Erwin Lazar's tradition at the Curative Education Clinic of the University of Vienna Children's Hospital; Asperger later explained that Schröder and Heinze, as leaders of the "Leipzig school of child psychiatry," had "railed against Lazar" because Lazar did not share their "established expressions" such as *Gemüt*.[19] Despite having begun his career in Lazar's clinic, Asperger sided with Schröder and Heinze in 1944. He cited Hans Heinze—the top euthanasia leader—in his first reference to *Gemüt* on the third page of his treatise.

Asperger then built from Heinze's "On the Phenomenology of *Gemüt*" to shower attention on Paul Schröder, discussing him on five of the eight pages of his introduction. Explaining how "the assessment of *Gemüt* is of central importance to Schröder's work," Asperger adopted Schröder's definition of *Gemüt* as "that spiritual side 'that contains relations with other people, the ability to take an interest in others, to empathize, to be with them.' "[20]

In an informal aside, Asperger joked that Schröder, "in discussions of *Gemüt*, always returns to the word and term '*Agape!*' " This was a Greek word for selfless love, which had taken on theological meaning with early Christians' agape feasts, a ritual meal celebrating Christian or brotherly love. Schröder used *Agape* as a term to convey children's aptitude for attachment, affection, empathy, generosity of spirit, and community feeling, a social and spiritual outgrowth of healthy *Gemüt*. Heinze, too, was concerned with children's "lack of *Agape*" [*Agapemangel*].[21]

Before his 1944 thesis, *Gemüt* had been fairly peripheral to Asperger's work. Although Asperger progressively invoked the functional goal of Nazi child psychiatry—integration into the collective—he had seldom invoked this signature term. In his articles from 1938–1943, Asperger had cited *Gemüt* most often in describing Hamburger's theory of "thymogen automatism." Hamburger claimed that the superior *Gemüt* of the educator could transfer to the *Gemüt* of the child, as though it was something one could catch.[22] Hamburger also advocated transmitting *Gemüt* among individuals in society through state institutions such as the Hitler Youth and the military. Since Hamburger stated that *Gemüt* even led to "changes in our bodies"—improving skin, musculature, and heart function—he instructed that it was doctors' responsibility to bestow

Gemüt for a "healthy psychic climate in greater Germany."[23]

Asperger's own pronouncements on *Gemüt* were rather minimal before 1944. He did not mention it at all in his 1937 article. Asperger's 1938 article mentioned it in passing; he said that the level of *Gemüt* might be one of several factors in deciding a child's sterilization, and criticized some children's "*gemüt*-less malice." His 1942 article mentioned *Gemüt* in the context of Schröder's priorities, that "qualities of *Gemüt*" were of "decisive importance" to a child's "social prognosis." His 1943 article, "Experience and Personality," went a little further to note that "qualities of *Gemüt*" were a "decisive question" in the "evaluation of each personality."[24]

But in his 1944 treatise, Asperger asserted that *Gemüt* was of highest importance. He went so far as to argue, "A person's whole personality speaks from the *Gemüt*." Asperger even placed *Gemüt* at the heart of his diagnosis of autistic psychopathy. As he put it, "It is a qualitative otherness, a disharmony of feeling, of *Gemüt*, often completely surprising contradictions, that brings about the disorder of adaptation."[25]

In elevating the role of *Gemüt*, Asperger was reflecting how the ideas of his senior colleagues in Nazi child psychiatry evolved over the Third Reich. After Heinze and Schröder had disseminated the concept of *Gemüt* in the early and mid-1930s, figures prominent in Nazi euthanasia killings deemed *Gemüt* a critical characteristic. In 1939, leading child psychiatrist Werner Villinger, who would soon become a T4 "expert" selecting adults for euthanasia killings, dissected children's "community competence" [*Gemeinschaftsfähigkeit*] and developed a three-by-four matrix of "characterology" that singled out those who were "less approachable, cool to cold natures," determined by the quality of one's "*Gemüt*."[26] Psychiatrist and neurologist Friedrich Panse, also a T4 "expert," wrote in 1940 about the prevailing ideas of "*Gemüt*-less psychopaths."[27] Gerhard Kujath—a proponent of curative education who was a head doctor at the euthanasia clinic of Wiesengrund in Berlin-Wittau—sought to redress "*Gemüt*-defect." As he claimed in articles in 1942, curative education meant "teaching community," awakening the "collective soul within the individual" and children's "fundamental urge to assimilate and align with the we-gestalt." Depending on their capacity, youths would be sorted into institutions ranging from reformatory homes to detention centers to concentration camps. Kujath himself presided over medical experiments and the deaths of at least eighty-one children.[28] But drawing on the compassionate rhetoric common to Nazi psychiatry, Kujath urged his colleagues to "approach each child impartially, with full

335

pedagogical faith, holding that the impossible might still be possible." With "closer inspection," the psychiatrist can discover a child's "various talents" and "*Gemüt*-ful aspects."[29]

Over the 1940s, euthanasia leaders in Vienna also deemed *Gemüt* central to one's worth. As director of Spicgelgrund, Erwin Jekelius asked attendees of the first meeting of the Vienna Society for Curative Education in 1941: "Of what use is the greatest intelligence and greatest fortitude if one has a complete poverty of *Gemüt* [*Gemütsarmut*] and antisocial drive?"[30] Jekelius even referred one teenager for potential death at Steinhof because of her "antisocial personality with dissocial traits (cheeky, unruly)" that added up to a "poverty of *Gemüt*."[31]

Ernst Illing, succeeding Jekelius as medical director of Spiegelgrund, likewise insisted that children possess *Gemüt*. In an address to Vienna's Society for Racial Hygiene at the University of Vienna, published in 1943, Illing cited Schröder and Heinze when defining *Gemüt* as the ability to forge "any emotional connection with other people." In Illing's opinion, one could spot children with a shortage of *Gemüt* [*Gemütsmangel*] from age three or four. Although such youths might be intellectually "gifted," they "lacked the ability to be considerate of others. They have no real friends, they know neither ties to relatives nor to objective values. They have no attachment, no need for affection, no compassion."[32]

To Illing, children's lack of social feeling translated into a lack of collective spirit. This posed a problem for the Reich. The children would not feel part of the national community, without "patriotism and love of Fatherland." Soldiers, in particular, required *"well-defined qualities of Gemüt"* (emphasis in original) for "enthusiasm, upstanding attitudes, absolute reliability and loyalty, genuine fellowship, human compassion." After all, having *Gemüt* was what it meant to be German. Illing held that members of the *Volk* possessed a depth of *Gemüt* [*gemütstiefe*] that "the British and Anglo-Americans" did not; "Bolsheviks" lacked *Gemüt* [*gemütsarm*], or were "at least considerably stunted."[33]

Illing suggested dire consequences for sixteen-year-old Raimund H., who he described as "rudely lacking *Gemüt* [*gemütsarm*], exhibiting no bond to people nor things." This meant Raimund was too detached from his surroundings; the boy was "objectively disinterested" and his "mood is consistently indifferent." Illing recommended his transfer to the brutal SS Juvenile Protection Camp at Moringen.[34] Illing also denounced twelve-year-old Friedrich Zawrel at Spiegelgrund in 1943 because of "his monstrous poverty of *Gemüt*." Then Spiegelgrund doctor Heinrich Gross found Illing's 1943 pronouncement important enough to use, verbatim, in his expert opinion on Zawrel three decades later, in 1975.[35]

While Asperger adopted his colleagues' emphasis on *Gemüt* in his 1944 thesis, he gave *Gemüt* greater dimensionality. Rather than seeing *Gemüt* as a straightforward trait that children either had or lacked, Asperger argued that "*Gemüt* is not a constant, which is simply present in different people to different quantities." *Gemüt* was "an extremely complex function" that had "great qualitative differences among various personalities."[36]

In Asperger's view, it was not a lack of *Gemüt*, but anomalous *Gemüt*, that caused autistic psychopathy. This may sound generous of Asperger, granting autistic children at least some form of *Gemüt*, but his actual descriptions of youths' *Gemüt* were much more disturbing. Asperger cautioned readers at the outset of his treatise just how much "Parents, guides, and friends must endure, or better, learn—how different the *Gemüt* of the autistic psychopaths is."[37]

Yet Asperger contradicted himself on whether autistic psychopathy was about different *Gemüt* or the deficit of *Gemüt*. In his introduction, Asperger insisted that "If you want to judge *Gemüt*, contradictions are impossible to classify or measure with the terms 'poverty of *Gemüt* [*Gemütsarmut*] or 'richness of *Gemüt*'

[*Gemütsmreichtum*]." But later in the paper he judged that autistic children's "wickedness and cruelty speak clearly to poverty of *Gemüt* [*Gemütsarmut*]."[38] This discrepancy suggests that Asperger may not exactly have thought through his adoption of *Gemüt* in 1944. Also, he might not have felt as charitably toward autistic children as he later claimed.

Asperger built upon ideas of *Gemüt* in his thesis to reflect Nazi psychiatry's overriding concern with community feeling, stressing the importance of collective belonging, and progressively identifying children who he believed to lack social spirit. Whereas the "normal child," Asperger said, "interacts appropriately with others as an integrated member of his community," children who did not integrate with the larger community had autistic psychopathy. They might behave "impossibly badly" when "in a group, which is meant to follow a common command," or "completely lack any respect for the other person."[39] Autistic youths could endanger the community with their egocentrism, as they "follow[ed] only their own wishes, interests and spontaneous impulses, without considering restrictions or prescriptions imposed from outside."[40] They were incapable of joining the *Volk*.

So as Nazism insisted that the individual must be brought into (or excised from) the community, Asperger maintained that an autistic child "is like an alien, oblivious to the surrounding noise and movement, and inaccessible in his preoccupation."[41] The youth was inaccessible, Asperger insisted, because "the fundamental disorder of autistic individuals is the limitation of their relationship with their environment." This cut off the child from others so that the child appeared "alone in the world," and lived "among people as if a stranger."[42]

Asperger was describing, in short, the mind trapped within itself. On the final page of his thesis, Asperger went so far as to say that "Introversion, if it is a restriction of the self and a narrowing of the relations to the environment, may well be autism (*Autismus*) in essence."[43] He was, essentially, defining autism and Nazism as inverse states of being. While the root of fascism (*fascio*) was the bundle, or group, the root of autism was *autos*, the condition of self. As an expert in Greek and Latin, Asperger may well have had this opposition in mind when sharpening his definitions of autistic psychopathy throughout the Third Reich.

What explains the shifts in Asperger's definitions of autistic psychopathy? Psychiatric diagnoses are often influenced by trends in society—such as historical diagnoses of hysteria and homosexuality—and definitions evolve. But in Asperger's case, the changes were swift and pronounced. Between 1938 and 1944, his diagnosis of autistic psychopathy became so aligned with his senior associates in Nazi child psychiatry that it would seem to be the result of his immediate circumstances rather than of the evolution of autonomous research and independent thought.

It is unclear whether Asperger was convinced by his own changes in the definition of autistic psychopathy, or even by Nazi child psychiatry in general. The end of the Third Reich would bring massive transformations in Asperger's approaches to both.

10

Reckoning

THE FALL OF the Third Reich did not bring a happy ending for the children who suffered at the hands of Nazi psychiatry. As the Soviet army entered Vienna in April 1945, while Asperger was in Yugoslavia, Spiegelgrund staff told children to fear the worst, issuing hair-raising warnings of Nazi propaganda such as "They will come and cut off your nose or your ears."[1] The Soviet invasion was a terrifying, tumultuous time, though some Spiegelgrund survivors remembered Red Army soldiers as nicer and more generous than their fellow countrymen at Spiegelgrund, as offering bread, apples, and even cigarettes, a valuable commodity at the time.

Many parents of children held at Spiegelgrund came to take them back home. When Alois Kaufmann's father arrived, Kaufmann estimated that he was around twenty-five pounds under-weight. He recounted that he could not walk across the Spetter Bridge, and implored, " 'Dad, I cannot, I cannot. I am scared of the br[idge].' " After he started crying, Kaufmann said, his father "took me in his arms and lifted me, and so we went across." Ernst Pacher had to remain at

Spiegelgrund, which continued to operate, albeit in a less murderous manner. He noted that most children were picked up, "But a few remained, and my mother did not pick me up, she just told me: 'You were taken care of well enough there.' " However, Pacher added, "We met them again later on, the same female and male orderlies were again in the institutions."[2]

Cruelty and violence continued. It was suspected that doctors and nurses deliberately neglected some children to death. Conditions looked different from the outside, for the public— but inside, youths still confronted a nightmarish reality. Even when Spiegelgrund was closed in 1950, the children and staff were simply transferred to nearby Wilhelminenberg Castle. Little changed; the children's blankets still bore the inscription "SPIEGELGRUND."[3]

The specter of Spiegelgrund remained a conceptual reality long after it closed. Caregivers at Vienna's children's homes would threaten to send children there, as if Spiegelgrund still existed. As one woman who had been institutionalized recalled, "Always when something happened, which would of course happen in that atmosphere, yes? What then? 'You all are going to Spiegelgrund!' No idea what Spiegelgrund was. I knew it existed and must be something real."[4] Threatening unruly children with Spiegelgrund even became a bit of a Viennese idiom, wholly abstracted; decades after the war, schoolteachers would scare misbehaving pupils with the grisly prospect.

Spiegelgrund survivors continued to suffer after their release. For Franz Pulkert, life did not improve much. "The violence, that was commonplace at the time, I mean, with my parents this wasn't different either, because my mother wasn't any better." Friedrich Zawrel recalled, "My father continued drinking. At home, it was as bad as before." Karl Hamedler, who was in his mid-teens, was bitter. "At that age you just don't know what do with yourself. There you are in the world, and nobody gives a shit about you, to put it bluntly." Even Leopoldine Maier, whose mother had journeyed to Spiegelgrund every week and rescued her, was troubled. She confessed, "I also very often ran away from my mother. I always had my bag with leftover food so I would not starve."[5]

Alois Kaufmann emphasized the enduring trauma and stigma of Spiegelgrund. "We were ashamed, literally ashamed to say that we had been in a youth correctional institution, in a euthanasia [facility], we did not let it pass our lips." He said his stepmother chided him, " 'Don't you dare tell anybody. There is nothing to be proud of.' " Kaufmann carried the horror of Spiegelgrund through his life. "I was not able to walk the streets, I just could not walk,"

Kaufmann repeated, "I was always afraid and cried continuously." Kaufmann allowed that "it took years, years" for his anxiety to improve. Even then, "It is fear that is my daily companion to this day. A cruel fear of death."

Other survivors stated that they distanced themselves from their childhood experiences. Alfred Grasel expunged them from his memory, explaining, "I have everything, how shall I put it, I erased it from my brain. I repressed everything. Because it's pointless." Grasel presented his forgetting as a survival strategy: "Look, I came to Vienna, I was all alone. And now I have to live." Ernst Pacher depicted a more layered relationship with his past. "What I saw myself runs by me like a movie," he reflected. "My wife tells me frequently that I cry out at night. I do not know why, and I just can't say why. [. . .] It is sheer madness. All of this means that, what the psychologists say, that these things come back in a powerful way as you get older, that's really true. At times this torments me, it's madness. . . ."[6] Rudolf Karger, too, reexperienced his Spiegelgrund trauma later in life. Upon reading his Spiegelgrund file as an adult, Karger described how the pain hit him suddenly, in full force:

It was a disaster for me. For one year, I was unable to say anything. I completely

346

retreated from everything, I was weeping like a child because I couldn't understand that people could be so mean and send us there, and they knew what was going on there, at Spiegelgrund. [. . .] I was knocked out. For a year, I was knocked out.[7]

Friedrich Zawrel was even more startled as he confronted his Spiegelgrund ordeal face to face—literally. Zawrel was sent to a court-appointed psychiatrist when he was arrested for theft in 1975. He found himself before Spiegelgrund doctor Heinrich Gross. The man responsible for killing hundreds of children had become a celebrated doctor who issued thousands of expert opinions for the Austrian state.

Zawrel admitted, "my first thought was: Heinrich, you got fat." Then, he said he castigated Gross: "But are you at all able to sleep peacefully, didn't you hear the little children crying on the balcony outside, you never heard it?! Those who were murdered. . . ." Zawrel narrated, "He recoiled big time. He turned white as the ceiling. Then he leaned forward, he looked as if he had aged by 50 years. 'You were up there?' I say: 'Where do you think I know you from?!' "

Gross got even with Zawrel in his court opinion. Gross not only recommended that Zawrel serve a long prison sentence, but he also reused a line written by Ernst Illing in Zawrel's

Spiegelgrund's records three decades earlier: "The examined individual originates from a genetically-sociologically inferior family."[8] Zawrel was not to be deterred, however, and launched a decades-long effort to bring Gross to court.

For Leopoldine Maier, legal recognition was cold comfort. She was still "crippled by these childhood memories," she explained. "When I do not watch myself, I always pull my neck in as if I were in constant fear of being hit in the neck with a stick or something else. [. . .] Whenever I wake up in the morning, I tell myself that I am old and it is over and that to me it will never happen again. This is my ritual each and every morning. I tell myself it is over and I survived it."

Maier dedicated her life to sustaining life. She became a nurse in Vienna and, she said, "I would have loved to have a child just to spare the child what I had to go through." But Maier found that her fallopian tubes were blocked. Although there is no record of it in her files, she suspects she was sterilized during the Third Reich. Haunted by Spiegelgrund's physical and mental abuse, Maier confided, "The term 'unworthy life' is still ringing in my ears. There is still a sign above my life that says: strictly speaking, you have no right to live."

AS SPIEGELGRUND SURVIVORS struggled in their later lives, most Spiegelgrund perpetrators got off easily after the war. A wave of public outrage immediately after 1945 targeted only a few prominent figures, not the legions of other Spiegelgrund personnel who continued to work with children in city homes. Three doctors stood trial on July 15–18, 1946: Marianne Türk, Margarethe Hübsch, and Ernst Illing. *New Austria* splashed a photograph of the three physicians sitting with arms folded, looking away from the camera, with the headline "The Child Killers from Steinhof in the Dock."[9] The People's Court sentenced Illing to death, Türk to ten years' imprisonment (she served only two), and acquitted Hübsch for lack of evidence. In April 1948, Spiegelgrund nurse Anna Katschenka was sentenced to eight years in prison for manslaughter (she served only two).[10] Meanwhile, Erwin Jekelius, who led Spiegelgrund from 1940 through the end of 1941, was captured by Soviet forces, sentenced in Moscow to twenty-five years' incarceration, and died of bladder cancer in prison in 1952. Ironically, one of Jekelius's fellow prisoners reportedly called Jekelius "the best comrade you can imagine! He gave consolation to everybody. He lived up to the highest conceivable moral standard."[11]

Many other perpetrators emerged virtually unscathed. Even top Reich-level euthanasia figures, Hans Heinze and Werner Villinger, had flourishing postwar careers as Germany's leading psychiatrists. Franz Hamburger, who had become emeritus in 1944, never faced trial.[12] The enormous role Hamburger's Children's Hospital played in the killing system also went unrecognized. Hamburger's student, Elmar Türk, who had conducted tuberculosis experiments on children with Hamburger, practiced through the 1990s and drew on his human experiments from the Third Reich. The body parts of children killed at Spiegelgrund continued to circulate among Vienna's research laboratories, the basis of its physicians' publications for decades.[13]

Spiegelgrund doctor Heinrich Gross published thirty-eight articles over twenty-five years—several based on the preserved brains of over four hundred children that he had harvested at Spiegelgrund during the Third Reich, collaborating with associates (such as Andreas Rett, who named Rett syndrome).[14] Gross became a preeminent physician in Austria and was awarded the government's Honorary Cross for Science and Art in 1975. Despite court proceedings against him in 1948 and 1981, Gross managed to evade conviction for murder. A rock solid case against Gross finally headed to court in 2000, but Gross was deemed unfit to stand trial due to advanced dementia—a condition many observers disputed. Gross died in 2005 at age ninety.[15]

Survivors of Spiegelgrund only began to gain recognition and compensation in the 1990s, as a liberalizing political and social climate in Germany and Austria led to greater scrutiny of the Third Reich. Media attention on Gross's trial also did much to raise awareness.[16] In 2002, the remains of Spiegelgrund's victims were buried and memorialized—including the brains Gross had collected, which were discovered in Spiegelgrund's basement, in neatly stacked glass jars. There were exhibitions, books, and symposia about Spiegelgrund, now regarded as one of Austria's major crimes of the Third Reich. Spiegelgrund was even the subject of a live-streamed opera in the Austrian Parliament building in 2013, featuring adults in caged cribs and subjected to torture. There has been, indeed, a partial reckoning with Nazi psychiatry.

ASPERGER WAS CLEARED of wrongdoing after the war. Most of Asperger's colleagues who had been in the Nazi Party were disqualified from leadership positions in the immediate postwar period; Asperger benefited from the vacuum and was appointed interim director of the University of Vienna Children's Hospital from 1946 to 1949.[17]

The Curative Education Clinic was rebuilt. It had been destroyed by Allied bombing on September 10, 1944, that killed head nurse Viktorine Zak, her arms around a child, after she had ushered other children from the clinic

Hans Asperger, around 1956.

to an air raid shelter. The reconstruction was meticulous. Former staff physician Georg Frankl, who had emigrated in 1937, visited the clinic in 1949 and found it eerie that the ward was "unchanged." Frankl explained that the clinic was "restored with photographic accuracy [. . .] You can not imagine how strange, absolutely physically identical."[18]

Asperger's intuitive approach to children, too, remained unchanged. He continued Hamburger's tradition of emotional and personal pediatrics rather than returning the Children's Hospital to Pirquet's emphasis on systematic science. Asperger also continued to advocate instinct over intellect in treating children's conditions and

352

characters. He enjoyed a long career. In 1957, Asperger was named director of the University of Innsbruck Children's Hospital; in 1962, Asperger followed in Hamburger's footsteps as permanent director of the University of Vienna Children's Hospital. Asperger wrote a textbook, *Heilpädagogik*, which found success in several editions—and his field of "curative education" expanded and shifted toward mainstream "special education."[19]

The Curative Education Clinic sent children to Spiegelgrund's successor institution, Wilhelminenberg. One was Erika Thaler—who recounted how, in 1951, personnel there considered her Jewish because of her dark hair, and repeatedly beat her and locked her in solitary confinement. Thaler was hospitalized multiple times from her injuries. Anna Theresia Kimmel, seen in Asperger's clinic, later described her encounter with Asperger. "I stood facing a tall, tall man in a white coat. Light-haired. The size difference was enormous. And I only know that he greeted my mother, and then he looked at me and punched me in the stomach with full force. Yes? My reaction was: no howling, nothing, but I probably looked at him angrily. And so he told me, he told my mother that I had aggression." Kimmel said she was institutionalized, held in a caged bed for a month. Afterward, Kimmel reflected, "I never heard from Asperger again. I don't know, was I a test subject? Was I a person? Was I a piece of wood? A guinea pig? I have no idea."[20]

One caregiver from Vienna's welfare Child Intake Office explained that Asperger's Curative Education Clinic had a reputation for severity in their referrals. She had dealt regularly with Asperger's staff; their discussions would become so "terrible," she felt, that "often" she and the institution's psychologist would "walk out." She said that up through the 1970s Asperger's clinic would "focus on the trouble-makers," which she thought was "backward." The opinions of Asperger himself, in her view, were "not the worst," but he "had blinders on."[21]

ASPERGER STATED AFTER the war that he had resisted the Nazi child euthanasia program, which he called "totally inhuman."[22] As he declared in a 1977 interview—in the third person—"the black [Catholic] Asperger did not report those with cerebral injuries for extermination."[23]

He claimed that his refusal to report children had put him in jeopardy during the Third Reich, saying in 1974: "I was never willing [. . .] to notify the Health Office of feeble-minded children, as we were instructed, this was a truly dangerous situation for me."[24] Asperger claimed in the same interview that he twice faced arrest by the Gestapo, but that Hamburger, despite ideological differences, had defended him. Hamburger, who was "a convinced National Socialist [. . .] knew my attitude but he protected me with his whole being, I credit him greatly for that."[25] While so far no record of these incidents has been found, Asperger developed a reputation as a Nazi resister, even as a victim of the regime. He asserted in 1977, "If the Nazis had won the war, it would have cost me my head."[26]

While Asperger may well have endeavored to protect some children who could face death, it is nevertheless documented that he recommended the transfer of others to Spiegelgrund, dozens of whom were killed. Asperger may well also have felt, as he said, he was in a "truly dangerous situation," and pressured into participation in the euthanasia program. Anyone in his milieu, with colleagues like his, would have felt pressured. That said, Asperger chose his milieu and colleagues. He had numerous, volitional ties to the euthanasia program, and it pervaded his professional world.

If Asperger was in grave danger or suffered persecution during this period, it does not seem to have hindered his career, which prospered. Remaining outside the party did not prevent Asperger from holding academic and state leadership positions in Vienna. And while Asperger asserted that his anti-Nazi reputation had delayed his promotion to *Dozent*, or associate professor, he still attained the position in October 1943 at thirty-seven, a young age.[27]

Asperger's unequivocal claims that he was a resister of Nazism raises questions about how he came to terms with his actions during the Third Reich. His postwar publications may provide some insight into how he understood his role in the euthanasia system, suggesting how he perhaps wrestled with and ultimately came to terms with it. Asperger wrote a great deal about children's souls, childhood death, and free will. He was focusing on youths who were terminally ill or on the brink of natural death—not on healthy children deemed to be disabled. Linking Asperger's postwar articles to the Reich's killing system is purely speculative; yet his meditations are nonetheless revealing of his attitudes toward the parameters of childhood death and morality.

In 1969, Asperger wrote an unusual article entitled "Early Spiritual Completion in Terminally Ill Children" that linked his religious concerns to early childhood death. He argued there was "a lawfulness of the life course, there is no chance when it comes to sickness and death." Even deaths brought by "accident or war," Asperger said, were "included in this law."[28] He held that the deaths of children, too, emerged from "internal laws."[29]

Asperger held that the souls of terminally ill youths "were always very different from the 'normal.'" As he put it, "Their fine spiritual differentiation results from a weakening in their primitive vitality through the existing disease—a consequence of the disease."[30] In other words, illness changed children's souls and prematurely aged them, completing their development. It was appropriate that they perished earlier than others. In his 1975 article, "The Dying Child," Asperger invoked scripture to conclude the point, citing the Wisdom of Solomon: children who die young "live a long life in a short span of time."[31]

"Incurable" diagnoses discussed in the Third Reich had nothing to do with terminal illness, but Asperger may have justified to himself a broader definition of what it meant to be terminally ill. If Asperger applied the idea of "early spiritual completion in terminally ill children" to children he deemed incurable, that would mean the child's soul was at the end of its life. The child would be ready for death: that was the "lawfulness of the life course." This reasoning may have helped Asperger square the circle of religiosity and killing. Since Asperger claimed the child's death "lays in God's hands," Asperger's fatalism removed responsibility for the child's fate from the doctor.[32] In Asperger's view, the doctor's role was to guide the child and his or her parents, particularly the grieving mother, down the path of death—to "fulfill his noble duty as guide into the realm of the natural."[33]

In his 1975 article, "The Dying Child," Asperger

also wrote that the doctor should "serve in death."
It is unclear exactly what Asperger meant by the
phrase, but he juxtaposed it with what he called
"active euthanasia." Whereas Asperger said the
"active euthanasia" of children meant "interfering
with the mechanisms of life with a sacrilegious
hand," he maintained immediately afterward that
a doctor might nevertheless offer a guiding hand:

> And there are situations where we must,
> for a dying child, serve in death [*dem
> Kind im Sterben, zum Sterben dienen*]—
> the doctor, the nurse, the parents, yes all
> of us, when we are called to do so. This
> is a difficult duty—but humaneness is
> difficult.[34]

Asperger was oblique about what to "serve
in death" exactly entailed. It might have
meant simply providing the child comfort.
Yet Asperger's comparison of it and "active
euthanasia" is curious, and it could be that to
"serve in death" might indeed involve something
more, especially since it was "a difficult duty."
It is perhaps telling that Asperger was at pains
to distinguish between the two types of actions,
condemning "active euthanasia" while lauding the
"humaneness" of "serv[ing] in death." Of course,
it is a stretch to apply Asperger's 1975 article to
his participation in the euthanasia program thirty

years earlier, especially since they seem to apply to entirely different categories: the terminally ill versus the allegedly difficult or disabled. It is possible, however, that Asperger considered children he deemed uneducable or severely impaired as terminally ill. So when he sent them to Spiegelgrund, Asperger might have believed—or wanted to believe in retrospect—that this was what it meant to "serve in death." He was aiding God, not playing God.

Asperger's postwar publications on personal values are likewise intruiging. In contrast to his work during the Third Reich, Asperger wrote a great deal about morality, choice, and religion in the postwar period. As he moved away from Nazi-era vocabulary and disavowed the "genetic determinism" of Nazi racial hygiene and psychiatric research, criticizing modernization, technology, and changing social norms, he extolled the values and virtues of traditional society.[35]

He began to incorporate religious themes in his work, citing scripture, appealing to his readers as Christians, regarding caregivers as Christians, and explaining medical outcomes by God's will.[36] Repeatedly citing Martin Luther's idea of the "freedom of a Christian," Asperger wrote in 1948, just three years after the fall of the Reich, that one could be absolved for an immoral act if one admitted to oneself it was wrong.[37] In his article "Determinants of Free Will: A Scientific Finding," Asperger argued that individuals had limited freedom of action, and thus limited free will. Yet since the individual had full freedom of thought, thoughts were the true measure of the person. Recanting an immoral act—to oneself—was more significant than committing the immoral act itself. As Asperger explained:

There is a freedom that is much less restricted than that of action, which is why we consider it an even greater duty: freedom, afterwards, when the act is done, to take a position on it. [. . .] It is about a decision: if one accepts the moral principle, submits to it, and takes responsibility—or if one rejects it from spite or deceiving oneself, which never works. Therein lies the ultimate vindication or condemnation, the last measure of one's value as a human being [. . .] this is about an internal decision, externally one does not need to do anything, no action, no word, no gesture.[38]

So Asperger held that what ultimately mattered was not doing wrong, but knowing it was wrong. It was about an internal state of mind, without need for external atonement. Three years after the fall of the Nazi regime, amid the purges and disgraces of his Nazi colleagues, he was concerned about the parameters of personal integrity.

Whether or not Asperger's postwar articles related to the Third Reich and euthanasia program, it is clear that questions of early childhood death, "active euthanasia" versus "serv[ing] in death," free will, morality, and atonement were on Asperger's mind. It is also clear that Asperger was trying to devise a framework for judging individuals in these realms, and that he seemed to think judgment was necessary.

PERHAPS MORE THAN any other period in history, the Nazi era invites judgment of individuals. It is tempting to classify people's actions as moral or immoral, innocent or criminal, rating each deed on a balance sheet with a positive or negative accounting at the end.

For many people living under Nazism, however, life was not lived in terms of abstract principles. Rather than inhabiting a world of black and white, most individuals in the Reich operated in shades of gray. People confronted countless decisions each day. One might walk by a "Jews unwanted" sign at a local store and not say anything—only to shop at a Jewish-owned store on the next block for its favorable prices. One might help a neighbor threatened by the regime—only to look away as another neighbor disappeared.

People navigated daily choices as they presented themselves, extemporizing in their personal and professional spheres. Caught in the swirl of life, one might conform, resist, and even commit harm all in the same afternoon. The cruelty of the Nazi world was inescapable.

Given the endless and unthinking decisions of everyday life, it can be misleading to classify people too neatly, including those whose actions might appear to be clear-cut on the surface. There were too many facets to living under Nazism. Also, life in the Third Reich kept changing. Decisions made right after the Nazi seizure of power did not necessarily have the same meaning a few years later, when the terms of Nazi rule were set, nor the same meaning after the war began. Those choosing to join the Nazi Party, for example, faced a shifting political landscape. The closer one looks, the more variation one sees.

People charted unique paths through the regime, accumulating choices and habits that added up to improvised lives. This element of improvisation meant that the Third Reich was not an inexorable, static, and abstract regime; it was composed of individuals making their way, making decisions about other individuals.

Observers have grappled with evaluating personal guilt and responsibility since the moment the Third Reich fell. In 1945, legal actions categorized different levels of accountability within the population. The Nuremberg Trials, the world's first international tribunal, focused on judging Nazi leaders for "crimes against humanity." Meanwhile, "denazification" proceedings targeted the entirety of the population—millions of Nazi Party members and high-profile citizens—as potentially complicit in the regime. Local denazification boards, using questionnaires, investigations, and character witnesses, catalogued individuals on a scale of 1 to 5, ranging from "major offenders" to "exonerated." In reality, few were held accountable. More than 90 percent of those tried in the western Allied occupation zones of Germany were deemed "fellow travelers" (the second-to-least culpable) or "exonerated"; similarly, denazification measures in Austria deemed over 90 percent of 487,067 former Nazi Party members "lesser offenders" [*Minderbelastet*].[39]

Historians, too, have tried to assess culpability in the Third Reich. In contrast to legal judgments, which often came down to individual responsibility and quantifying the level of harm, scholars have focused on context and individual agency—asking to what extent individuals took initiative, or to what extent were they caught up in circumstances, or even coerced. They assess the parameters of the possible.

There are a number of well-known frameworks of Holocaust perpetration. Christopher Browning, for example, described the transformation of "ordinary men," following how Germans on the eastern front perpetrated mass shootings of Jews—although it was possible to opt out of the killings—as they deferred to orders, felt group pressure, became desensitized over time, and consumed copious amounts of alcohol.[40] Jan Gross described the transformation of "neighbors" in one community in Poland, where inhabitants slaughtered Jews not because they were under orders but, in the course of successive Soviet and Nazi occupations, were swept away by collective violence in the context of war.[41] Primo Levi described a "gray zone" in which Holocaust victims were turned into perpetrators, such as Jewish concentration camp inmates who participated in the *Sonderkommandos*—special squads who helped operate the gas chambers and crematoria.[42] At the other extreme, Hannah Arendt described the detached "desk murderers" who worked in the bureaucracy of the camp system, running the machinery of the Holocaust through what she called the "banality of evil."[43]

These are all powerful paradigms. The actions of child euthanasia perpetrators, though, fit rather uneasily within Holocaust categories. Doctors and nurses in the special children's wards were neither fevered nor faceless—nor themselves potentially victims to violence. Whereas the Nazi state had decided that Jews were to be annihilated as a race, in an indiscriminate genocide, child euthanasia personnel had a godlike autonomy to determine a child's worthiness to exist, deciding life and death on an intimate, individual basis. Doctors and nurses were not following a clear rulebook, but were themselves setting the standards in a diagnosis regime that fostered individual improvisation.

While the facts of Asperger's life are well documented, their meaning is subject to interpretation. Readers might differ in their judgments. Even the extent to which one could, or should, make moral judgments is an open question. Asperger was a minor figure in the Nazi child euthanasia program, nowhere near as active as some of his associates. He was not personally involved in killing, and the number of deaths in which Asperger was involved might seem slight compared to the millions of people who died during the Holocaust. Those who have examined Asperger's relationship to the Third Reich and euthanasia system have viewed him in a range of ways: as a resister who rescued children, as a determined perpetrator, or as a passive follower.[44] Herwig Czech, a Viennese historian most familiar with Asperger's work, sees Asperger as "a part of the apparatus."[45]

These are each compelling interpretations. Yet Asperger's actions were perhaps less straightforward than any of these labels suggest. He navigated decisions in a proactive, individual way, making conscious choices to resist some aspects of the regime, and conscious choices to participate in others. His decisions not to join the Nazi Party and to remain a dedicated Catholic were difficult and unusual choices for someone in Asperger's position, yet he opted to participate in myriad organizations and institutions that promoted the political tenets, racial hygiene policies, and systematic killings of the Third Reich. High-ranking Nazi Party officials and colleagues deemed Asperger reliable and trusted him with sensitive information. Top euthanasia figures in Vienna included Asperger in their inner circle as well as in the leadership of their field. What emerges is not a type of person but an individual, who must be judged in his accumulations of decisions, evolving and fluctuating over time.

When it came to the child euthanasia program, Asperger does not appear as a submissive figure, working within a system beyond his influence. Nor does he appear to have been coerced, since many of his choices were elective. While knowing of the euthanasia program, Asperger publicly urged his colleagues to send children to Spiegelgrund; he participated in numerous Reich offices that sent children to Spiegelgrund; and he sent children to Spiegelgrund directly from his clinic. He met many of the youths one-on-

one, talked with their parents, and studied them closely over time. Available records suggest that Asperger sent dozens of children to Spiegelgrund who perished, and sent numerous children to Spiegelgrund who risked death but survived. None of these were simple or ordinary actions. They required initiative, determination, and improvisation.

Asperger's actions are perhaps more reflective of the nature of perpetration in the Third Reich than those of more prominent figures. The Reich's systems of extermination depended upon people like Asperger, who maneuvered themselves, perhaps uncritically, within their positions. Individuals such as Asperger were neither committed killers nor even directly involved in the moment of death. Yet, in the absence of murderous convictions, they made the Reich's killing systems possible.

Ultimately, the choice to cooperate in an exterminationist program was a critical moral moment shared by all Reich perpetrators, regardless of the specific role. Contrary to Asperger's postwar image, he was far from an insular researcher, secluded in his clinic and immune from Nazi influence. Rather, Asperger was active in his milieu; on any given day, he had multiple points of contact with the regime. The magnitude of his actions might seem small, yet when considering a system of systematic killing, it is debatable whether the exact number of those who perished as a direct result of his decisions even matters. One can not escape the fact that Asperger worked within a system of mass killing as a conscious participant, very much tied to his world and to its horrors.

Epilogue

After the fall of the Third Reich, Asperger moved away from his Nazi-era work on autistic psychopathy. While Asperger wrote over three hundred articles in the postwar period, very few of them were on the diagnosis for which he later became famed. Asperger does not appear to have conducted additional systematic research on the condition; at least he did not mention any in thirty-five years, up through his last publication on the topic in 1979. Scanning Asperger's long list of publications, one would never guess that autistic psychopathy was his primary contribution to psychiatry.[1]

Asperger recycled two works on autistic psychopathy after 1945 that he reissued in a handful of publications. The first was a 27-page section of his 306-page textbook, *Heilpädagogik*.[2] Published in 1952, the vast majority of the section was taken verbatim from his 1944 autism thesis, albeit rearranged with the names of the boys in his case studies removed. Subsequent editions of *Heilpädagogik*—in 1956, 1961, 1965, and 1968—were largely the same.

Asperger's diagnosis remained little known outside of his immediate professional network;

he published in German and did not travel widely to international conferences. It was Leo Kanner's definition of autism, published in the United States in 1943, that was used in the English-speaking world. Psychiatrists applied Kanner's autism diagnosis to children and adults seen to have significant cognitive impairments, less verbal and socially interactive than the children Asperger described.

International recognition of Asperger's work came slowly. He developed a second, shorter version of his work on autistic psychopathy for a special 1968 edition of *Acta Paedopsychiatrica*, the official journal of the International Association for Child and Adolescent Psychiatry and Allied Professions. The volume, with ten contributors, addressed the state of research on autism. Leo Kanner kicked off the discussion with an exhaustive article; Asperger followed with an article a quarter of the length that compared his idea of autistic psychopathy to others' work in general terms. Asperger then republished this material in abbreviated forms in five short articles over the next decade. Two of them appeared in newsletters, and one was a talk to the Swiss Association of Parents with Autistic Children in Fribourg.[3]

In his 1977 address to the Swiss parents' association, Asperger admitted that he had not been working on, let alone thinking about, autistic psychopathy. He told the audience that the invitation to speak "gives me the opportunity to think through this fascinating problem again, to attain greater clarity for myself as well as help clarify for others."[4]

Asperger's later articles on autistic psychopathy did differ from his Nazi-era work in two major respects, however. First, Asperger distanced himself from Nazi child psychiatry's idea of *Gemüt*. In 1962, he even criticized what he called the "the Schröder School's idea of the 'poverty of *Gemüt*,' " saying it was too "simple."[5] After the war, he no longer cited Paul Schröder and Hans Heinze, the leader in the child euthanasia program who had authored "On the Phenomenology of *Gemüt*," even though their work had been prominent in his 1944 thesis.[6]

Likewise, Asperger's post-1968 articles are far less critical of the children he diagnosed with autistic psychopathy than the work he produced in the Third Reich. While describing children's difficulties, his writing is orders of magnitude more benevolent, and overwhelmingly stresses children's special abilities. If Asperger had highlighted the skills of autistic children during the Third Reich in order to protect them from the child euthanasia program, it is striking that his praise of autistic children became more hyperbolic after the war, when their lives were no longer at stake.

Perhaps for Asperger personally, something was indeed at stake. In his articles on autistic psychopathy, Asperger sought to distinguish his diagnosis from Kanner's better-known idea of "early infantile autism." Asperger insisted that the children he studied were superior to those Kanner described. Although Asperger did allow that the two groups of children had certain traits in common, namely atypical social contact, his articles repeated that "Kanner's early infantile autism is a near psychotic or even a psychotic state," whereas "Asperger's typical cases are very intelligent children with extraordinary originality of thought and spontaneity of activity."[7]

Asperger also downplayed his Nazi-era idea of autistic psychopathy as a psychopathy. He now called the condition a "character anomaly" or "character variant."[8] He said *anyone* might "behave autistically"—especially if in a state of depression or in "a state of great creativity and mental activity."[9] By contrast, Kanner's autism was a "severely pathological condition."[10]

While Asperger did not draw on additional empirical research in these articles, he did make some small qualifications to his diagnosis. He claimed that autistic psychopathy was more pronounced in cities than in the countryside because individuals had greater opportunities to develop their individual interests, with more resources for their "cultural and artistic achievements," and could thus "accomplish outstanding things for which their character predestines them."[11] Also, though Asperger continued to say autistic psychopathy was an "extreme variant" of male intelligence, present "only in boys" in Austria, he did allow that there were some cases in girls in the United States, where women had become more "masculinized."[12]

That Asperger wrote little on autistic psychopathy after the Third Reich and did not engage in additional systematic research raises questions about the extent to which he may have believed in his Nazi-era work in the first place. Had international scholars not discovered and compared Asperger's diagnosis to Kanner's in the 1960s, one wonders whether Asperger would even have published his later articles on autistic psychopathy. Of course, Asperger's interests and convictions may have evolved over time. Yet given how rapidly Asperger adopted the language of Nazi child psychiatry and sharpened his definitions of the diagnosis between 1937 and 1944, it is possible that Asperger, at least to some extent, had shaped his 1944 thesis to the ideology of his times without full conviction in his work.

How unexpected, then, that while Asperger seems to have no longer stood by his 1944 definition of autistic psychopathy in the postwar period, others did.

• • •

BRITISH PSYCHIATRIST LORNA Wing publicized Asperger's diagnosis of autistic psychopathy almost forty years later, in 1981. Wing had switched fields to child psychiatry when her daughter, Susie, was diagnosed with autism. Having conducted extensive research on youths who she felt did not quite fit into Kanner's idea of autism, Wing was intrigued when she heard of Asperger's work.[13] She tracked down Asperger's 1944 thesis—which her husband translated for her—and recognized in Asperger's descriptions behaviors she had studied in a number of children. Wing saw Kanner and Asperger as describing different aspects of the same condition, their work fitting together in an autism "spectrum."

Asperger disagreed with Wing. In the late 1970s, he and Wing met in the cafeteria of London's Maudsley Hospital and discussed the matter "over tea." Wing described how "Professor Asperger listened with great courtesy to my arguments and we cordially agreed to differ." Asperger wanted a clearer distinction between the children he described, who he said had "extraordinary" abilities, and the potentially "psychotic" children Kanner described.[14]

Wing held that Kanner and Asperger were describing different parts of the same autism. Ironically, though, the title of her seminal 1981 article on the subject, "Asperger's Syndrome:

A Clinical Account," wound up establishing Asperger's syndrome as its own category. Naming the syndrome after Asperger was somewhat of a professional courtesy, as Wing had published far more extensively in the field than had Asperger. But Asperger had died the year before, in 1980, and Wing saw an advantage to distinguishing the type of child she believed he was describing. However, Wing later said that coining the term *Asperger's syndrome* was like "opening Pandora's box," because there was such discussion over it as a potentially separate diagnosis.[15]

Another critical aspect of Wing's title was the word *syndrome*. While Asperger had called autism a "psychopathy," Wing believed he meant "abnormality of personality," not "sociopathic behavior." She wanted to use a "neutral term," and thus selected the word *syndrome*. Yet Asperger had not used a neutral term. Psychopathy in German psychiatry had long connoted social deviance and recalcitrance—which were embedded in his Nazi-era diagnosis.[16] So when Asperger's work went mainstream, it was cleansed of its historical context. Or rather, maybe it went mainstream because it was cleansed of its historical context.

Over the 1980s, Asperger's syndrome became increasingly well known within the British psychiatric community. Uta Frith, a German-born developmental psychologist working in London, published an English translation of Asperger's

1944 treatise in 1991.[17] Frith's translation also softened the historical context of Asperger's diagnosis. She, like Wing, eschewed Asperger's term of "autistic psychopathy" and translated the diagnosis instead as "autism," which he did not use. Also, Frith did not include Asperger's preface to his thesis, which engaged with Nazi child psychiatrists and situated the diagnosis within the intellectual framework of the Third Reich.

The idea of Asperger's syndrome took off in the 1990s. In 1992, the World Health Organization included it as a distinct diagnosis in its *International Classification of Diseases, Tenth Revision* (ICD-10), and in 1994, the American Psychiatric Association added Asperger's disorder to its *Diagnostic and Statistical Manual of Mental Disorders* (DSM-IV). Neither body, it would seem, thoroughly vetted Asperger's life during the Third Reich before giving the diagnosis his name. Organizations typically research historical figures before designating eponymous diagnoses in order to avoid naming a condition after a person who has engaged in ignominious actions. The ethics of diagnostic labels has been much discussed, and numerous conditions named after Nazi-era doctors who were implicated in programs of extermination now go by alternative names.[18]

The introduction of Asperger's work expanded notions of an autism spectrum to encompass many different types of children. The DSM-IV's

1994 definitions became quite complicated. The broad category of pervasive development disorder (PDD) included autism, Asperger's disorder, and pervasive developmental disorder—not otherwise specified (PDD-NOS). In shorthand, professionals and parents began slotting youths as having "low-functioning," "mid-functioning," or "high-functioning" autism, replicating the hierarchy Asperger laid out in his thesis. Since Asperger's disorder increasingly came to be seen as a form of "high-functioning" autism in the United States, the American Psychiatric Association dissolved the diagnosis (and PDD-NOS) and presented only the umbrella diagnosis of autism spectrum disorder in the DSM-V in 2013.

As the idea of the autism spectrum expanded criteria, rates of diagnosis shot up. Autism became the fastest-growing developmental disability in the United States. Statistical sources are debated, but according to the United States Centers for Disease Control and Prevention (CDC), a common measure, the number of children diagnosed with an autism spectrum disorder rose 6 percent to 15 percent a year in the 2000s, up to one in sixty-eight children in 2016. Youths labeled with the condition might bear very little resemblance to each other, either in type of disability or in personality. According to the DSM-V, what they shared were "deficits in social communication and social interaction" and "restricted, repetitive patterns of behavior, interests, or activities."[19] These were rather broad criteria—the common denominator of which was Asperger's concept of not fitting into a social community.

Ultimately, Lorna Wing regretted how she brought Asperger's ideas to the English-speaking world and changed the face of autism. She said before her death in 2014: "I wish I hadn't done it. I would like to throw all labels away today, including Asperger's syndrome, and move towards the dimensional approach. Labels don't mean anything, because you get such a wide variety of profiles."[20]

ASPERGER'S NAME IS now part of our daily lives. It is a term we apply to loved ones, an adjective people use to describe those they regard as socially awkward, and even a personality archetype in popular culture. While Asperger's disorder is no longer an official psychiatric diagnosis in the American Psychiatric Association's DSM-V, the term will likely persist as a social label. And internationally, Asperger's syndrome remains an official diagnosis in the ICD-10.[21]

But Asperger's original definition of autistic psychopathy can not be removed from its historical context. It was a product of its age, forged in a series of political and intellectual upheavals. The socialism of Red Vienna in the

1920s led to the interventionist social work that established Asperger's clinic. In the 1930s, Austrofascism led to the isolation of Asperger's hospital on the far right. The staff at his Curative Education Clinic collectively developed the term "autistic" as a descriptor—not a pathology—of children with social challenges. Yet just months after the Nazi takeover of Austria in 1938, Asperger, who had previously argued against applying diagnoses to children, introduced autism as a psychopathy. Following his senior colleagues in Nazi child psychiatry, Asperger sharpened the diagnosis year by year and progressively identified children who he believed to lack social spirit, developing the concept of autism as the psychological opposite of Nazism.

Seen as a whole, the full history of Asperger, autism, and Vienna exposes a tragic trajectory in the science of selfhood. Sigmund Freud's generation of famed psychoanalysts and psychiatrists gave birth to a generation of children among the most surveilled, regulated, and persecuted in history. The social workers of interwar Vienna created a renowned welfare system that ultimately destroyed the children it cared for. The darker elements of Viennese psychiatry and welfare came to the fore, so that by the Third Reich, new standards created a diagnosis regime in which defining ever more defects required ever more invasive measures.

This was a self-fulfilling prophecy that resulted, for some children, in intensive remediation—and, for others, in extermination.

Philosopher Ian Hacking has described how diagnoses lead to "making up people."[22] Definitions of diagnoses emerge from the cumulative interactions of doctors, patients, and social forces, and, in a continual feedback loop, change over time. Multiple factors have shaped our current approaches to autism, such as research funding, disability legislation, public services, school policies, parent activism, awareness drives, nonprofit organizations, and media representations. Then, the terms of a diagnosis can influence perceptions of people who are diagnosed; the actions of a child diagnosed with autism, for example, might be read through the lens of the diagnosis as something intrinsically autistic, which can obscure the uniqueness of the child as an individual. It has been shown that treating a child based on a set of assumptions can affect the behavior of the child. Before long, children's evolving behaviors affect evolving perceptions of a diagnosis, which further affect children's behaviors, and so on.

The Third Reich was "making up people" in the most extreme sense. In its elaborate diagnosis regime, child psychiatrists based their diagnoses more on ideological concerns of the *Volk* than the actual characteristics of the children who stood before them. As with the Nazi state overall, Nazi psychiatry was a strategy of reshaping humanity by denying humanity. Nazi child psychiatry had the power, quite literally, to unmake people.

Studies of the Holocaust have revealed how social death preceded individuals' physical death, tracing the creep of generalizations, exclusions, and dehumanization of Jews that made mass murder possible.[23] Child euthanasia involved a similar progression. Nazi psychiatry effaced the individuality of thousands of children, pronouncing them irredeemable, removing them from friends and family, and isolating them in nightmarish institutions that paved the way toward their biological death.

The story of Asperger and his diagnosis points to the elasticity and improvisation behind Reich policies and individuals' actions. Asperger's life and work channeled the historical threads of his era, incorporating its values and pressures bit by bit. Yet while Asperger's definitions of autistic psychopathy were fluid, his final 1944 description has had a lasting impact. His words live on, shaping the lives and the self-images of millions of individuals.

THE WAYS IN which Asperger's work connects to the present is an open question. This book has no definitive answers, but brings historical facts and perspectives to light, ideally providing a broader context for conversations about autism today.

Why did Asperger's idea of autism take off in the mid-1990s? How did a diagnosis born in Nazi ideals of conformity and social spirit resonate with an individualistic society in the late twentieth century? Leaving aside the possible medical factors behind the rise of autism diagnosis (a topic this book does not explore) it would seem that the 1990s gave rise to its own kind of diagnosis regime, in which growing scrutiny of children led to greater numbers of labels for defects.[24] Accelerating pressures in the culture of parenting, mental health care, and school counseling led to higher standards for children's development. Youths' failure to hit prescribed milestones fed a growth in psychiatric diagnoses, most notably attention deficit hyperactivity disorder (ADHD) and attention deficit disorder (ADD)—giving rise to a generation of children raised on Ritalin and other psychiatric medications. The expansion of child psychiatry also became manifest in the idea of an "autism spectrum" that included children with ever milder challenges.

Today, as for Asperger and his contemporaries, the idea of autism draws on anxieties about integration into a perfectionist and fast-changing world. The autism spectrum exaggerates the range of a child's possible places in society. On one end, a youth with autism might face a lifetime of severe disability and isolation, and on the other, adapt and be perceived to have superior abilities. With the prevalence of technology in our daily lives, autism preys upon fears of detachment and inability to adjust—as well as dreams of skills coveted in these new times, of savant engineers, scientists, and coders. We project a bifurcated two-dimensional spectrum, maintaining Asperger's distinction between those who might be assimilated and those who might not. A diagnosis of autism suggests problems, whereas Asperger's disorder or "high-functioning autism" suggests those who might be incorporated and be productive, even superior. The conception of an ever-broadening spectrum taps into our greatest hopes and fears for our children, and for society.

Other aspects of Asperger's work have endured, too. The idea of autism is still primarily about boys. Just as Asperger proclaimed autism "is an extreme variant of male intelligence," and "of the male character," the ratio of boys to girls diagnosed with autism is almost 5:1, and there is even an "extreme male brain theory" of autism.[25] In treatment, Asperger's clinic used an intensive cognitive and relationship-based approach that lies at the core of therapies today. It stresses the importance of social feeling and the potential to transform children. The goal of imbuing youths with different feelings, thoughts, and interactions with the world is central to common visions of the diagnosis. Some talk of "curing" or "recovering" children. This hope of wholesale metamorphosis was not often present with other childhood diagnoses such as intellectual disability, which decreased as rates of autism diagnosis increased. One 2015 study suggests that reclassification of diagnoses could account for 64 percent of the increase in autism rates from 2000–2010.[26] Diagnostic substitution suggests happier outcomes, since implicit in the idea of autism, for many, is a promise of progress, and a sense of potential power and control over the mind.

Most significantly, autism is often a diagnosis of behavior, not of an underlying physiological condition. Indeed, science increasingly recognizes that autism is heterogeneous: while children with autism share characteristics, they can have different biological causes. Researchers suggest that autism likely encompasses many different physiological conditions that one day will be split into different diagnoses. Right now, *autism* serves as an expansive umbrella diagnosis.

A catchall term from the nineteenth and early twentieth century that lumped together disparate biological conditions—ranging from epilepsy to anxiety to schizophrenia to syphilis—was female hysteria. There was a wide spectrum of presumed manifestations of hysteria. But what the women diagnosed with hysteria all had in common, the medical establishment then believed, was the inability to control their emotions. At a time when women were asserting visible roles in public life, the image of the hysterical woman captured the public mind.[27]

As with hysteria, individuals diagnosed with autism can bear little resemblance to one another. Public debates around autism also seem to be about navigating gender, cultural, generational, and social norms as they undergo profound change. While hysteria was a diagnosis of supposedly overemotional women, autism could be seen as a diagnosis of supposedly under-emotional boys. Although children classified with the condition can have very dissimilar forms of disability, media images often stereotype them. Like women diagnosed with hysteria, boys with autism are often depicted as disconnected from society, as solitary figures predominantly from the white middle class trapped in their own minds. Popular images often obscure the diversity of people behind the labels.

The heterogeneity of the hysteria and autism labels shows the challenges of classifying another person's mind. Society plays a role in developing diagnoses that define others. Specific individuals and professions may name these conditions, but they are not simply foisted upon us. We accept them, perpetuate them, and participate in their creation. When we invoke the autism label, it should be with full knowledge of its origins and implications.

Society is becoming increasingly sensitive to nuance in issues of race, religion, gender, sexuality, and nationality. As appreciation of neurodiversity now grows, we might begin to see the perils of a totalizing label based on varying traits, since labels affect the treatment of individuals, and treatment affects their lives. The history of Asperger and autism should underscore the ethics of respecting every child's mind, and treating those minds with care—showing how a society can shape a diagnosis.

Acknowledgments

I am grateful to the many individuals who have supported this book over the years.

Margaret Lavinia Anderson, John Connelly, Robert Moeller, and James Sheehan encouraged me to pursue what at first seemed an unlikely topic. As I began my research in Vienna, Kathrin Hippler, Roxanne Sousek, Herwig Czech, Katja Geiger, Thomas Mayer, and Carola Sachse generously introduced me to the world of Vienna psychiatry. For research assistance, I thank Berthold Konrath and Rudolf Jerabek at the Austrian State Archives, Andrew Simon and Susanne Fritsch-Rübsamen at the Vienna City and Regional Archives, and Thomas Maisel at the University of Vienna Archives. I also thank Kathleen M. Smith of Stanford Libraries, as well as Mary Louise Munill, who managed to locate sources I did not think existed.

This book benefited greatly from academic exchanges. A Stanford Humanities Fellowship facilitated a yearlong dialogue with colleagues in multiple disciplines. Research at Stanford's Spatial History Project, under the guidance of Zephyr Frank, Jason Heppler, and Matt Bryant, enabled me and Michelle Kahn to pursue digital approaches. This book also owes much to the faculty and students who engaged in presentations of the work, notably Tara Zahra, Michael Geyer, Eleonor Gilburd, and Stephen Haswell Todd at the University of Chicago; Gary Cohen, Howard Louthan, Daniel Pinkerton at the University of Minnesota; Astrid Eckert and Sander Gilman at Emory and the Atlanta Science Festival, as well as Ami Klin at the Marcus Autism Center; Jennifer Allen and Stefan-Ludwig Hoffmann at the German history working group at the University of California, Berkeley, and Norma Feldman and Beverly Kay Crawford at the Center for German and European Studies at the University of California, Berkeley.

I am indebted to colleagues who offered extensive suggestions on the manuscript: James T. Campbell, Gary Cohen, Sander Gilman, James C. Harris, David Holloway, Norman Naimark, Robert Proctor, and Richard Roberts. J. P. Daughton read and brainstormed numerous drafts. Greg Eghigian, Emily Banwell, and Nastassja Myer offered material help with the project. Agent Don Fehr was instrumental in bringing the book to publication, and editor Alane Mason offered absolutely inspired revisions. I extend particular thanks to my close academic interlocutors Anne Lester, Alan Mikhail, Tara Zahra, and Lisa Zwicker. And I am thankful for the spirited, invaluable discussions with my graduate students, Ian Beacock, Michelle Chang, Benjamin

Hein, Samuel Huneke, and Michelle Kahn.

I had hoped my late father, Robert Replogle, could have seen the publication of this book. As a physician, he believed deeply in its mission. I am grateful to Patricia and Alan Sheffer for their ongoing engagement and advice—and to my mother, Carol Replogle, who has lived this manuscript with me in multiple ways, reading every draft with words of love and wisdom. I treasure the unconditional support and insights of my husband, Scott, as well as the enthusiasm of my daughter, Alice, who sat with me while I wrote and tried to brighten what she called a very depressing topic.

My beloved son, Eric, wanted me to dedicate the book to him; I do so with pleasure. Eric was diagnosed with autism when he was seventeen months old. He struggled with great difficulties over the years, and showed more gumption and tenacity than I have seen in anyone else. At thirteen, Eric chafes against the idea of autism. While many, of course, identify with the diagnosis, Eric wanted to add his voice to this book:

> Autism is not real; we all have issues. However, some are more noticeable than others. Autism is not a disability or diagnosis, it is a stereotype for certain individuals. People with autism should be

treated like everyone else, because if they are not, it will make them be even less social. Parents of all children, whether or not they are autistic, should think of their children's perspective and help their children based on their perspectives.

In fourth grade, I saw autism represented as a cartoon of a child playing around with toy trains, I thought, *that's kind of like me* because of the symptoms I noticed such as lack of eye contact, and lack of social behavior. It made me feel humiliated, and I wanted to put an end to the label of autism.

As this is a book about the act of classification, Eric's words suggest the effect labels can have on those who are labeled. Whether or not others share Eric's perspective, we can agree that labels are powerful, with histories and consequences that reach far beyond the individuals who issue them.

Abbreviations

VIENNA CITY AND REGIONAL ARCHIVES

Wiener Stadt- und Landesarchiv
1.3.2.202.A5 Personalakten 1. Reihe / Asperger. *WStLA 1.3.2.202.A5 P: A*
1.3.2.202.A5 Personalakten 1. Reihe / Franz Hamburger. *WStLA 1.3.2.202.A5 P: H*
1.3.2.209.1.A47 prov-Kinderklinik; Heilpädagogische Station: Krankengeschichten, Christine Berka. *WStLA 1.3.2.209.1.A47 HP: CB*
1.3.2.209.1.A47 prov-Kinderklinik; Heilpädagogische Station: Krankengeschichten, Elfriede Grohmann. *WStLA 1.3.2.209.1.A47 HP: EG*
1.3.2.209.1.A47. B.H.2-B.J.A.2/L. prov-Kinderklinik; Heilpädagogische Station: Krankengeschichten, Margarete Schaffer. *WStLA 1.3.2.209.1.A47 HP: MS*
3.13.A1-A. Biographical File, Hans Asperger. *WStLA 3.13.A1-A: A*

AUSTRIAN STATE ARCHIVES

Österreichischen Staatsarchiv
(AdR) K 10/02. Bundesministerium für Unterricht/
Personalakten, Prof. Dr. Hans Asperger, vols.
D, I & II. *ÖStA (AdR) K 10/02 BfU: A*
(AdR 02) Zl36.055. Gauakt—Asperger. *ÖStA
(AdR 02) Zl36.055. G: A*

UNIVERSITY OF VIENNA ARCHIVES

Archiv der Universität Wien
MED PA 17 Personnel file, Dean of the Medical
Faculty

SELECTED JOURNALS

American Journal of Orthopsychiatry (AJO)
Archiv für Kinderheilkunde (AfK)
Der Erbarzt (DE)
Der Nervenarzt (DN)
Die deutsche Sonderschule (dS)
Erziehung und Unterricht (EU)
Heilpädagogik (HP)
Heilpädagogische Schul- und Elternzeitung (HS-E)
International Council of Nurses (ICN)
Journal of Child Neurology (JCN)
Journal of Pediatrics (JP)
Kinderärztliche Praxis (KP)
Klinische Wochenschrift (KW)

Medizinische Klinik (MK)
Monatsschrift für Kinderheilkunde (MfK)
Monatsschrift für Psychiatrie und Neurologie
(MfPN)
Münchner Medizinische Wochenschrift (MMW)
Österreichische Zeitschrift für Kinderheilkunde
und Kinderfürsorge (OZfKK)
Praxis der Kinderpsychologie und Kinder-
psychiatrie (PdKK)
Psychiatrisch-Neurologische Wochenschrift (P-NW)
Wiener Archiv für Innere Medizin (WAfIM)
Wiener klinische Wochenschrift (WkW)
Wiener Medizinische Wochenschrift (WMW)
Zeitschrift für die gesamte Neurologie und
Psychiatrie (ZfNP)
Zeitschrift für Heilpädagogik (ZfH)
Zeitschrift für Kinderforschung (ZfK)
Zeitschrift für Kinderpsychiatrie (ZfKp)
Zeitschrift für Kinderschutz und Familien- und
Berufsfürsorge (ZfKFB)
Zeitschrift für Kinderschutz und Jugendfürsorge
(ZfKJ)
Zeitschrift für Pädagogik (ZfP)

Notes

INTRODUCTION

1. Asperger, Hans. "Die 'Autistischen Psychopathen' im Kindesalter." *Archiv für Psychiatrie und Nervenkrankheiten* 117 no. 1 (1944): 76–136; 99 (54). Most English quotations of Asperger's treatise in this book are from the standard English translation by Uta Frith, with page references in parentheses: Asperger, Hans. " 'Autistic Psychopathy' in Childhood," (1944). In *Autism and Asperger Syndrome*, edited and translated by Uta Frith, 37–92. Cambridge: Cambridge UP, 1991. Citations that lack parenthesis are the author's own translations. This book translates the title of Asperger's thesis as: "The 'Autistic Psychopaths' in Childhood."

2. Asperger, " 'Psychopathen,' " 135 (89).
3. Asperger, " 'Psychopathen,' " 96, 97 (50).
4. Asperger, " 'Psychopathen,' " 100, 133 (55, 88).
5. Asperger, " 'Psychopathen,' " 101, 102, 97 (56, 57, 52).
6. Asperger, " 'Psychopathen,' " 132, 118, 135, 132 (87, 74, 90).

7. Asperger, " 'Psychopathen,' " 99 (54).
8. Bleuler, Eugen. *Dementia praecox, oder Gruppe der Schizophrenien.* Leipzig: Deuticke, 1911. Overview: Feinstein, Adam. *A History of Autism: Conversations with the Pioneers.* Chichester, West Sussex, UK; Malden: Wiley-Blackwell, 2010, 4–8. Soviet psychiatrist Grunya Sukhareva has received the most attention for her work on "schizoid psychopathy," which she later called "autistic (pathological avoidant) psychopathy." Ssucharewa, Grunya Efimovna [name misspelled in original]. "Die schizoiden Psychopathien im Kindesalter." *MfPN* 60 (1926): 235–61.
9. Kanner, Leo. "Autistic Disturbances of Affective Contact." *Nervous Child* 2 (1943): 217–50.
10. World Health Organization. *International Statistical Classification of Diseases and Related Health Problems, Tenth Revision,* (ICD-10). 1992–2017. "Asperger's Syndrome," Diagnosis code 84.5.
11. Baoi, Jon. "Prevalence of Autism Spectrum Disorder Among Children Aged 8 Years— Autism and Developmental Disabilities Monitoring Network, 11 Sites, United States, 2010." *Morbidity and Mortality Weekly Report.* [United States Centers for Disease Control] 63, SS02 (2014): 1–21.

12. Asperger, "Die 'Autistischen Psychopathen,' " 120–21, 136 (77, 90). American Psychiatric Association. *Diagnostic and Statistical Manual of Mental Disorders* (DSM-5). Arlington, VA: American Psychiatric Association, 2013, 299.00 (F 84.0).

13. e.g., Silberman, Steve. *NeuroTribes: The Legacy of Autism and the Future of Neurodiversity.* New York: Avery; Random House, 2015, 141; Attwood, Anthony. *The Complete Guide to Asperger's Syndrome.* London: Jessica Kingsley, 2006, 10, 341; Schirmer, Brita. "Hans Aspergers Verteidigung der 'autistischen Psychopathen' gegen die NS-Eugenik." *Neue Sonderschule* 6 (2002): 450–54.

14. e.g., ORF Radio Österreich 1. "Interview mit dem Kinderarzt und Heilpädagogen Hans Asperger" [24 December 1974]. Rebroadcast 28 March 1978. http://www.mediathek.at/atom/01782B10-0D9-00CD5-00000BEC-01772EE2.

15. Herwig Czech has also conducted extensive research on Asperger's activities. His work is credited throughout this book, and has also been noted in John Donvan's and Caren Zucker's *In a Different Key: The Story of Autism.* New York: Crown, 2016.

16. Asperger, " 'Psychopathen,' " 132, 133 (87, 88).

17. Burleigh, Michael, and Wolfgang Wippermann. *The Racial State: Germany 1933–1945*. Cambridge: Cambridge UP, 1991. Debate: Pendas, Devin, Mark Roseman, and Richard F. Wetzell, eds. *Beyond the Racial State: Rethinking Nazi Germany*. New York: Cambridge UP, 2017.

18. Fritzsche, Peter. *Life and Death in the Third Reich*. Cambridge, MA: Belknap, 2008, 113–14.

19. Kater, Michael H. *Doctors under Hitler*. Chapel Hill: UNC Press, 1990; Müller-Hill, Benno. *Murderous Science: Elimination by Scientific Selection of Jews, Gypsies, and Others, Germany 1933–1945*, translated by George Fraser. Oxford: Oxford UP, 1988; Aly, Götz, Peter Chroust, and Christian Pross. *Cleansing the Fatherland: Nazi Medicine and Racial Hygiene*. Translated by Belinda Cooper. Baltimore: Johns Hopkins UP, 1994; Proctor, Robert. *Racial Hygiene: Medicine under the Nazis*. Cambridge, MA: Harvard UP, 1988, and Proctor, Robert. *The Nazi War on Cancer*. Princeton, NJ: Princeton UP, 1999; Weindling, Paul. *Health, Race, and German Politics between National Unification and Nazism, 1870–1945*. Cambridge: Cambridge UP, 1989; Szöllösi-Janze, Margit. *Science in the Third Reich*. Oxford: Berg, 2001.

20. Kondziella, Daniel. "Thirty Neurological Eponyms Associated with the Nazi Era." *European Neurology* 62 no. 1 (2009): 56–64.

21. Nazi psychiatry: Beddies, Thomas, and Kristina Hübener, eds. *Kinder in der NS-Psychiatrie*. Berlin-Brandenburg: Be.bra, 2004; Hamann, Matthias, Hans Asbek, and Andreas Heinz, eds. *Halbierte Vernunft und totale Medizin: zu Grundlagen, Realgeschichte und Fortwirkungen der Psychiatrie im Nationalsozialismus*. Berlin; Göttingen: Schwarze Risse; Rote Strasse, 1997; Blasius, Dirk. *Einfache Seelenstörung: Geschichte der deutschen Psychiatrie, 1800–1945*. Frankfurt: Fischer, 1994; Klee, Ernst. *Irrsinn Ost—Irrsinn West: Psychiatrie in Deutschland*. Frankfurt: Fischer, 1993; Brink, Cornelia. *Grenzen der Anstalt: Psychiatrie und Gesellschaft in Deutschland 1860–1980*. Göttingen: Wallstein, 2010, 270–359.

22. Eley, Geoff. *Nazism as Fascism: Violence, Ideology, and the Ground of Consent in Germany 1930–1945*. London: Routledge, 2013; Paxton, Robert O. *The Anatomy of Fascism*. New York: Knopf, 2004; Griffin, Roger. *The Nature of Fascism*. London: Routledge, 1993.

23. Leiter, Anna. "Zur Vererbung von asozialen

Charaktereigenschaften." *ZfNP* 167 (1939): 157–60.

24. By the summer of 1941, the T4 program claimed to have "disinfected" the Reich of 70,273 unfit adults.

25. Megargee, Geoffrey P., ed. *The United States Holocaust Memorial Museum Encyclopedia of Camps and Ghettos, 1933–1945*, vols. 1 & 2. Bloomington: Indiana UP, 2009–2012.

CHAPTER 1—ENTER THE EXPERTS

1. Asperger, " 'Psychopathen,' " 76.
2. von Goethe, Johann Wolfgang, *Faust,* Part II, V/IV; Felder, Maria Asperger. " 'Zum Sehen geboren, zum Schauen bestellt': Hans Asperger (1906–1980: Leben und Werk)." In *Hundert Jahre Kinder- und Jugendpsychiatrie*, edited by Rolf Castell, 99–119. Göttingen: Vandenhoeck & Ruprecht, 2008; Felder, Maria Asperger. " 'Zum Sehen geboren, zum Schauen bestellt,' " 38–43; Sousek, Roxanne. "Hans Asperger (1906–1980)—Versuch einer Annäherung," 15–23, 21. Both in *Auf den Spuren Hans Aspergers*, edited by Arnold Pollack. Stuttgart: Schattauer, 2015. Stuttgart: Schattauer 2015, 21.
3. ORF Radio, Asperger, 1974. "Lebenslauf," 1b, WStLA 1.3.2.202.A5. P: A.

4. Felder, Maria Asperger. "Foreword." In *Asperger Syndrome: Assessing and Treating High-functioning Autism Spectrum Disorders*, edited by James McPartland, Ami Klin, and Fred Volkmar. New York: Guilford, 2014, x; Zweymüller, E. "Nachruf für Herrn Dr. H. Asperger." *WkW* 93 (1981): 33–34; 33; ORF Radio, Asperger, 1974.

5. Felder, " 'Sehen,' " (2015), 38–39; Frith, Uta. "Asperger and his Syndrome." In *Autism and Asperger Syndrome*, 1–36; 9–10; ORF Radio, Asperger, 1974; Asperger, Hans. "Problems of Infantile Autism." *Communication* (1979): 45–52; 49; Asperger, Hans. *Probleme des kindlichen Autismus*. Lüdenscheid: Gerda Crummenerl, 1977, 2; Asperger, Hans. "Die Jugendgemeinschaften als Erziehungsfaktor." In *Jugend in Not*, edited by Alfred Brodil, 121–36. Vienna: Schriften zur Volksbildung des BfU, 1959, 130.

6. Felder, " 'Sehen,' " (2008), 100. They married in July 1935. Fragebogen für den Personalkataster, Abteilung V., 27 November 1940. WStLA 1.3.2.202.A5, P: A.

7. Sousek, "Hans Asperger," 20–21; Lyons, Viktoria, and Michael Fitzgerald. "Did Hans Asperger (1906–1980) have Asperger Syndrome?" *Journal of Autism and Developmental Disorders* 37 no. 10 (2007): 2020–21;

Asperger, "Infantile Autism," 49; also "Frühkindlicher Autismus." *MK* 69 no. 49 (1974): 2024–27; 2026.

8. Felder, " 'Sehen,' " (2008), 101. Also: ORF Radio, Asperger, 1974.
9. Schorske, Carl. *Fin-de-siècle Vienna: Politics and Culture.* New York: Knopf, 1979; Kandel, Eric. *The Age of Insight: The Quest to Understand the Unconscious in Art, Mind, and Brain, from Vienna 1900 to the Present.* New York: Random House, 2012.
10. Healy, Maureen. *Vienna and the Fall of the Habsburg Empire: Total War and Everyday Life in World War I.* Cambridge: Cambridge UP, 2004; Maderthaner, Wolfgang, and Lutz Musner. *Unruly Masses: The Other Side of Fin-de-Siècle Vienna.* New York: Berghahn, 2008; Boyer, John. *Political Radicalism in Late Imperial Vienna: Origins of the Christian Social Movement, 1848–1897.* Chicago: University of Chicago Press, 1981; Boyer, John. *Culture and Political Crisis in Vienna: Christian Socialism in Power, 1897–1918.* Chicago: University of Chicago Press, 1995; Judson, Pieter. " 'Where our Commonality is Necessary . . .': Rethinking the End of the Habsburg Monarchy." *Austrian History Yearbook* 48 (2017): 1–21; Judson, Pieter M. *The Habsburg Empire: A New History.* Cambridge, MA: Belknap,

2016; Deak, John. *Forging a Multinational State: State Making in Imperial Austria from the Enlightenment to the First World War.* Stanford: Stanford UP, 2015.

11. Wasserman, Janek. *Black Vienna: The Radical Right in the Red City, 1918–1938.* Ithaca: Cornell UP, 2014.

12. McEwen, Britta. "Welfare and Eugenics: Julius Tander's Rassenhygienische Vision for Interwar Vienna." *Austrian History Year book* 41 (2010): 170–90; Gruber, Helmut. *Red Vienna: Experiment in Working-Class Culture, 1919–1934.* New York: Oxford UP, 1991.

13. Löscher, Monika. *"—der gesunden Vernunft nicht zuwider—?": katholische Eugenik in Österreich vor 1938.* Innsbruck: Studien, 2009; Wolf, Maria. *Eugenische Vernunft: Eingriffe in die reproduktive Kultur durch die Medizin 1900–2000.* Vienna: Böhlau, 2008; Baader, Gerhard, Veronika Hofer, and Thomas Mayer, eds. *Eugenik in Österreich: biopolitische Strukturen von 1900–1945.* Vienna: Czernin, 2007; Logan, Cheryl. *Hormones, Heredity, and Race: Spectacular Failure in Interwar Vienna.* New Brunswick, NJ: Rutgers UP, 2013; Gabriel, Eberhard, and Wolfgang Neugebauer, eds. *Vorreiter der Vernichtung?: Eugenik, Rassenhygiene und Euthanasie in der österreichischen*

Diskussion vor 1938. Zur Geschichte der NS-Euthanasie in Wien, vol. 3. Vienna: Böhlau, 2005.

14. Tandler, Julius. *Gefahren der Minderwertigkeit*. Vienna: Verlag des Wiener Jugendhilfswerks, 1929, and *Ehe und Bevölkerungspolitik*. Vienna: Perles, 1924; McEwen, "Welfare," 187, and *Sexual Knowledge: Feeling, Fact, and Social Reform in Vienna, 1900–1934*. New York: Berghahn, 2012, 145; Turda, Marius. *The History of East-Central European Eugenics, 1900–1945: Sources and Commentaries*: London: Bloomsbury, 2015, 21.

15. Gruber, Helmut. "Sexuality in 'Red Vienna': Socialist Party Conceptions and Programs and Working-Class Life, 1920–34." *International Labor and Working-Class History* 31 (1987): 37–68; Sieder, Reinhard. "Housing Policy, Social Welfare, and Family Life in 'Red Vienna,' 1919–34." *Oral History* 13 no. 2 (1985): 35–48; Gruber, Helmut, and Pamela Graves. "The 'New Woman': Realities and Illusions of Gender Equality in Red Vienna." In *Women and Socialism, Socialism and Women: Europe between the two World Wars*, edited by Helmut Gruber and Pamela Graves, 56–94. New York: Berghahn, 1998; Wegs, Robert. *Growing up Working Class: Continuity and*

Change among Viennese Youth, 1890–1938. University Park: Pennsylvania State UP, 1989.

16. Dickinson, Edward Ross. *The Politics of German Child Welfare from the Empire to the Federal Republic.* Cambridge, MA: Harvard UP, 1996, 48–79. International: Dekker, Jeroen. *The Will to Change the Child: Re-Education Homes for Children at Risk in Nineteenth Century Western Europe.* Frankfurt: Peter Lang, 2001; Rosenblum, Warren. *Beyond the Prison Gates: Punishment and Welfare in Germany, 1850–1933.* Chapel Hill: UNC Press, 2012. Foucault, Michel. *History of Madness*, edited by Jean Khalfa. London: Routledge, 2006, and *Madness and Civilization: A History of Insanity in the Age of Reason.* New York: Pantheon, 1965; Blackshaw, Gemma, and Sabine Wieber, eds. *Journeys into Madness: Mapping Mental Illness in the Austro-Hungarian Empire.* New York: Berghahn, 2012.

17. Fadinger, Biljana. "Die vergessenen Wurzeln der Heilpädagogik: Erwin Lazar und die Heilpädagogische Station an der Universitäts-Kinderklinik in Wien." University of Vienna, 1999, 91; Lazar, Erwin. "Die heilpädagogische Abteilung der k. k. Universitäts-Kinderklinik in Wien

und ihre Bedeutung für die Jugendfürsorge." *ZfKJ* 5 no. 11 (1913): 309–13; Bruck, Valerie, Georg Frankl, Anni Weiß, and Viktorine Zak. "Erwin Lazar und sein Wirken." *ZfK* 40 (1932): 211–18; 211–12.

18. Biewer, Gottfried. *Grundlagen der Heilpädagogik und inklusiven Pädagogik.* Stuttgart: UTB, 2010; Moser, Vera. "Gründungsmythen der Heilpädagogik." *ZfP* 58 no. 2 (2012): 262–74. Foundational: Georgens, Jan, and H. Deinhardt. *Die Heilpädagogik: mit Berücksichtigung der Idiotie und der Idiotenanstalten.* Leipzig: Fleischer, 1863; Heller, Theodor. *Grundriss der Heilpädagogik.* Leipzig: Engelmann, 1904.

19. Frankl, Georg. "Die Heilpädagogische Abteilung der Wiener Kinderklinik." *ZfKFB* 29 no. 5–6 (1937): 33–38; 33; Heller, Theodor. "Nachruf, Erwin Lazar." *ZfK* 40 (1932): I–III; Heller, Theodor. "Fürsorgeerziehung und Heilpädagogik in Deutschland und Österreich." *Zentralblatt für Jugendrecht und Jugendwohlfahrt* 22 no. 10/11 (1931): 369–75.

20. Schröder, Paul. "Kinderpsychiatrie und Heilpädagogik," *ZfK* 49 (1943): 9–14; 10; Asperger, Hans. "Tagungsbericht: Erziehungsfragen im Rahmen der Kinderkundlichen Woche." *DN* 14 no. 2 (1941):

28–31; 29. Asperger on history: "Pädiatrie—Kinderpsychiatrie—Heilpädagogik." *WkW* 87 (1975): 581–82; "Heilpädagogik in Österreich." *HP* 1 (1958): 2–4; "Die medizinische Grundlagen der Heilpädagogik." *MfK* 99 no. 3 (1950): 105–7.

21. Wagner, Richard. *Clemens von Pirquet: His Life and Work*. Baltimore: Johns Hopkins, 1968, 118; Neuburger, Max. "The History of Pediatrics in Vienna," translated by Robert Rosenthal. *Medical Record* 156 (1943): 746–51.

22. von Pirquet, Clemens Peter. "Die Amerikanische Schulausspeisung in Österreich." *WkW* 31 no. 27 (1921): 323–24; von Pirquet, Clemens Peter. "Die Amerikanische Kinderhilfsaktion in Österreich." *WMW* 70 nos. 19 and 20 (1920): 854, 858; 908–9; Obrowsky, Louis. *Historische Betrachtung der sozialmedizinischen Einrichtungen in Wien vom Beginn des 20. Jahrhunderts bis zum Ende der Ersten Republik*. Frankfurt: Lang, 2005, 74–81; Schick, Béla. "Pediatric Profiles: Pediatrics in Vienna at the Beginning of the Century." *JP* 50 no. 1 (1957): 114–24, 121.

23. Hubenstorf, Michael. "Pädiatrische Emigration und die 'Hamburger Klinik' 1930–1945," 69–220; 78, and Gröger, Helmut. "Der Entwicklungsstand der Kinderheilkunde

in Wien am Beginn des 20. Jahrhunderts," 53–68, both in *90 Jahre Universitäts-Kinderklinik in Wien,* edited by Kurt Widhalm and Arnold Pollak. Vienna: Literas-Universitätsverlag, 2005.

24. Rudolph, Clarissa, and Gerhard Benetka. "Kontinuität oder Bruch? Zur Geschichte der Intelligenzmessung im Wiener Fürsorgesystem vor und in der NS-Zeit." In *Verfolgte Kindheit: Kinder und Jugendliche als Opfer der NS-Sozialverwaltung,* edited by Ernst Berger and Else Rieger, 15–40. Vienna: Böhlau, 2007, 36 (34–39); Lazar, Erwin. "Die Aufgaben der Heilpädagogik beim Jugendgericht." *HS-E* 10 Nr. 1–2 (1919): 1–9; Fadinger, "Wurzeln," 39–137; Brezinka, Wolfgang. "Heilpädagogik in der Medizinischen Fakultät der Universität Wien: ihre Geschichte von 1911–1985." *ZfP* 43 no. 3 (1997): 395–420; Fadinger, "Wurzeln"; Skopec, Manfred, and Helmut Wyklicki. "Die Heilpädagogische Abteilung der Universitätsklinik in Wien." *HP* 24 no. 1 (1981): 98–105.

25. Bruck, Frankl, Weiß, and Zak, "Erwin Lazar," 212; Zak, Viktorine. "Die Entwicklung der klinischen Heilpädagogik in Wien." *ICN* 3 no. 4 (1928): 348–57; 356; Malina, Peter. "Zur Geschichte des Spiegelgrunds." In *Verfolgte Kindheit,* 159–92; 183; Malina,

Peter. "Im Fangnetz der NS-'Erziehung':
Kinder- und Jugend- 'Fürsorge' auf dem
'Spiegelgrund' 1940–1945." In *Von der
Zwangssterilisierung zur Ermordung—zur
Geschichte der NS-Euthanasie in Wien*, vol.
2, edited by Eberhard Gabriel and Wolfgang
Neugebauer, 77–98. Vienna: Böhlau, 2002,
91–92.

26. *Neue deutsche Biographie*, 14, "Lazar,
Erwin," 8–9; Teller, Simone. "Zur Heil-
pädagogisierung der Strafe: oder Geschichte
der Wiener Jugendgerichtshilfe von 1911 bis
1928." University of Vienna, 2009.

27. Rudolph and Benetka, "Kontinuität,"
35; Lazar, Erwin. "Über die endogenen
und exogenen Wurzeln der Dissozialität
Jugendlicher." *HS-E* 4 (1913). Part 1:
no. 11, 199–205; Part 2: no. 12, 218–25;
Lazar, Erwin. *Medizinische Grundlagen
der Heilpädagogik*. Vienna: Springer, 1925.
A comprehensive history of the clinic is
underway in a dissertation by Ina Friedmann,
"Hans Asperger und die Heilpädagogische
Abteilung der Wiener Universitäts-
Kinderklinik. Konzepte und Kontinuitäten
im 20. Jahrhundert." University of Vienna.

28. Dorffner, Gabriele, and Gerald Weippl.
*Clemens Freiherr von Pirquet: ein
begnadeter Arzt und genialer Geist*.
Strasshof-Vienna: Vier-Viertel, 2004, 143.

29. Feldner, Josef. "Wer war Lazar?" *ZfH* 24 (1932): 36–38; 36, 37; Frankl, Georg. "Die Heilpädagogische Abteilung der Wiener Kinderklinik." *ZfKFB* 29 no. 7–8 (1937): 50–54; 51.

30. Groh, Ch., E. Tatzer, and M. Weninger. "Das Krankengut der Heilpädagogischen Abteilung im Wandel der Zeit." *HP* 24 no. 4 (1981): 106–111; 108; Bruck, Frankl, Weiss, and Zak, "Erwin Lazar," 212. Quoted: Wolf, *Vernunft*, 434. Bruck, Valerie. "Die Bedeutung der Heilpädagogik für die Jugendgerichtshilfe." In *Festschrift der Wiener Jugendgerichtshilfe zur Erinnerung an die 25. Wiederkehr ihrer Gründung*, 26–27. Vienna, 1937, 37.

31. Löscher, *Eugenik*; Wolf, *Vernunft*; Baader, Gerhard, Hofer, and Mayer, eds., *Eugenik*; Logan, *Hormones*.

32. Sieder, Reinhard, and Andrea Smioski. "Gewalt gegen Kinder in Erziehungsheimen der Stadt Wien: Endbericht." Stadt Wien, Amtsführender Stadtrat Christian Oxonitsch, 2012, 27–29. Terms: *Verwahrlosung, Gefährdung, Asozialität, Erziehung-sschwierig-keiten.*

33. Sieder and Smioski, "Gewalt," 40. Wolfgruber, Gudrun. *Zwischen Hilfestellung und Sozialer Kontrolle: Jugendfürsorge im Roten Wien, dargestellt am Beispiel der*

Kindesabnahme. Vienna: Ed. Praesens, 1997.

34. Baader, Gerhard, Hofer, and Mayer, eds., *Eugenik*.

35. Quoted: Midgley, Nick. *Reading Anna Freud*. London: Routledge, 2012, 5.

36. Danto, Elizabeth Ann. *Freud's Free Clinics: Psychoanalysis & Social Justice, 1918–1938*. New York: Columbia UP, 2005, 17.

37. Danto, *Clinics*, 4.

38. Aichhorn, August. *Verwahrloste Jugend: die Psychoanalyse in der Fürsorgeerziehung: zehn Vorträge zur ersten Einführung*. Internationaler Psychoanalytischer Verlag, 1925, 123, 124, 144; Adler, Alfred. *Guiding the Child: On the Principles of Individual Psychology*. London: Routledge, 2013.

39. German-language psychiatry: Engstrom, Eric. *Clinical Psychiatry in Imperial Germany: A History of Psychiatric Practice*. Ithaca: Cornell UP, 2003; Blasius, *Seelenstörung*; Brink, *Grenzen*; Schaffner-Hänny, Elisabeth. *Wo Europas Kinderpsychiatrie zur Welt kam: Anfänge und Entwicklungen in der Region Jurasüdfuss*. Dietikon: Juris Druck + Verlag, 1997; Engstrom, Eric, and Volker Roelcke. *Psychiatrie im 19. Jahrhundert: Forschungen zur Geschichte von psychiatrischen Institutionen, Debatten und Praktiken im deutschen Sprachraum*.

411

Basel: Schwabe, 2003; Roelcke, Volker. "Continuities or Ruptures? Concepts, Institutions and Contexts of Twentieth-Century German Psychiatry and Mental Health Care." In *Psychiatric Cultures Compared: Psychiatry and Mental Health Care in the Twentieth Century: Comparisons and Approaches*, edited by Marijke Gijswijt-Hofstra, Harry Oosterhuis, and Joost Vijselaar, 162–82: Amsterdam: Amsterdam UP, 2005, 163–65; Müller-Küppers, Manfred. "Die Geschichte der Kinder- und Jugendpsychiatrie unter besonderer Berücksichtigung der Zeit des Nationalsozialismus." *Forum der Kinder- und Jugendpsychiatrie und Psychotherapie* 11 no. 2 (2001).

Transnational linkages: Eghigian, Greg. *From Madness to Mental Health: Psychiatric Disorder and its Treatment in Western Civilization*. New Brunswick: Rutgers UP, 2010; Remschmidt, Helmut, and Herman van Engeland. *Child and Adolescent Psychiatry in Europe: Historical Development, Current Situation, Future Perspectives*. Darmstatt: Steinkopff, 1999; Berrios, German, and Roy Porter. *A History of Clinical Psychiatry: The Origin and History of Psychiatric Disorders*. London: Athlone, 1995; Roelcke, Volker, Paul Weindling, and Louise Westwood, eds. *International Relations in Psychiatry: Britain, Germany, and the United States to World War II.* Rochester: University of Rochester Press, 2010; Eghigian, Greg. "Deinstitutionalizing the History of Contemporary Psychiatry." *History of Psychiatry* 22 (2011): 201–14. Austrian neurology: Jellinger, Kurt A. "Highlights in the History of Neurosciences in Austria—Review." *Clinical Neuropathology* 5 (2006): 243–52; Jellinger, Kurt A. "A Short History of Neurosciences in Austria." *Journal of Neural Transmission* 113: 271–82.

40. Intersections: Hoffmann-Richter, Ulrike. "Die Wiener akademische Psychiatrie und die Geburt der Psychoanalyse." In *Gründe der Seele: die Wiener Psychiatrie im 20. Jahrhundert*, edited by Brigitta Keintzel and Eberhard Gabriel, 49–72. Vienna: Picus, 1999; Benetka, Gerhard. *Psychologie in Wien: Sozial- und Theoriegeschichte des Wiener Psychologischen Instituts, 1922–1938.* Vienna: WUV-Universitätsverlag, 1995, and *Zur Geschichte der Institutionalisierung der Psychologie in Österreich: die Errichtung des Wiener Psychologischen Instituts.* Vienna: Geyer-Edition, 1990.

41. These findings stem from a digital history project at Stanford's Spatial History Project conducted by Edith Sheffer and

Michelle Kahn, "Forming Selves: The Creation of Child Psychiatry from Red Vienna to the Third Reich and Abroad." Research tracked professional and personal connections among fifty leading figures in Vienna, indexing their schooling, training, organizational memberships, and social circles in a database spanning the 1920s, 1930s, and 1940s.

42. Hubenstorf, Michael. "Tote und/oder Lebendige Wissenschaft: die intellektuellen Netzwerke der NS-Patientenmordaktion in Österreich." In *Zwangssterilisierung zur Ermordung*, vol. 2, 237–420; 287–88; Gröger, "Entwicklung"; Danto, *Clinics*.

43. *Neue deutsche Biographie*, "Lazar, Erwin," 8; Skopec and Wyklicki, "Abteilung," 102; Fadinger, "Wurzeln," 91.

44. Frankl, "Abteilung," 34, 35; Frankl, Georg. "Die Wirkungskreis der ärztlichen Heilpädagogik." *Volksgesundheit* 6 (1932): 180–85.

45. Roazen, Paul. *Helene Deutsch: A Psychoanalyst's Life*. New Brunswick: Transaction, 1992, 102, 106. Child psychoanalyst Rosetta Hurwitz also worked for a time at the Curative Education Clinic, as did, according to Asperger, Hermine Hug-Hellmuth, an eminent child psychoanalyst. Asperger, "Erwin Lazar und seine Heilpädagogische

Abteilung der Wiener Kinderklinik." *HP* 3 (1962): 34–41; 39.

46. Details: Hubenstorf, "Emigration," 80–86; Wagner, *von Pirquet.*

47. Mayer, Thomas. "Akademische Netzwerke um die 'Wiener Gesellschaft für Rassenpflege (Rassenhygiene)' von 1924 bis 1948." University of Vienna, 2004, 94–95, 98.

48. *Der Abend*, 15 March 1929, 3, Quoted: Dorffner and Weippl, *von Pirquet*, 282 (succession debates: 275–82).

49. Berger, Karin. *Zwischen Eintopf und Fliessband: Frauenarbeit und Frauenbild im Faschismus, Österreich, 1938–1945.* Vienna: Gesellschaftskritik, 1984; Bischof, Günter, Anton Pelinka, and Erika Thurner, eds. *Women in Austria.* New Brunswick: Transaction, 1988; Hamburger, Franz A. "Lebenslauf von Univers.-Professor Dr. Hamburger, Vöcklabruck." *MmW* 96 no. 33 (1954): 928.

50. "100 Jahre Wiener Kinderklinik." *Medical Tribune*, 11 May 2011; Hamburger, Franz A., "Lebenslauf," 928.

51. Hamburger, Franz. "Festvortrag: Nationalsozialismus und Medizin." *WkW* 52 (1939): 133–38; 137.

52. Hubenstorf, "Emigration," 99, 93.

53. Hubenstorf, "Wissenschaft," 320.

54. "Lebenslauf," 1b, 4b, WStLA 1.3.2.202.A5. P: A. ORF Radio, Asperger, 1974.

55. "Lebenslauf," 1b, 4b, WStLA 1.3.2.202. A5. P: A. Asperger, "Erlebtes Leben," 216. Asperger's personnel file at the University of Vienna: MED PA 17.

56. Quoted: Felder, " 'Sehen,' " (2008), 101. Asperger, Hans. "Erlebtes Leben: fünfzig Jahre Pädiatrie." *Pädiatrie und Pädagogie* 12 (1977): 214–23; 216.

57. Löscher, *Eugenik*, 18, 217; Gröger, Helmut. "Zur Ideengeschichte der medizinischen Heilpädagogik." In *Auf den Spuren Hans Aspergers*, 30–37; 31. "Lebenslauf," 1b, 4b, WStLA 1.3.2.202.A5 P: A.

58. Hubenstorf, "Emigration," 108. Jekelius's National Socialist affiliations: Ertl, Karin Anna. "NS-Euthanasie in Wien: Erwin Jekelius—der Direktor vom 'Spiegelgrund' und seine Beteiligung am NS-Vernichtungsprogramm." University of Vienna, 2012, 134–35; early career: 113–15. Connections with Asperger: Hubenstorf, "Tote," 319–20.

59. Ertl, "NS-Euthanasie," 114.

60. Bischof, Günther, Anton Pelinka, and Alexander Lassner, eds. *The Dollfuss-Schuschnigg Era in Austria: A Reassessment.* New Brunswick: Transaction, 2003; Lewis, Jill. *Fascism and the Working Class in Austria, 1918–1934: The Failure of Labour in the First Republic.* New York: Berg, 1991; Lauridsen, John. *Nazism and the Radical*

Right in Austria, 1918–1934. Copenhagen: Royal Library, Museum Tusculanum, 2007; Beniston, Judith, and Robert Vilain, eds. *Culture and Politics in Red Vienna*. Leeds: Maney, 2006; Holmes, Deborah, and Lisa Silverman, eds. *Interwar Vienna: Culture between Tradition and Modernity*. Rochester: Camden House, 2009.

61. Large, David Clay. *Between Two Fires: Europe's Path in the 1930s*. New York: W. W. Norton, 1991, 77.

62. Thorpe, Julie. *Pan-Germanism and the Austrofascist State, 1933–38*. New York: Oxford UP, 2011, 91. Nazi Party in Austria: Pauley, Bruce. *Hitler and the Forgotten Nazis: A History of Austrian National Socialism*. Chapel Hill: UNC Press, 1981.

63. Burgwyn, James. *Italian Foreign Policy in the Interwar Period, 1918–1940*. Westport: Praeger, 1997, 88.

64. Member number B 134831. "Lebenslauf," 1b, WStLA 1.3.2.202.A5. P: A.

65. Dr. Asperger Hans, 7 October 1940. WStLA 1.3.2.202.A5. P: A. Ernst, Edzard. "A Leading Medical School Seriously Damaged: Vienna 1938." *Annals of Internal Medicine* 122 no. 10 (1995): 789–92; 790.

66. Löscher, Monika. "Eugenics and Catholicism in Interwar Austria." In *"Blood and Homeland": Eugenics and Racial*

Nationalism in Central and Southeast Europe, 1900–1940, edited by Marius Turda and Paul Weindling, 299–316. Budapest: Central European UP, 2007, 308–9.

67. Löscher, "Eugenics," 308–9. Memberships: Czech, Herwig. "Hans Asperger und die 'Kindereuthanasie' in Wien—mögliche Verbindungen." In *Auf den Spuren Hans Aspergers*, 24–29; Hager, Christa, "Hans Asperger—'Er war Teil des Apparats.'" Interview of Herwig Czech. *Wiener Zeitung*, 31 March 2014; Beniston, Judith, and Ritchie Robertson. *Catholicism and Austrian Culture*. Edinburgh: Edinburgh UP, 1999.

68. Asperger, "Erlebtes Leben," 215.

69. Chart: Hubenstorf, "Tote," 271.

CHAPTER 2—THE CLINIC'S DIAGNOSIS

1. Frith, "Asperger," 9; Felder, " 'Sehen,' " (2015), 40–41. Rosenmayr, E. "Gedanken zur Pirquet'schen Klinik und ihrem Umfeld." In *90 Jahre Universitäts-Kinderklinik*, 31–39; 34. *Neue deutsche Biographie*, 14, "Lazar, Erwin," 8.

2. Asperger, Hans. "Erwin Lazar—der Mensch und sein Werk." *EU* (1958): 129–34; 130, 133; Asperger, "Erwin Lazar," 38.

3. Zak, "Entwicklung," 355, 366.

4. Zak, Viktorine. "Die heilpädagogische

Abteilung unter Lazar." *ZfH* 24 (1932): 38–40; 40, 39; Mühlberger, Theresa. "Heilpädagogisches Denken in Österreich zwischen 1945 und 1980." University of Vienna, 2012, 45.

5. Zak, "Heilpädagogische Abteilung," 39, 40.

6. Asperger, Hans. *Heilpädagogik: Einführung in die Psychopathologie des Kindes für Ärzte, Lehrer, Psychologen und Fürsorgerinnen.* Vienna: Springer, 1952 [1956, 1961, 1965, and 1968], iv; Asperger, Hans. "Schwester Viktorine Zak." *EU* (1946): 155–58; 157.

7. Asperger, "Schwester Zak," 157.

8. Asperger, "Erwin Lazar–Mensch," 131.

9. Asperger, "Schwester Zak," 156.

10. Hubenstorf, "Emigration," 118–19.

11. Bruck, Frankl, Weiß, and Zak, "Erwin Lazar," 213. Hamburger's portrayal: Hamburger, Franz. "Prof. Erwin Lazar (Nachruf zum Tode von Erwin Lazar)." *WkW* 45 (1932): 537–38. Bruck, "Bedeutung," 37. Bruck-Biesok, Valerie, Clemens von Pirquet, and Richard Wagner. "Rachitisprophylaxe." *KW* 6 no. 20 (1927): 952.

12. Frankl, "Wirkungskreis," 185. Georg Frankl is not to be confused with philosopher and psychoanalyst George Frankl, who was also from Vienna but escaped to England in 1939 after being sent to Dachau.

13. Braiusch-Marrain, A., and Hans Asperger.

"Über den Einfluss von Ultraviolett-bestrahlung auf die Pirquet- und die Schickreaktion." *MK* 2 (1932): 1310–12; Siegl, Josef, and Hans Asperger. "Zur Behandlung der Enuresis," *AfK* (1934): 88–102; Asperger, Hans. "Leuzin und Tyrosin im Harn bei Lungengeschwulsten." *WkW* 43 (1930): 1281–84; Risak, Erwin, and Hans Asperger. "Neue Untersuchungen über das Auftreten von Melaninreaktionen im Menschlichen Harn nach Sonnen-bestrahlung." *KW* 11 no. 4 (1932): 154–56; Löscher, *"Katholische Eugenik,"* 217. In 1939: Asperger, Hans. "Eczema Vaccinatum." *WkW* 52 (1939): 826.

14. Asperger, "Erwin Lazar," 38; Asperger, "Erwin Lazar—Mensch," 130. Feldner's typologies: Feldner, Josef. "Gesellschafts-feindliche Schulkinder." In *Festschrift der Wiener Jugendgerichtshilfe zur Erinnerung an die 25. Wiederkehr ihrer Gründung,* 24–26. Vienna, 1937.

15. Michaels, Joseph. "The Heilpedagogical Station of the Children's Clinic at the University of Vienna." *AJO* 5 no. 3 (1935): 266–75; 266, 271.

16. Michaels, "Heilpedagogical Station," 274, 275.

17. Michaels, "Heilpedagogical Station," 266; Zak, "Entwicklung," 354.

18. Michaels, "Heilpedagogical Station," 268.
19. Michaels, "Heilpedagogical Station," 271.
20. Michaels, "Heilpedagogical Station," 272.
21. Michaels, "Heilpedagogical Station," 274, 267.
22. Quoted: Felder, " 'Sehen,' " (2008), 102.
23. Michaels, "Heilpedagogical Station," 270.
24. Frankl, Georg. "Befehlen und Gehorchen." *ZfK* 42 (1934): 463–74; 478.
25. Frankl, Georg. "Über postenzephalitischen Parkinsonismus und verwandte Störungen im Kindesalter." *ZfK* 46 no. 3 (1937): 199–249; 208, 212, 247, 244–45; Frankl, Georg. "Triebhandlungen bei Dissozialität nach Encephalitis epidemica und anderen psychopathischen Störungen des Kindesalters." *ZfK* 46 no. 5 (1937): 401–48; 423, 425. Also: Frankl, "Heilpädagogische Abteilung," 54.
26. Weiss, Anni B. "Qualitative Intelligence Testing as a Means of Diagnosis in the Examination of Psychopathic Children." *AJO* 5 no. 2 (1935): 154–79; 155.
27. Weiss, "Qualitative Intelligence," 155.
28. Weiss, "Qualitative Intelligence," 158, 156.
29. Weiss, "Qualitative Intelligence," 160, 167, 156.
30. Weiss, "Qualitative Intelligence," 160, 161, 157, 160.
31. Weiss, "Qualitative Intelligence," 173.

32. Tramer, Moritz. "Einseitig talentierte und begabte Schwachsinnige." *Schweizerische Zeitschrift für Gesundheitspflege* 4 (1924): 173–207.

33. Asperger, " 'Psychopathen,' " 118 (75).

34. Teachers College, Columbia University. *Teachers College Record* 37, no. 3 (1935): 252; 38, no. 2 (1936): 161–62. Teachers College, Columbia University. *Advanced School Digest* 1–6, (1936).

35. Teachers College, Columbia University. *The Advanced School Digest* 7 (1941): 18. Jewish emigration and Reich policy: Zahra, Tara. *The Great Departure: Mass Migration from Eastern Europe and the Making of the Free World*. New York: W. W. Norton, 2016.

36. Robison, John. "Kanner, Asperger, and Frankl: A Third Man at the Genesis of the Autism Diagnosis." *Autism* (September 2016): 1–10; Silberman, *NeuroTribes*, 167–69.

37. Kanner, Leo. *Child Psychiatry*. Springfield, IL: Charles C. Thomas, 1935.

38. Silberman, *NeuroTribes*, 141; Feinstein, *History*, 10–12; Schirmer, Brita. "Autismus—von der Außen—zur Innenperspektive." *Behinderte in Familie, Schule und Gesellschaft* 3 (2003): 20–32.

39. Druml, Wilfried. "The *Wiener klinische Wochenschrift* from 1938 to 1945: On the

50th Anniversary of its Reappearance." *WkW* 110 no. 4–5 (1998): 202–5; 202, 203; Birkmeyer, W. "Über die Vererbung der Nervenkrankheiten—aus den Schulungsabenden der Ärzteschaft des SS-Oberabschnittes 'Donau.' " *WkW* 51 no. 46 (1938): 1150–51; 1051.

40. Silberman, *NeuroTribes*, 168; Robison, "Kanner," 4.
41. e.g., Kanner, Leo. "Play Investigation and Play Treatment of Children's Behavior Disorders." *JP* 17 no. 4 (1940): 533–46.
42. Kanner, "Autistic Disturbances," 219–21.
43. Robison, "Kanner," 6. Kanner, "Autistic Disturbances"; Frankl, George. "Language and Affective Contact." *Nervous Child* 2 (1943): 251–62.
44. Frankl, "Language," 261.
45. Frankl, "Language," 261, 258, 260.
46. Frankl, "Language," 258, 260, 256.

CHAPTER 3—NAZI PSYCHIATRY AND SOCIAL SPIRIT

1. Quoted: Felder, " 'Sehen' " (2008), 102–3.
2. Rempel, Gerhard. *Hitler's Children: The Hitler Youth and the SS.* Chapel Hill: UNC Press, 1989; Reese, Dagmar. *Growing up Female in Nazi Germany.* Ann Arbor: University of Michigan Press, 2006; Kater,

Michael H. *Hitler Youth*. Cambridge, MA: Harvard UP, 2004.

3. Kuhn, Hans-Werner, Peter Massing, and Werner Skuhr. *Politische Bildung in Deutschland: Entwicklung, Stand, Perspektiven*. Opladen: Leske + Budrich, 1990, 90.

4. Fritzsche, *Life*, 113–14.

5. Tornow, Karl, and Herbert Weinert, *Erbe und Schicksal: von geschädigten Menschen, Erbkrankheiten und deren Bekämpfung*. Berlin: Metzner, 1942, 159.

6. *Richtlinien für die Leibeserziehung in Jungenschulen*. Berlin: Weidmann'sche Verlagsbuchhandlung, 1937, 7–8.

7. "Führer." *Deutsches Lesebuch für Volksschulen. 3. u. 4. Schuljahr*. Munich: Oldenbourg, 1937, 272.

8. *Deutsches Lesebuch für Volksschulen. 5. u. 6. Schuljahr*. Nuremberg: F. Korn, 1936, 361–63.

9. Razumovsky, Maria, Dolly Razumovsky, and Olga Razumovsky. *Unsere versteckten Tagebücher, 1938–1944: drei Mädchen erleben die Nazizeit*. Vienna: Böhlau, 1999, 16.

10. Williams, John A. *Turning to Nature in Germany: Hiking, Nudism, and Conservation, 1900–1940*. Stanford: Stanford UP, 2007, 203. Kater, *Hitler Youth*.

11. Cesarani, David, and Sarah Kavanaugh.

Holocaust: Hitler, Nazism and the "Racial State." London: Routledge, 2004, 371.

12. Good, David, Margarete Grandner, and Mary Jo Maynes, eds. *Austrian Women in the Nineteenth and Twentieth Centuries: Cross-Disciplinary Perspectives.* Providence: Berghahn, 1996; Bischof, Pelinka, and Thurner, eds., *Women*; Bischof, Günter, Anton Pelinka, and Dagmar Herzog, eds. *Sexuality in Austria.* New Brunswick: Transaction, 2007.

13. Tantner, Anton. *"Schlurfs": Annäherungen an einen subkulturellen Stil Wiener Arbeiterjugendlicher.* Morrisville: Lulu, 2007; Mejstrik, Alexander. "Urban Youth, National-Socialist Education and Specialized Fun: The Making of the Vienna Schlurfs, 1941–44." In *European Cities, Youth and the Public Sphere in the Twentieth Century*, edited by Axel Schildt and Detlef Siegfried, 57–89. Aldershot: Ashgate, 2005.

14. Fritz, Regina. "Die 'Jugendschutzlager' Uckermark und Moringen im System nationalsozialistischer Jugendfürsorge." In *Verfolgte Kindheit*, 303–26; 314; Malina, Peter. "Verfolgte Kindheit. Die Kinder vom 'Spiegelgrund' und ihre 'Erzieher.' " In *Totenwagen: Kindheit am Spiegelgrund von Alois Kaufmann*, edited by Robert Sommer, 94–115. Vienna: Uhudla, 1999,

102; Schikorra, Christa. "Über das Zusammenspiel von Fürsorge, Psychiatrie und Polizei bei der Disziplinierung auffälliger Jugendlicher." In *Kinder in der NS-Psychiatrie*, edited by Thomas Beddies and Kristina Hübener, 87–106. Berlin-Brandenburg: Be.bra, 2004, 93–95.

15. Steinberg, Holger, "Rückblick auf Entwicklungen der Kinder- und Jugendpsychiatrie: Paul Schröder." *PdKK* 48 (1999): 202–6, 204; Ettrich, K. U., "Gottlieb Ferdinand Paul Schröder—wissenschaftliches Denken und praktische Bedeutung." In *Bewahren und Verändern. 75 Jahre Kinder- und Jugendpsychiatrie an der Universität Leipzig,* edited by K. U. Ettrich, 14–25. Leipzig: Klinik und Poliklinik für Psychiatrie, Psychotherapie und Psychosomatik, 2002; Laube, S. "Zur Entwicklung der Kinder- und Jugendpsychiatrie in Deutschland von 1933 bis 1945." Leipzig: MD thesis, 1996.

16. Bürger-Prinz, Hans. *Ein Psychiater berichtet.* Hamburg: Hoffmann und Campe, 1971, 113; Steinberg, "Rückblick," 205; Thüsing, Carina. "Leben und wissenschaftliches Werk des Psychiaters Paul Schröder unter besonderer Berücksichtigung seines Wirkens an der Psychiatrischen und Nervenklinik der Universität Leipzig." University of Leipzig, 1999, 27.

17. Dahl, Matthias. "Aussonderung und Vernichtung—der Umgang mit 'lebensunwerten' Kindern während des Dritten Reiches und die Rolle der Kinder- und Jugendpsychiatrie." *PdKK* 50 no. 3 (2001): 170–91; 185. Steinberg, Holger and M. C. Angermeyer. "Two Hundred Years of Psychiatry at Leipzig University: An Overview." *History of Psychiatry* 13 no. 51 (2002): 267–83; 277; Castell, Rolf, and Uwe-Jens Gerhard. *Geschichte der Kinder- und Jugendpsychiatrie in Deutschland in den Jahren 1937 bis 1961*. Göttingen: Vandenhoeck & Ruprecht, 2003, 441. Thüsing, "Leben," 47–50.

18. Schepker, Klaus, and Heiner Fangerau. "Die Gründung der Deutschen Gesellschaft für Kinderpsychiatrie und Heilpädagogik." *Zeitschrift für Kinder- und Jugendpsychiatrie und Psychotherapie* 44 no. 3 (2016): 180–88; 181–82.

19. Schepker and Fangerau, "Gründung," 182, 183.

20. Asperger, Hans. " 'Jugendpsychiatrie' und 'Heilpädagogik.' " *MmW* 89 no. 16 (1942): 352–56.

21. Rudert, Johannes. "Gemüt als charakterologischer Begriff." In *Seelenleben und Menschenbild*, edited by Adolf Daümling and Philipp Lersch, 53–73. Munich: Barth,

1958; Scheer, Monique. "Topographies of Emotion," 32–61; 44, and Gammerl, Benno. "Felt Distances," 177–200; 195, both in *Emotional Lexicons: Continuity and Change in the Vocabulary of Feeling, 1700–2000*, edited by Monique Scheer, Anne Schmidt, Pascal Eitler, et al. Oxford: Oxford UP, 2014.

22. *Dictionary of Untranslatables: A Philosophical Lexicon*, edited by Barbara Cassin, Emily Apter, Jacques Lezra, Michael Wood. Princeton, NJ: Princeton UP, 2014, 374. Scheer, "Topographies," 49, 56; Bonds, Mark Evan. *Absolute Music: The History of an Idea*. New York: Oxford UP, 2014, 150, 151.

23. Frevert, Ute. "Defining Emotions: Concepts and Debates over Three Centuries." In *Emotional Lexicons*, 1–31; 26–28; Rudert, "Gemüt," 55.

24. Diriwachter, Rainer, and Jaan Valsiner, eds. *Striving for the Whole: Creating Theoretical Syntheses*. New Brunswick: Transaction, 2011, 26–27.

25. Ash, Mitchell G. *Gestalt Psychology in German Culture, 1890–1967: Holism and the Quest for Objectivity*. Cambridge: Cambridge UP, 1998, 342.

26. Goebbels, Joseph. *Die Tagebücher von Joseph Goebbels*, Part 1, vol. 1, Munich: K. G. Saur, 2004, 110.

27. Asperger, "Problems of Infantile Autism," 45–52, 46, and *Probleme des kindlichen Autismus*, 3. Asperger's citations of Klages in his 1944 thesis: Klages, Ludwig. *Die Grundlagen der Charakterkunde.* Leipzig: Barth, 1936, and Klages, Ludwig. *Grundlegung der Wissenschaft vom Ausdruck.* Leipzig: Barth, 1936; Lebovic, Nitzan. *The Philosophy of Life and Death: Ludwig Klages and the Rise of a Nazi Biopolitics.* New York: Palgrave Macmillan, 2013; Ash, *Gestalt,* 345.

28. Geuter, Ulfried. *The Professionalization of Psychology in Nazi Germany.* Cambridge; New York: Cambridge UP, 1992, 169. Asperger's citations: Jaensch, Erich. *Der Gegentypus: Psychologisch-anthropologische Grundlagen deutscher Kulturphilosophie.* Leipzig: Barth, 1938, and Jaensch, Erich. *Grundformen menschlichen Seins.* Berlin: Elsner, 1929.

29. Wetzell, Richard F. *Inventing the Criminal: A History of German Criminology, 1880–1945.* Chapel Hill: UNC Press, 2000, 181, 297; Schneider, Kurt. *Die psychopathischen Persönlichkeiten.* Leipzig: Deuticke, 1923.

30. Stumpfl, Friedrich. "Kriminalität und Vererbung." In *Handbuch der Erbbiologie des Menschen,* vol. 2, edited by Günther Just, 1223–72. Berlin: J. Springer, 1939–

1940; 1257; Wetzell, *Inventing*, 151,152; 191–208.

31. Frevert, "Defining," 26; Bailey, Christian. "Social Emotions," In *Emotional Lexicons,* 201–29; 207. Another translation: Scheer, "Topographies," 50.

32. Speech to SS Group Leaders' Meeting at Posen (4 October 1943), in Röttger, Rüdiger. *Davon haben wir nichts gewusst: jüdische Schicksale aus Hochneukirch/Rheinland 1933–1945.* Düsseldorf: DTP, 1998, 181.

33. Bailey, "Social," 201–29, 216, 225–26 (1933); Scheer, "Topographies," 55.

34. Schröder, Paul, and Hans Heinze. *Kindliche Charaktere und ihre Abartigkeiten, mit erläuternden Beispielen von Hans Heinze.* Breslau: Hirt, 1931, 30, 33.

35. Schröder, Paul. "Kinderpsychiatrie." *MfPN* 99 (1938): 269–93; 287, 291. Schröder's terminology: Nissen, Gerhardt. *Kulturgeschichte seelischer Störungen bei Kindern und Jugendlichen.* Stuttgart: Klett-Cotta, 2005, 455–56; Thüsing, "Leben," 32–37, characterology: 80–84; Rudert, "Gemüt," 57.

36. Quoted: Felder, " 'Sehen,' " (2008), 102.

37. Felder, " 'Sehen,' " (2015), 39, and (2008), 102–3.

38. Schröder and Heinze, *Kindliche Charaktere*, 33.

39. Schröder and Heinze, *Kindliche Charaktere*; Asperger, "Erwin Lazar," 37.

40. Heinze, Hans. "Zur Phänomenologie des Gemüts." *ZfK* 40 (1932): 371–456; Asperger, "'Psychopathen,'" 78.

41. Heinze, "Phänomenologie," 395, 384–85, and "Psychopathische Persönlichkeiten. Allgemeiner und klinischer Teil." *Handbuch der Erbkrankheiten* 4 (1942): 154–310; 179–84.

42. Schultz, Heinz. "Die hypomanischen Kinder: Charakter, Temperament und soziale Auswirkungen." *ZfK* 45 (1936): 204–33. Leiter, "Zur Vererbung," and "Über Erbanlage und Umwelt bei gemütsarmen, antisozialen Kindern und Jugendlichen." *ZfK* 49 (1943): 87–93.

43. Kramer, Franz, and Ruth von der Leyen. "Entwicklungsverläufe 'anethischer, gemütloser' psychopathischer Kinder." *ZfK* 43 (1934): 305–422. Exchange with Schröder: *ZfK* 44 (1935): 224–28.

44. Lange, Klaus, Susanne Reichl, Katharina Lange, Lara Tucha, and Oliver Tucha. "The History of Attention Deficit Hyperactivity Disorder." *Attention Deficit and Hyperactivity Disorders* 2 no. 4 (2010): 241–55; 247–48; Müller-Küppers, "Geschichte," 23; Neumärker, Klaus-Jürgen. "The Kramer-Pollnow Syndrome: A Contribution on

the Life and Work of Franz Kramer and Hans Pollnow." *History of Psychiatry* 16 no. 4 (2005): 435–51; Fuchs, Petra, and Wolfgang Rose. "Kollektives Vergessen: die Diagnose Psychopathie und der Umgang mit dem schwierigen Kind im Verständnis von Franz Kramer und Ruth von der Leyen." *In Kinder- und Jugendpsychiatrie im Nationalsozialismus und in der Nachkriegszeit: zur Geschichte ihrer Konsolidierung*, edited by Heiner Fangerau, Sascha Topp, and Klaus Schepker, 187–208. Berlin: Springer, 2017.

45. German returns were 99.08 percent. Bukey, Evan Burr. *Hitler's Austria: Popular Sentiment in the Nazi Era, 1938–1945*. Chapel Hill: UNC Press, 2000, 38.
46. Bukey, *Hitler's Austria*, 74, 55; Tálos, Emmerich, Ernst Hanisch, Wolfgang Neugebauer, and Reinhard Sieder, eds. *NS-Herrschaft in Österreich*. Vienna: öbv & htp, 2000.
47. Bukey, *Hitler's Austria*, 131. Pauley, Bruce F. *From Prejudice to Persecution: A History of Austrian Anti-Semitism*. Chapel Hill: UNC Press, 1992; Vyleta, Dan. *Crime, Jews and News: Vienna, 1895–1914*. New York: Berghahn Books, 2012.
48. ORF Radio, Asperger, 1974.
49. Pernkopf, "Nationalsozialismus und

Wissenschaft," *WkW* 51 No. 20 (1938): 547–48. Quoted: Medizinische Universität Wien. http://www.meduniwien.ac.at/geschichte/anschluss/an_pernkopf.html. Neugebauer, "Racial Hygiene."

50. Malina, Peter, and Wolfgang Neugebauer. "NS-Gesundheitswesen und-Medizin." In *NS-Herrschaft in Österreich. Ein Handbuch*, edited by Emmerich Tálos, Ernst Hanisch, and Wolfgang Neugebauer, 696–720. Vienna: öbv & htp, 2000. Of the 173 faculty dismissals, 26 were for political reasons.

51. Two-thirds of the dismissed physicians emigrated to the United States and 15 percent to the United Kingdom; others committed suicide or were deported and killed in concentration camps. Ernst, "Medical School," 790; Merinsky, Judith. "Die Auswirkungen der Annexion Österreichs durch das Deutsche Reich auf die Medizinische Fakultät der Universität Wien im Jahre 1938." University of Vienna, 1980; Lehner, Martina. "Die Medizinische Fakultät der Universität Wien 1938–1945." University of Vienna, 1990.

52. Hubenstorf, "Emigration," 71–72, 132. Seidler, Eduard. "Das Schicksal der Wiener jüdischen Kinderärzte zwischen 1938 und 1945." *WkW* 111 no. 18 (1999): 754–63, and *Jüdische Kinderärzte,*

1933–1945: Entrechtet/geflohen/ermordet. Basel: Karger, 2007; Feikes, Renate. "Veränderungen in der Wiener jüdischen Ärzteschaft 1938." University of Vienna, 1993. Specifics: Gröger, Helmut. "Zur Vertreibung der Kinderheilkunde: zwischen 1918 und 1938 lehrende Privatdozenten für Kinderheilkunde der Universität Wien." In *100 Jahre Universitätsklinik für Kinder- und Jugendheilkunde*, edited by Arnold Pollak, 55–66. Vienna, 2011.

53. Kater, *Doctors*, 58. Viennese science: Ash, Mitchell G., and Alfons Söllner, eds. *Forced Migration and Scientific Change: Emigré German-Speaking Scientists and Scholars after 1933*. New York: Cambridge UP, 1995; Heiss, Gernot, Siegfried Mattl, Sebastian Meissl, Edith Saurer, and Karl Stuhlpfarrer, eds. *Willfährige Wissenschaft: die Universität Wien 1938–1945*. Vienna: Gesellschaftskritik, 1989; Ash, Mitchell G., Wolfram Niess, and Ramon Pils, eds. *Geisteswissenschaften im Nationalsozialismus: das Beispiel der Universität Wien*. Göttingen: V & R Unipress; Vienna UP, 2010; Stadler, Friedrich, ed. *Kontinuität und Bruch 1938–1945–1955: Beiträge zur österreichischen Kultur- und Wissenschaftsgeschichte*. Vienna: Jugend und Volk, 1988.

54. Hubenstorf, "Tote," 258.

55. Mühlleitner, Elke, and Johannes Reichmayr. "The Exodus of Psychoanalysts from Vienna." In *Vertreibung der Vernunft: The Cultural Exodus from Austria*, edited by Peter Weibel and Friedrich Stradler. Vienna: Löcker, 1993, 111; Peters, Uwe Henrik. *Psychiatrie im Exil: die Emigration der Dynamischen Psychiatrie aus Deutschland 1933–1939*. Düsseldorf: Kupka, 1992, 65–103; Ash, Mitchell G. "Diziplinentwicklung und Wissenschaftstransfer—deutschsprachige Psychologen in der Emigration." *Berichte zur Wissenschaftsgeschichte* 7 (1984): 207–26.

56. Mühlleitner, Elke, and Johannes Reichmayr. "Following Freud in Vienna: The Psychological Wednesday Society and the Viennese Psychoanalytical Society 1902–1938." *International Forum of Psychoanalysis* 6 no. 2 (1997): 73–102; 79, 80; Reichmayr, Johannes, and Elke Mühlleitner. "Psychoanalysis in Austria after 1933–34: History and Historiography." *International Forum of Psychoanalysis* 12 (2003): 118–29.

57. Geuter, *Professionalization*; Ash, Mitchell G., and Ulfried Geuter. *Geschichte der deutschen Psychologie im 20. Jahrhundert: ein Überblick*. Opladen: Westdeutscher Verlag, 1985; Cocks, Geoffrey. *Psycho-*

therapy in the Third Reich: The Göring Institute. New Brunswick: Transaction, 1997; Ash, Mitchell G., and Thomas Aichhorn, *Psychoanalyse in totalitären und autoritären Regimen.* Frankfurt: Brandes & Apsel, 2010; Goggin, James, and Eileen Brockman Goggin. *Death of a "Jewish Science": Psychoanalysis in the Third Reich.* West Lafayette: Purdue UP, 2001; Fallend, Karl, B. Handlbauer, and W. Kienreich, eds. *Der Einmarsch in die Psyche: Psychoanalyse, Psychologie und Psychiatrie im Nationalsozialismus und die Folgen.* Vienna: Junius, 1989.

58. König, Karl. *The Child with Special Needs: Letters and Essays on Curative Education.* Edinburgh: Floris, 2009, 41; Brennan-Krohn, Zoe. "In the Nearness of Our Striving: Camphill Communities Re-Imagining Disability and Society." Brown University, 2009; Mühlberger, "Heilpädagogisches Denken," 44.

59. Asperger, Hans, 7 October 1940. WStLA 1.3.2.202.A5. P: A.

60. Asperger's activities: ÖStA (AdR) K 10/02 BfU: A. Czech, "Hans Asperger"; Hager, "Hans Asperger;" Feinstein, *History*, 15; Hubenstorf, "Emigration." 76, 120.

61. Hamburger, "Festvortrag," 134; Hubenstorf, "Emigration," 111.

62. Asperger, Hans. "Das psychisch abnorme Kind." *WkW* 50 (1937): 1460–61; 1461.

63. Asperger, Hans. "Das psychisch abnorme Kind." *WkW* 49/51 (1938): 1314–17; 1316.

64. Mejstrik, Alexander. "Die Erfindung der deutschen Jugend. Erziehung in Wien, 1938–1945." In *NS-Herrschaft in Österreich*, edited by Tálos, Hanisch, Neugebauer, and Sieder, 494–522; Gehmacher, Johanna. *Jugend ohne Zukunft: Hitler-Jugend und Bund Deutscher Mädel in Österreich vor 1938*. Vienna: Picus, 1994.

65. "News and Comment." *Archives of Neurology & Psychiatry* 37, no. 5 (1937): 1171; "News and Notes." *American Journal of Psychiatry* 94, no. 3 (1937): 720–36, 727, 729; Castell and Gerhard, *Geschichte*, 48–49, 45–46; Schröder, "Kinderpsychiatrie," 9; Dahl, "Aussonderung," 186; Schepker and Fangerau, "Gründung," 183. Moritz Tramer of Switzerland was selected General Secretary.

66. Asperger, "Das psychisch abnorme Kind" (1938), 1314.

67. Asperger, "Das psychisch abnorme Kind" (1938), 1314.

68. Asperger, "Das psychisch abnorme Kind" (1938), 1314, 1317. Asperger also raved in a book review about Franz Günther von Stockert's 1939 *Introduction to the*

Psychopathology of Childhood, which staunchly advocated sterilization and outlined conditions for it. Asperger, "Bücherbesprechungen: F. G. v. Stockert, *Einführung in die Psychopathologie des Kindesalters*." *AfK* 120 (1940): 48; Castell and Gerhard, *Geschichte*, 48.

69. Asperger, "Das psychisch abnorme Kind" (1938), 1314.
70. Asperger, "Das psychisch abnorme Kind" (1938), 1317, 1314.
71. Asperger, "Das psychisch abnorme Kind" (1938), 1316.
72. Asperger, "Das psychisch abnorme Kind" (1938), 1316.
73. Asperger, "Das psychisch abnorme Kind" (1938), 1316.
74. Asperger, "Das psychisch abnorme Kind" (1938), 1316.
75. Eghigian, Greg. "A Drifting Concept for an Unruly Menace: A History of Psychopathy in Germany." *Isis* 106 no. 2 (2015): 283–309; Schmiedebach, Heinz-Peter. *Entgrenzungen des Wahnsinns: Psychopathie und Psychopathologisierungen um 1900*. Berlin: Walter de Gruyter, 2016.
76. Schneider, *Persönlichkeiten*, 16.
77. Wetzell, *Inventing*, 149–52; 203–5. Steinberg, Holger, Dirk Carius and Hubertus Himmerich. "Richard Arwed Pfeifer—

A Pioneer of 'Medical Pedagogy' and an Opponent of Paul Schröder." *History of Psychiatry* 24 no. 4 (2013): 459–76; 471.

78. Asperger, "Das psychisch abnorme Kind" (1938), 1314.

79. Asperger, "Das psychisch abnorme Kind" (1938), 1315.

80. Asperger, "Das psychisch abnorme Kind" (1938), 1315.

81. Asperger, "Das psychisch abnorme Kind" (1938), 1316.

82. Asperger, "Das psychisch abnorme Kind" (1938), 1315.

83. Schröder, "Kinderpsychiatrie," 9. Proceedings: Hanselmann, Heinrich, and Therese Simon, eds. *Bericht über den I. Internationalen Kongress für Heilpädagogik.* Zürich: Leemann, 1940, 11, 201; Asperger, Hans. "Kurze Geschichte der Internationalen Gesellschaft für Heilpädagogik." *HP* 14 (1971): 50–52; 50. Summaries: Hanselmann, Heinrich. "Erster Internationaler Kongreß für Heilpädagogik." *ZfK* 48 (1940): 142–48; Castell and Gerhard, *Geschichte*, 367–77; 375.

CHAPTER 4—INDEXING LIVES

1. Bornefeld, Adele. "Entstehung und Einsatz des Gesundheitswagens." *WkW* 53 (1940):

704–5; Czech, Herwig. "Zuträger der Vernichtung? Die Wiener Universitäts-Kinderklinik und die NS-Kindereuthanasieanstalt 'Am Spiegelgrund.'" In *100 Jahre Universitätsklinik*, 23–54; 40; Hubenstorf, "Emigration," 152–61. Mother Advice Centers in Vienna: Czech, Herwig. "Geburtenkrieg und Rassenkampf: Medizin, 'Rassenhygiene' und selektive Bevölkerungspolitik in Wien 1938 bis 1945." *Jahrbuch des Dokumentationsarchivs des österreichischen Widerstandes* (2005): 52–95; 59–61.

2. Hans Asperger to H. Hoberstorfer, Verwaltung des Reichsgaues Wien. Gesundheitsamt, 14 September 1940, 3a. WStLA 1.3.2.202.A5. P: A.

3. Hamburger, Franz. "Der Gesundheitswagen (Motorisierte Mütterberatung)." *WkW* 53 (1940): 703–4; 704; Goll, Heribert. "Erfahrungen mit dem ersten Gesundheitswagen im Kreise Zwettl, Niederdonau." *WkW* 53 (1940): 705–9; 705; Asperger to Hoberstorfer, 14 September 1940, 3a. WStLA 1.3.2.202.A5. P: A.

4. Goll, "Erfahrungen." In 1940, there were twenty-five similar advising initiatives in the Lower Danube District, fifteen in the Upper Danube District, and thirty-seven elsewhere in Austria. Wolf, *Vernunft*, 351–53.

5. Hubenstorf, "Emigration." 156–58; Koszler, Viktor. "Franz Hamburger 70 Jahre." *WkW* 57 no. 31/32 (1944): 391–92; 391; Hamburger, "Gesundheitswagen," 704.

6. Bornefeld, "Entstehung," 704.

7. Goll, "Erfahrungen," 705.

8. Asperger to Hoberstorfer, 14 September 1940; Hubenstorf, "Emigration," 158.

9. Häupl, *Kinder*, 118.

10. Asperger, Hans. "Zur Erziehungstherapie in der Jugendfürsorge." *MfK* 87 (1941): 238–47; 240.

11. Asperger, "Zur Erziehungstherapie," 240.

12. Asperger, "Das psychisch abnorme Kind." (1938), 1315.

13. Asperger, "Zur Erziehungstherapie," 240, 245, and "Tagungsbericht: Erziehungsfragen im Rahmen der Kinderkundlichen Woche." *DE* 14 no. 2 (1941): 28–31; 28–29.

14. Hamburger, "Festvortrag," 134.

15. SS-Sturmbahnführer (Jahrmann) to Gemeindeverwaltung des Reichsgaues Wien, Personalamt, 14 November 1940, 11. WStLA 1.3.2.202.A5. P: A.

16. Ertl, "NS-Euthanasie," 12.

17. Felder, " 'Sehen,' " (2008), 104.

18. e.g., Asperger to Hauptgesundheitsamt der Stadt Wien, WStLA 1.3.2.202.A5. P: A. Donvan and Zucker, *Different*, 341: citing Herwig Czech.

19. SS-Sturmbahnführer to Gemeindeverwaltung des Reichsgaues Wien, 14 November 1940.

20. Parkinson, Fred. *Conquering the Past: Austrian Nazism Yesterday & Today*. Detroit: Wayne State UP, 1989, 139; Spicer, Kevin. "Catholic Life under Hitler." In *Life and Times in Nazi Germany*, edited by Lisa Pine, 239–62. London: Bloomsbury, 2016, 241.

21. Gauamt für Volksgesundheit, "Politische Beurteilung," 2 May 1939. ÖStA (AdR 02) Zl36.055. G: A.

22. Kamba (Gauhauptstellenleiter, Gauleitung Wien) to Scharizer (Stellvertretenden Gauleiter), 11 July 1940, 36. Similar: Marchet. 1938. Both: ÖStA (AdR 02) Zl36.055. G: A.

23. ÖStA (AdR 02) Zl36.055. G: A; WStLA 1.3.2.202.A5, 7.

24. SS-Sturmbahnführer to Gemeindeverwaltung des Reichsgaues Wien, 14 November 1940, 11.

25. "Schwer erziehbare Jugend findet zur Gemeinschaft." *Neues Wiener Tagblatt*, 7 August 1940.

26. Asperger to Hauptgesundheitsamt der Stadt Wien, 1 October 1940, 4a; Gemeindeverwaltung des Reichsgaues Wien, Personalamt, 9 November 1940, 6a. WStLA 1.3.2.202.A5. P: A. Asperger's activities: ÖStA (AdR) K 10/02 BfU: A. Hüntelmann,

Axel, Johannes Vossen, and Herwig Czech. *Gesundheit und Staat: Studien zur Geschichte der Gesundheitsämter in Deutschland, 1870–1950.* Husum: Matthiesen, 2006.

27. Gemeindeverwaltung des Reichsgaues Wien, Personalamt, 9 November 1940, 6a; Vellguth, Stadtmedizinaldirektor, Hauptgesundheits- und Sozialamt to Personalamt, Abteilung 2, 10 October 1940, 4c; Erneuerung des Dienstvertrages, 25 October 1954. WStLA 1.3.2.202.A5. P: A. Evans, Richard. *The Third Reich at War.* New York: Penguin, 2008, 429.

28. Czarnowski, Gabriele. "The Value of Marriage for the '*Volksgemeinschaft*': Politics towards Women and Marriage under National Socialism. In *Fascist Italy and Nazi Germany*, edited by Richard Bessel, 94–112. Cambridge: Cambridge UP, 1996, 98.

29. Malina and Neugebauer, "NS-Gesundheitswesen." Häupl, *Massenmord*, 23.

30. Czech, Herwig. "Venereal Disease, Prostitution, and the Control of Sexuality in World War II Vienna." *East Central Europe* 38 (2011): 64–78; 71.

31. Burleigh, *Death*, 56.

32. With five thousand and ten thousand as the lower and upper estimates. Malina and Neugebauer, "NS-Gesundheitswesen"; Neugebauer, Wolfgang. "Zwangssteri-

lisierung und 'Euthanasie' in Österreich 1940–1945." *Zeitgeschichte* 19 no. 1/2 (1992): 17–28. Vienna: Spring, Claudia. *Zwischen Krieg und Euthanasie: Zwangssterilisationen in Wien 1940–1945.* Vienna: Böhlau, 2009. Reich: Bock, Gisela. *Zwangssterilisation im Nationalsozialismus: Studien zur Rassenpolitik und Frauenpolitik.* Opladen: Westdeutscher Verlag, 1986.

33. Aly, Götz, and Karl Heinz Roth. *The Nazi Census: Identification and Control in the Third Reich.* Translated by Edwin Black and Assenka Oksiloff. Philadelphia: Temple UP, 2004, 104.

34. Fritzsche, *Life*, 117. Proctor, *Racial Hygiene*, 106 [*Hitlerschnitt*].

35. Gellately, Robert, and Nathan Stoltzfus, eds. *Social Outsiders in Nazi Germany.* Princeton, NJ: Princeton UP, 2001, 149. In Austria, 43.2 percent were sterilized for "feeble-mindedness" (two-thirds of them women), 28 percent for schizophrenia, 17.8 percent with epilepsy, and 37 percent with manic depression, as well as small percentages labeled with physical malformations, deafness, blindness, and alcoholism. Spring, Claudia. " 'Patient tobte und drohte mit Selbstmord': NS-Zwangssterilisationen in der Heil- und Pflegeanstalt Am Steinhof und deren Rechtfertigung der Zweiten Republik."

In *Zwangssterilisierung zur Ermordung,* vol. 2, 41–76; 56.

36. Torrey, E. Fuller, and Robert Yolken. "Psychiatric Genocide: Nazi Attempts to Eradicate Schizophrenia." *Schizophrenia Bulletin* 36 no. 1 (2010): 26–32. Around 132,000 people diagnosed with schizophrenia were sterilized.

37. Dr. A. Marchet, 1938; Hauptstellenleiter Stowasser to Gemeindeverwaltung des Reichsgaues Wien, 1 November 1940, 7. WStLA 1.3.2.202.A5. P: A.

38. Asperger, Hans. "Über einen Fall von Hemichorea bei einem eineiigen Zwillingspaar." *DE* 6 (1939): 24–28; Asperger, Hans, and Heribert Goll. "Über einen Fall von Hemichorea bei einem eineiigen Zwillingspaar; Gleichzeitung ein Beitrag zum Problem der Individualität bei erbleichen Zwillingen." *AfK* 116–18 (1939): 92–115; Löscher, *Eugenik,* 217–19; Proctor, *Racial Hygiene,* 104–6.

39. Asperger, "Das psychisch abnorme Kind" (1938), 1315.

40. "Nimm ein haarsieb und spare—auch mit Menschenseelen!" *Das Kleine Volksblatt,* 11 September 1940, 8.

41. Asperger, "Zur Erziehungstherapie," 239, 245–46; Asperger, " 'Jugendpsychiatrie,' " 353.

42. Full list: Aly and Roth, *Nazi Census*, 2–3.
43. Czarnowski, "Value," 99.
44. Spring, " 'Patient,' " 51. Overview of Reich efforts: Roth, Karl Heinz. " 'Erbbiologische Bestandsaufnahme': ein Aspekt 'ausmerzender' Erfassung vor der Entfesselung des Zweiten Weltkrieges." In *Erfassung zur Vernichtung: von der Sozialhygiene zum "Gesetz über Sterbehilfe,"* edited by Karl Heinz Roth, 57–100. Berlin: Verlagsgesellschaft Gesundheit, 1984; Nitschke, Asmus. *Die "Erbpolizei" im Nationalsozialismus: zur Alltagsgeschichte der Gesundheitsämter im Dritten Reich.* Berlin: Springer, 2013.
45. "Erbbestandsaufnahme: Meldungen der Universitätskliniken an die Gesundheitsämter." *Deutsche Wissenschaft, Erziehung und Volksbildung: Amtsblatt des Reichsministeriums für Wissenschaft, Erziehung und Volksbildung und der Unterrichtsverwaltungen der Länder* (5, 1939): 289–90; 289.
46. "Erbbestandsaufname," *Deutsche Wissenschaft, Erziehung und Volksbildung,* 290.
47. *WAfIM* 34–35 (1940): 327, 328.
48. Kresiment, Max. "Massnahmen durch Staat und Gemeinden: Erbbestandsaufnahme," 76–79 (1940). In *Carl Flügge's Grundriss der Hygiene: für Studierende und Praktische*

Ärzte, Medizinal- und Verwaltungsbeamte, edited by Carl Flügge, Hans Reiter, and Bernhard Möllers. Berlin, Heidelberg: Springer, 2013, 79.

49. Wolf, *Vernunft,* 359. Malina and Neugebauer, "NS-Gesundheitswesen."

50. Czech, Herwig. "Die Inventur des Volkskörpers: die 'erbbiologische Bestandsaufnahme' im Dispositiv der NS-Rassenhygiene in Wien." In *Eugenik in Österreich,* edited by Baader, Hofer, and Mayer, 284–311; 291–98; Czech, Herwig. "From Welfare to Selection: Vienna's Public Health Office and the Implementation of Racial Hygiene Policies under the Nazi Regime." In *"Blood and Homeland,"* 317–33; 324–25.

51. Czech, "Inventur," 304–5; Czech, *Selektion und Auslese,* 55–59; Aly and Roth, *Nazi Census,* 106–7.

52. Czech, "Welfare," 325.

53. *WAfIM* 34–35 (1940): 326.

CHAPTER 5—FATAL THEORIES

1. Burleigh, Michael. *Death and Deliverance: "Euthanasia" in Germany c. 1900–1945.* Cambridge: Cambridge UP, 1994, 105.

2. Overviews: Beddies and Hübener, eds., *Kinder*; Benzenhöfer, Udo. *Der gute Tod? Geschichte der Euthanasie und Sterbehilfe.*

Göttingen: Vandenhoeck & Ruprecht, 2009; Benzenhöfer, *Der Fall Leipzig (alias Fall Kind Knauer) und die Planung der NS-Kindereuthanasie.* Münster: Klemm & Oelschläger, 2008; Benzenhöfer, *Kinderfachabteilungen und NS-Kindereuthanasie.* Wetzlar: GWAB, 2000; Burleigh, *Death*, 101–3; Friedlander, Henry. *The Origins of Nazi Genocide: from Euthanasia to the Final Solution.* Chapel Hill: UNC Press, 1995; Aly, Götz. *Aktion T4, 1939–1945: die "Euthanasie"-Zentrale in der Tiergartenstrasse 4.* Berlin: Hentrich, 1987; Lifton, Robert Jay. *The Nazi Doctors: Medical Killing and the Psychology of Genocide.* New York: Basic, 1988; 2000; Mostert, Mark. "Useless Eaters: Disability as Genocidal Marker in Nazi Germany." *Journal of Special Education* 36 no. 3 (2002): 157–70; Schmidt, Gerhard, and Frank Schneider. *Selektion in der Heilanstalt 1939–1945.* Berlin: Springer, 2012.

3. Mende, Susanne. "Die Wiener Heil- und Pflegeanstalt am Steinhof in der Zeit des NS-Regimes in Österreich." In *NS-Euthanasie in Wien,* vol. 1, edited by Eberhard Gabriel and Wolfgang Neugebauer, 61–73. Vienna: Böhlau, 2000; Schwartz, Peter. "Mord durch Hunger: 'Wilde Euthanasie' und 'Aktion Brandt' am Steinhof

in der NS-Zeit." In *Zwangssterilisierung zur Ermordung*, vol. 2, 113-141; Kepplinger, Brigitte, Gerhart Marckhgott, and Hartmut Reese. *Tötungsanstalt Hartheim*. Vienna: OÖLA, 2008. The death toll at Hartheim Castle was reportedly 18,269 people. The total number of deaths from euthanasia in Austria, including children, was around 25,000. About 62 percent of patients in Austria's state psychiatric institutions died in the T4 program. Kepplinger, Brigitte. "The National Socialist Euthanasia Program in Austria: Aktion T4." In *New Perspectives on Austrians and World War II*, edited by Günther Bischof, Fritz Plasser, and Barbara Stelzl-Marx, 224–49. New Brunswick: Transaction, 2009, 238; Hartheim: Kepplinger, Brigitte, Irene Leitner, and Andrea Kammerhofer, eds. *Dameron Report: Bericht des War Crimes Investigating Teams No. 6824 der U.S. Army vom 17.7.1945 über die Tötungsanstalt Hartheim*. Innsbruck: Studien, 2012. "Wild euthanasia" in Austria: Czech, Herwig. "Vergessene Opfer der NS-Zeit: 'wilde Euthanasie' in psychiatrischen Anstalten in den 'Donau- und Alpenreichsgauen.' " *Pflegen: Psychosozial* 1 (2010): 42–47. Elderly in Austria: Arias, Ingrid, Sonia Horn, and Michael Hubenstorf, eds. *"In der Versorgung"*:

vom Versorgungshaus Lainz zum Geriatriezentrum "Am Wienerwald." Vienna: Verlagshaus der Ärzte, 2005. Maps: Häupl, Waltraud. *Der organisierte Massenmord an Kindern und Jugendlichen in der Ostmark 1940–1945: Gedenkdokumentation für die Opfer der NS-Euthanasie.* Vienna: Böhlau, 2008, 11–14.

4. Pavilion 17: Czech, Herwig. "Selektion und Auslese," In *Von der Zwangssterilisierung zur Ermordung*, vol. 2, 165–187. Vienna: Böhlau, 2002, 186. Over the next five years, Spiegelgrund would undergo a series of name changes, leadership changes, and structural changes. The institution began as the Vienna Municipal Youth Welfare Institution at Spiegelgrund [*Wiener Städtische Jugendfürsorgeanstalt "Am Spiegelgrund"*], and was run by Erwin Jekelius from 1940–1941. In the first half of 1942, Hans Bertha and Margarethe Hübsch became provisional directors of what was then renamed the Vienna Municipal Curative Education Clinic at Spiegelgrund [*Heilpädagogische Klinik der Stadt Wien "Am Spiegelgrund"*]. Ernst Illing ran Spiegelgrund from July 1, 1942, until 1945. In November 1942, Spiegelgrund was split into separate institutions. Pavilions 15 and 17, with 220 beds, became the Vienna Municipal Mental Clinic for

Children [*Wiener städtische Nervenklinik für Kinder "Am Spiegelgrund"*], which was overseen by city councilor Max Gundel. The other pavilions, with 680 beds, became the Vienna Municipal Reformatory at Spiegelgrund [*Wiener Städtische Erziehungsanstalt "Am Spiegelgrund"*]. Additional details: Neugebauer, Wolfgang. "Die Klinik 'am Spiegelgrund' 1940–1945— eine 'Kinderfachabteilung' im Rahmen der NS-'Euthanasie.' " *Jahrbuch des Vereins für Geschichte der Stadt Wien* 52/53 (1996/1997): 289–305; 294–97.

5. Dahl, Matthias. *Endstation Spiegelgrund: die Tötung behinderter Kinder während des Nationalsozialismus am Beispiel einer Kinderfachabteilung in Wien 1940 bis 1945.* Vienna: Erasmus, 1998, 97; Cervik, Karl. *Kindermord in der Ostmark: Kindereuthanasie im Nationalsozialismus 1938–1945.* Münster: Lit, 2001.

6. Interrogation of Ernst Illing, 22 October 1945. Quoted: Dahl, *Endstation*, 41.

7. Interrogation of Erwin Jekelius, 7 July 1948. Quoted: Ertl, "NS-Euthanasie," 151.

8. Häupl, *Kinder*, 14.

9. Häupl, Waltraud. *Die ermordeten Kinder vom Spiegelgrund: Gedenkdokumentation für die Opfer der NS-Kindereuthanasie in Wien.* Vienna: Böhlau, 2006, 537.

10. Häupl, *Kinder*, 154–55.
11. Häupl, *Kinder*, 476.
12. Stutte, Hermann. "30 Jahre Deutsche Vereinigung für Jugendpsychiatrie." *DN* 41 (1970): 313–17; 313.
13. Müller-Küppers, "Geschichte." Schröder, "Kinderpsychiatrie," 9; Castell and Gerhard, *Geschichte*, 46, 60–62; "Geschäftssitzung," *ZfK* 49 (1943): 118.
14. Schröder, "Kinderpsychiatrie," 11.
15. Schröder, "Kinderpsychiatrie," 12. Asperger, "Tagungsbericht," 29.
16. Schröder, "Kinderpsychiatrie," 14.
17. Asperger, "Tagungsbericht;" Steinert, T., and B. Plewe. "Psychiatrie in 'Der Nervenarzt' von 1928–2000." *DE* 76 no. 1 (2005): 93–102; 98; Pfeiffer, Martina. "Das Erbgesundheitsgesetz im Spiegel der Publikationen aus der Zeitschrift 'Der Nervenarzt' in den Jahren von 1928 bis 1945." Ludwig Maximilian University of Munich, 2008; Hübel, Stefan. "Vergleichende Darstellung der psychiatrischen und neurologischen Begutachtung in der Zeitschrift 'Der Nervenarzt' in den Jahren 1928 bis 1944." LMU Munich, 2006.
18. Asperger, "Tagungsbericht," 29.
19. Schröder, "Kinderpsychiatrie," 10; Asperger, "Tagungsbericht," 29.
20. "Bericht über die 1. Tagung der Deutschen

Gesellschaft für Kinderpsychiatrie und Heilpädagogik in Wien am 5. September 1940." *ZfK* 49 (1943): 1–118; 3.

21. V. B., "Ansprachen," *ZfK* 49 (1943): 4. Riedel, Heinz. "Kinderpsychiatrie und Psychotherapie in Wien." *MmW* 87 (1940): 1161–63. Reiter was later tried for war crimes at Nuremberg but was never convicted.

22. Asperger, "Tagungsbericht," 30.

23. The pediatrics meeting was September 1, 2, and 4, 1940, and the psychotherapy meeting was September 6, 1940. Proceedings: Goebel, F. "Verhandlungen der siebenundvierzigsten ordentlichen Versammlung der Deutschen Gesellschaft für Kinderheilkunde in Wien 1940." *MfK* 87 (1941): 1–307; Bilz, Rudolf. *Psyche und Leistung: Bericht über die 3.Tagung der Deutschen allgemeinen ärztlichen Gesellschaft für Psychotherapie in Wien, 6.–7. Sept. 1940.* Stuttgart: Hippokrates-Verlag Marquardt, 1941. Summaries: "Berichte Kinderärztlicher Gesellschaften—Kinderkundliche Woche in Wien vom 1.–7. September 1940." *KP* 12, no. 1 (1941): 25–29; no. 2 (1941): 57–60; no. 3 (1941): 89–93; no. 4 (1941): 121–24.

24. Schepker and Fangerau, "Gründung," 185; Hamburger, Franz. "Willkommen zur ersten Kinderkundlichen Woche in Wien!" *WkW* 53 no. 35 (1940).

25. "Tagesgeschichtliche Notizen." *MmW*, 87(30) 1940. Quoted: Schepker and Fangerau, "Gründung," 187.

26. "Glanzvoller Auftakt der Wiener Herbstmesse." *Wiener Illustrierte*, 11 September 1940, 4–5.

27. "Wiener Geschmack." *(Neuigkeits) Welt Blatt*, 5 September 1940, 4; Hofmann-Söllner, "Wiener Mode auf der Wiener Herbstmesse." *Wiener Illustrierte*, 11 September 1940, 23.

28. "Opfer der Jugend garantieren den Sieg." *Österreichische Volks-Zeitung*, 5 September 1940, 3.

29. "Mitteilung." *ZfK* 7 (1940): 63.

30. There is a vast literature on psychiatry and psychoanalysis in other authoritarian states. Overviews: Damousi, Joy, and Mariano Ben Plotkin, eds. *Psychoanalysis and Politics: Histories of Psychoanalysis under Conditions of Restricted Political Freedom*. New York: Oxford UP, 2012; Eghigian, Greg, Andreas Killen, and Christine Leuenberger, eds. *The Self as Project: Politics and the Human Sciences*. Chicago: University of Chicago Press, 2007; Ash and Aichhorn, *Psychoanalyse*.

31. Schröder, "Kinderpsychiatrie," 9; Schröder, Paul. "Gründung und Erste Tagung der Deutschen Gesellschaft für Kinder-

Psychiatrie und Heilpädagogik in Wien." *Zeitschrift für psychische Hygiene* 13 no. 5/6 (1940): 67–71; 68. Including the Vienna Board of Education, Vienna Public Health Office, the Office for the Health Guidance of the Reich Youth Leadership, the German Council of Municipalities, German Association of Juvenile Courts and Juvenile Court Services, the German Association for Public and Private Welfare, and the Central Committee of the Inner Mission.

32. Schröder, "Gründung," 68.
33. Huber, Wolfgang. *Psychoanalyse in Österreich seit 1933*. Vienna: Geyer-Ed., 1977, 60–3.
34. "Mitteilung," *ZfKp* 7 (1940): 63.
35. Summary: Riedel, "Kinderpsychiatrie." Scholarship: Castell and Gerhard, *Geschichte*, 63–76; Schmuhl, Hans-Walter. *Die Gesellschaft Deutscher Neurologen und Psychiater im Nationalsozialismus*. Berlin; Heidelberg: Springer, 2015, 344–47; Dahl, "Aussonderung," 185–87; Hänsel, Dagmar. *Karl Tornow als Wegbereiter der sonderpädagogischen Profession: die Grundlegung des Bestehenden in der NS-Zeit*. Bad Heilbrunn: Julius Klinkhardt, 2008, 273–82.
36. Liehr-Langenbeck, M., ed., *Kurt Isemann, Arzt und Heilpädagoge: ein Lebensbild;*

(*1886–1964*). Neuburgweier/Karlsruhe: Schindele, 1969, 121.

37. Schulte, Walter. [Kurt Isemann]. In *Kurt Isemann*, 21–32; 21.

38. Isemann, Kurt. "Aus der Praxis des Heilerziehungsheimes." In *Kind und Umwelt, Anlage und Erziehung*, edited by Arthur Keller, 230–38. Leipzig: Deuticke, 1930, 231.

39. Ritter von Stockert. "Kurt Isemanns ärztlich-pädagogische Aufgabe," 32–35; 33, and Spiekermann, F. Rosa Elisabeth, geb. Heckel, "Die Heckelgruppe," 61–65; 64, both in *Kurt Isemann*. Isemann, "Praxis," 233.

40. Isemann, Kurt, "Psychopathie und Verwahrlosung," *ZfK* 49 (1943): 43–53; 45, 51–52.

41. Isemann, Kurt. "Arzt und Erzieher," In *Bericht über den I. Internationalen Kongress für Heilpädagogik,* 258–67; 259, 260. Here Isemann refers to "autism" as a character trait, as the opposite of hysterical, and not as a standalone diagnosis.

42. Asperger, "Tagungsbericht," 29.

43. Leiter, "Erbanlage" and "Vererbung."

44. Ernst, Karl. "Psychiatrie des Kindes- und Jugendalters." In *Naturforschung und Medizin in Deutschland 1939–1946: Psychiatrie*, edited by Ernst Kretschmer, 215–240. Wiesbaden: Dietrich, 1948,

227, 229; Francke, Herbert. "Jugendkriminalität." *ZfK* 49 no. 3 (1943): 110–36; 111; Heinze, "Persönlichkeiten," 175, 236, 250; Dubitscher, Fred. "Leiter, Anna: zur Vererbung von asozialen Charaktereigenschaften." *Deutsche Zeitschrift für die gesamte gerichtliche Medizin* 33 no. 1 (1941): 80–81; Schorsch, Gerhard. "Psychopathische Persönlichkeiten und psychopathische Reaktionen." In *Fortschritte der Neurologie, Psychiatrie und ihrer Grenzgebiete*, edited by A. Bostoem and K. Beringer, 69–81. Leipzig: Thieme, 1942, 74; Schliebe, Georg, and Karl Seiler. "Internationaler Literaturbericht für Erziehungswissenschaft." *Internationale Zeitschrift für Erziehung* 13 no. 4/5 (1944): 211–270; 248; Lange-Cosack. "Zeitschriftenschau." *Monatsschrift für Kriminalbiologie und Strafrechtsreform* 32 no. 11/12 (1941): 336–42; 337–38; Hans Thomae, *Persönlichkeit: eine dynamische Interpretation*, Bonn: Bouvier, 1955, 77, 80.

45. Leiter, "Erbanlage," 91, 92; 88; 92, 91.
46. Leiter, Anna. "Über bisherige Tätigkeit und Erfolg des Jugendpsychiaters im BDM." *Die Ärztin* 17 (1941), 218–23; 220; 218, 219.
47. Leiter, "Erbanlage," 92.
48. Leiter, "Erbanlage," 88, 93.
49. Asperger, "Tagungsbericht," 30.

50. Steinberg, Carius, and Himmerich, "Pfeifer," 471; Busemann, Adolf, and Hermann Stutte. "Das Porträt: Werner Villinger, 65 Jahre alt." *Unsere Jugend* 4 (1952): 381–82; Holtkamp, Martin. *Werner Villinger (1887–1961): die Kontinuität des Minderwertigkeitsgedankens in der Jugend- und Sozialpsychiatrie.* Husum: Matthiesen, 2002.

51. Castell and Gerhard, *Geschichte*, 464, 468; Schmuhl, Hans-Walter. "Zwischen vorauseilendem Gehorsam und halbherziger Verweigerung: Werner Villinger und die nationalsozialistischen Medizinverbrechen." *DN* 73 no. 11 (2002): 1058–63; 1060.

52. Villinger, Werner. "Erfahrungen mit der Durchführung des Erbkrankenverhütungsgesetzes an männlichen Fürsorgezöglingen." *ZfK* 44 (1935): 233–48; 237, 245; Ellger-Rüttgardt, Sieglind. *Geschichte der Sonderpädagogik.* Munich: Reinhardt, 2008, 250; Klee, Ernst. *Die SA Jesu Christi: die Kirchen im Banne Hitlers.* Frankfurt: Fischer, 1989, 92; Schmuhl, "Gehorsam," 1060–61; Castell and Gerhard, *Geschichte,* 465–67.

53. Villinger, Werner. "Erziehung und Erziehbarkeit." *ZfK* 49 (1943): 17–27; 18, 21. e.g., Villinger, *Die biologischen Grundlagen des Jugendalters.* Eberswalde-Berlin: R. Müller, 1933, 32; Triebold, Karl, Karl Tornow,

and Werner Villinger. *Freilufterziehung in Fürsorge-Erziehungsheimen.* Leipzig: Armanen, 1938, 14.

54. Villinger, "Erziehung," 21–22, 22–23.
55. Villinger, "Erziehung," 22. Villinger, Werner. "Die Notwendigkeit eines Reichsbewahrungsgesetzes vom jugendpsychiatrischen Standpunkt aus." *ZfK* 47 (1939): 1–20, 17.
56. Villinger, "Erziehung," 26.
57. Asperger, "Tagungsbericht," 29.
58. Nedoschill, Jan. "Aufbruch im Zwielicht—die Entwicklung der Kinder- und Jugendpsychiatrie in der Zeit von Zwangssterilisation und Kindereuthanasie." *PdKK* 58 no. 7 (2009): 504–16; 509–10; Schmuhl, "Gehorsam," 1062; Castell and Gerhard, *Geschichte*, 469–80.
59. Villinger, "Notwendigkeit," 16.
60. Wolfisberg, Carlo. *Heilpädagogik und Eugenik: zur Geschichte der Heilpädagogik in der deutschsprachigen Schweiz (1800–1950).* Zurich: Chronos, 2002, 121–36; Gröschke, Dieter. *Heilpädagogisches Handeln: eine Pragmatik der Heilpädagogik.* Bad Heilbrunn: Klinkhardt, 2008, 148.
61. Moseley, Ray. *Mussolini's Shadow: The Double Life of Count Galeazzo Ciano.* New Haven, CT: Yale UP, 1999, ix–x; 254, 255.
62. Spieler, Josef, "Freiwillige Schweiger und

sprachscheue Kinder," *ZfK* 49 (1943): 39–43; 39–40, 43, 44.

63. Repond, André. "Der ärztliche heilpädagogische Dienst des Kantons Wallis." *ZfK* 49 (1943): 100–11; 105.

64. Asperger, " 'Jugendpsychiatrie,' " 352; Asperger, Hans, and Josef Feldner. "Bemerkungen zu dem Buche *Praktische Kinderpsychologie* von Prof. Charlotte Bühler." *ZfK* 47 (1939): 97–100. Asperger's postwar positions were little changed. Asperger, Hans. "Psychotherapie in der Pädiatrie." *OZfKK* 2 (1949): 17–25; 24.

65. Geuter, *Professionalization*; Ash and Geuter, *Geschichte*; Cocks, *Psychotherapy*; Göring , M. H. "Eröffnungsansprache." In *Psyche und Leistung,* edited by Bilz, 7–10.

66. Brill, Werner. *Pädagogik der Abgrenzung: die Implementierung der Rassenhygiene im Nationalsozialismus durch die Sonderpädagogik.* Bad Heilbrunn: Klinkhardt, 2011, 25–54, 120, 156; Ellger-Rüttgardt, *Geschichte*, 256–57; Poore, Carol. *Disability in Twentieth-Century German Culture.* Ann Arbor: University of Michigan Press, 2007, 84; Hänsel, Dagmar. *Die NS-Zeit als Gewinn für Hilfsschullehrer.* Bad Heilbrunn: Klinkhardt, 2006, 97–98.

67. Brill, *Pädagogik*, 55–86, 140–57; Hänsel, *NS-Zeit*; Hänsel, Dagmar. "Die Deutsche

Gesellschaft für Kinderpsychiatrie und Heilpädagogik im Nationalsozialismus als verkappte Fachgesellschaft für Sonderpädagogik." In *Kinder- und Jugendpsychiatrie*, 253–94.

68. Klee, Ernst. "Der blinde Fleck: wie Lehrer, Ärzte und Verbandsfunktionäre die 'Gebrechlichen' der Verstümmelung und der Vernichtung auslieferten." *Die Zeit*, 8 December 1995; Brill, *Pädagogik*, 169, 177.

69. Brill, *Pädagogik*; Poore, *Disability*, 84; Zwanziger, Fritz. "Betr. Brauchbarkeit ehemaliger Hilfsschüler im jetzigen Kriege," *dS* 7 (1940): 297.

70. Zwanziger, Fritz. "Die Beschulung des gehör- und sprachgebrechlichen Kindes im neuen Deutschland." *ZfK* 49 (1943): 14–17; 15, 16.

71. Lesch, Erwin. "Sichtung der Schulversager—eine heilpädagogische Aufgabe." *ZfK* 49 (1943): 111–15, 112, 114.

72. Bechthold, Eduard. "Die Lage auf dem Gebiete des Blindenwesens, *ZfK* 49 (1943): 71–76; 74, 73; Bechthold, Eduard. "Die Blindenanstalt im neuen Staat." *dS* 1, no. 1 (1934): 42–46, 43–44; Bechthold, Eduard. "Die Blindenfürsorge im neuen Staat," 496; Brill, *Pädagogik*, 169, 177.

73. Tornow, Karl. "Völkische Sonderpadagogik

und Kinderpsychiatrie." *ZfK* 49 (1943): 76–86; 81.

74. Ellger-Rüttgardt, *Geschichte*, 259–62; Hänsel, Dagmar. " 'Erbe und Schicksal': Rezeption eines Sonderschulbuchs." *ZfP* 55 no. 5 (2009): 781–95; Tornow and Weinert, *Erbe*, 208, 159.

75. Tornow, "Sonderpadagogik," 86.

76. Tornow, "Sonderpadagogik," 80–81, 77; Landerer, Constanze. "Das sprachheilpädagogische Arbeitsfeld im Wechsel der politischen Systeme 1929–1949." TU Dortmund, 2013, 25–28, 255; Eberle, Gerhard. "Anmerkungen zu einer These Hänsels über das Verhältnis Tornows und Lesemanns während und nach der NS-Zeit." *Empirische Sonderpädagogik* 1 (2010): 78–94.

77. Tornow, "Sonderpadagogik," 81.

78. Asperger, "Tagungsbericht," 30, 29.

79. Dickinson, *Politics*; Wetzell, *Inventing*.

80. Francke, Herbert. "Ansprachen und Begrüssungen," *ZfK* 49 (1943): 6–8; 6, 7.

81. Willing, Matthias. *Das Bewahrungsgesetz (1918–1967): eine rechtshistorische Studie zur Geschichte der deutschen Fürsorge.* Tübingen: Siebeck, 2003.

82. Peukert, Detlev. *Grenzen der Sozialdisziplinierung: Aufstieg und Krise der deutschen Jugendfürsorge von 1878 bis*

1932. Cologne: Bund, 1986, 251; Dickinson, *Politics*, 198–99.

83. A total of 137 children had passed through his facility between August 1934 and early 1936, of whom over 80 percent were girls.

84. Kuhlmann, Carola. *Erbkrank oder erziehbar?: Jugendhilfe als Vorsorge und Aussonderung in der Fürsorgeerziehung in Westfalen von 1933–1945.* Weinheim: Juventa, 1989, 44; Willing, *Bewahrungsgesetz,* 147, 117.

85. Fritz, " 'Jugendschutzlager,' " 314; Malina, "Kindheit," 102; Czech, "Selektion," 178. Schikorra, "Zusammenspiel," 93–95.

86. Dickinson, *Politics,* 221.

87. Hecker, Walther. "Neugliederung der öffentlichen Ersatzerziehung nach Erbanlage und Erziehungserfolg." *ZfK* 49 (1943): 28–39; 33–34.

88. Hecker, "Neugliederung," 33, 35; Köster, Markus. *Jugend, Wohlfahrtsstaat und Gesellschaft im Wandel: Westfalen zwischen Kaiserreich und Bundesrepublik.* Paderborn: F. Schöningh, 1999, 227, 227 fn 151.

89. Asperger, "Tagungsbericht," 29.

90. Hamburger, Franz. "Aussprache." *ZfK* 49 (1943): 116–17; 117.

91. Schröder, Paul. "Schluß," *ZfK* 49 (1943): 118.

92. Stutte, "30 Jahre," 314.

93. Stutte, "Anfänge," 190; Müller-Küppers, "Geschichte."

94. "Mitteilungen." *P-NW* 43 no. 21 (1941): 218; Rüden, Ernst, Pelte, and H. Creutz. "6. Jahresversammlung der Gesellschaft Deutscher Neurologen und Psychiater, Würzburg." *P-NW* 43 (1941): 359–60; 359; Schröder, Paul. "Zu diesjährigen Tagung der Deutschen Gesellschaft für Kinderpsychiatrie und Sonderpädagogik." *dS* 8 no. 4 (1941): 248. It was to be tacked on to the Sixth Annual Meeting of German Neurology and Psychiatry (October 5–7, 1941). Schröder, "Gründung."

95. Benzenhöfer, Udo. "Der Briefwechsel zwischen Hans Heinze (Görden) und Paul Nitsche (1943/44)." In *Dokumente zur Psychiatrie im Nationalsozialismus*, edited by Thomas Beddies and Kristina Hübener, 271–85. Berlin: Be.bra, 2003; Nedoschill, Jan, and Rolf Castell. "Der Vorsitzende der Deutschen Gesellschaft für Kinderpsychiatrie und Heilpädagogik im Zweiten Weltkrieg." *PdKK* 3 (2001): 228–37; Castell and Gerhard, *Geschichte*, 77–87; Schepker, Klaus, Sascha Topp, and Heiner Fangerau. "Wirren um Paul Schröder, Werner Villinger und Hans Heinze: die drei Vorsitzenden der Deutschen Gesellschaft für Kinderpsychiatrie und Heilpädagogik

zwischen 1940 und 1945," *DE* 88 no. 3 (2017): 282–90; Schmuhl, *Gesellschaft*, 347–54.

CHAPTER 6—ASPERGER AND THE KILLING SYSTEM

1. It bore little resemblance to the previous "Austrian Society for Curative Education" founded in 1935 by Theodor Heller, who had committed suicide with the Anschluss. Gröger, "Ideengeschichte," 34; Hubenstorf, "Emigration," 109; Ertl, "NS-Euthanasie," 127; Topp, Sascha. "Kinder- und Jugendpsychiatrie in der Nachkriegszeit." In *Kinder- und Jugendpsychiatrie*, 295–446; 309.
2. Ertl, "NS-Euthanasie," 132.
3. Czech, Herwig. *Erfassung, Selektion und "Ausmerze": das Wiener Gesundheitsamt und die Umsetzung der nationalsozialistischen "Erbgesundheitspolitik" 1938 bis 1945.* Vienna: Deuticke, 2003, 95.
4. Jekelius, Erwin. "Grenzen und Ziele der Heilpädagogik." *WkW* 55, no. 20 (1942): 385–86, 386.
5. Jekelius, "Grenzen," 385.
6. Ertl, "NS-Euthanasie," 6, 25. Hans Bertha was the other T4 "expert" in Vienna.
7. Ertl, "NS-Euthanasie," 72.

8. Dahl, *Endstation,* 35; Ertl, "NS-Euthanasie," 166; Frankl, Viktor E. *Man's Search for Meaning.* Boston: Beacon, 2006, 133.

9. "Schwer erziehbare Kinder sind noch lange nicht schlechte Kinder." *(Österreichische) Volks-Zeitung,* 20 October 1940, 4. Also: " 'Strawanzer' und 'Schulstürzer' sind noch keine Verbrecher." *Kleine Volks-Zeitung.* Sunday, 20 October 1940, no. 290, 9.

10. Schödl, Leo. "Borgia-Rummel in Lainz," *Völkischer Beobachter,* 2 November 1940, 7. Emphasis in original.

11. Dahl, *Endstation,* 33. *Luftpost* 19, 23 September 1941. Quoted: Czech, "Zuträger," 42.

12. Vörös, Lukas. "Kinder- und Jugendlicheneuthanasie zur Zeit des Nationalsozialismus am Wiener Spiegelgrund," University of Vienna, 2010, 47; Malina, " 'Fangnetz,' " 82; Neugebauer, Wolfgang. "Wiener Psychiatrie und NS-Verbrechen." Vienna: DÖW, 1997.

13. *Neues Österreich,* 18 July 1946. Quoted: Ertl, "NS-Euthanasie," 147.

14. Ertl, "NS-Euthanasie," 100. (Jekelius to Novak, 07.09.1941, DÖW 20 486/4). Hubenstorf, "Emigration," 159–60.

15. Ertl, "NS-Euthanasie," 127. Frankl, *Man's Search,* 133.

16. Jekelius Interrogation Protocol, 8 July

1948. Quoted: Ertl, "NS-Euthanasie," 149; Evans, Richard. *Lying about Hitler: History, Holocaust, and the David Irving Trial.* New York: Basic, 2001, 129; Knopp, Guido. *Geheimnisse des "Dritten Reichs,"* Munich: Bertelsmann, 2011, 38–9; "Journal Reveals Hitler's Dysfunctional Family." *The Guardian*, 4 August 2005.

17. Ertl, "NS-Euthanasie," 141–42. Jekelius after 1942: Hubenstorf, Michael. "Kontinuität und Bruch in der Medizingeschichte: Medizin in Österreich 1938 bis 1955." In *Kontinuität und Bruch*, 299–332; 328–29. T4 personnel in the Final Solution: Friedlander, Henry. "Euthanasia and the Final Solution." In *The Final Solution: Origins and Implementation*, edited by David Cesarani, 51–61: London; New York: Routledge, 2002, 54–5; Berger, Sara. *Experten der Vernichtung: das T4-Reinhardt-Netzwerk in den Lagern Belzec, Sobibor und Treblinka.* Hamburg: Hamburger Edition, 2013.

18. Personnel file: WStLA 1.3.2.202.A5 P: H.

19. Asperger, "Erlebtes Leben," 217.

20. Details: Hubenstorf, "Emigration," 149–51. Seidler, Eduard. ". . . vorausgesetzt, dass Sie Arier sind. . . . : Franz Hamburger (1874–1954) und die Deutsche Gesellschaft für Kinderheilkunde." In *90 Jahre Universitäts-Kinderklinik*, 44–52.

21. e.g., Hamburger, "Die Mütterlichkeit." *WkW* 55 no. 46 (1942): 901–5; "Die Väterlichkeit." *WkW* 56 no. 17/18 (1943): 293–95; "Schonung und Leistung." *WkW* 51 no. 37 (1938): 986–87; "Aufzucht und Erziehung unserer Kinder." *WkW* 55 no. 27 (1942): 522–26; Hubenstorf, "Emigration," 136–47; Wolf, *Vernunft*, 418–35.

22. Hamburger, Franz, "Kindergesundheitsführung," *WkW* 52 (1939): 33–35, 33. The birth rate tripled in Vienna from 1937–1940, from 10,032 per year to 30,330. Czech, "Welfare," 326.

23. Czech, "Zuträger," 35 (36–40).

24. Czech, Herwig. "Beyond Spiegelgrund and Berkatit: Human Experimentation and Coerced Research at the Vienna School of Medicine, 1939 to 1945." In Paul Weindling, ed. *From Clinic to Concentration Camp: Reassessing Nazi Medical and Racial Research, 1933–1945*. New York: Taylor & Francis, 2017, 141, 142; Türk, Elmar. "Vitamin-D-Stoß-Studien." *AfK* 125 (1942): 1–31.

25. Hamburger, Franz. "Protokoll der Wiener Medizinischen Gesellschaft." *WkW* 55, no. 14 (1942): 275–77, 275; Türk, Elmar. "Über BCG-Immunität gegen kutane Infektion mit virulenten Tuberkelbazillen." *MK* 38 no. 36 (1942): 846–47. Summary: Czech, "Beyond," 141.

26. "Fachgruppe für ärztliche Kinderkunde der Wiener medizinischen Gesellschaft—Sitzung vom 11. November 1942." *Medizinische Klinik* 39 (1943): 224–25; 224; Häupl, *Kinder*, 177–78.

27. This tuberculosis research was coordinated through the Vienna Public Health Office, and was part of a larger Reich initiative. Other major research sites were in Kaufbeuren and Berlin. Dahl, Matthias. "'... deren Lebenserhaltung für die Nation keinen Vorteil bedeutet.' Behinderte Kinder als Versuchsobjekte und die Entwicklung der Tuberkulose-Schutzimpfung." *Medizinhistorisches Journal* 37 no. 1 (2002): 57–90. Czech, Herwig. "Abusive Medical Practices on 'Euthanasia' Victims in Austria during and after World War II." In *Human Subjects Research after the Holocaust*, 109–26. Cham: Springer, 2014, 112–20.

28. "Fachgruppe für ärztliche Kinderkunde," 224. Also: Hamburger, "Verhandlungen," 275. Postwar: Türk, Elmar. "Pockenschutzimpfung—kutan oder subkutan?" *OZfKK* 10 no. 3–4 (1954): 322–29; Türk, Elmar. "Über die spezifische Dispositionsprophylaxe im Kindesalter (Tuberkulose-Schutzimpfung)." *Deutsches Tuberkulose-Blatt* 18 no. 2 (1944): 1–28.

29. Koszler, "Franz Hamburger," 391; Chiari.

"Lebensbild—Franz Hamburger zum 80. Geburtstag." *MmW* 96 no. 33 (1954): 928.

30. Quoted: Czech, "Beyond," 143.

31. Czech, "Beyond," 143–44. Goll, Heribert. "Zur Frage: Vitamin A und Keratomalazie beim Säugling." *MmW* 88 (1941): 1212–14; Goll, Heribert, and L. Fuchs. "Über die Vitamin A-Reserven des Säuglings." *MmW* 89 (1942): 397–400.

32. Hubenstorf, "Emigration," 120–1.

33. Franz A. Hamburger to Asperger, 5 October 1962. Quoted: Hubenstorf, "Emigration," 192.

34. H. O. Glattauer, "Menschen hinter grossen Namen," Salzburg 1977, WStLA 3.13.A1-A: A; ORF Radio, Hans Asperger, 1974.

35. Asperger, " 'Jugendpsychiatrie,' " 355.

36. Castell, *Geschichte*, 349.

37. Asperger, " 'Jugendpsychiatrie,' " 355.

38. Castell, *Geschichte*, 349; Friedlander, *Origins*, 57.

39. *Völkischer Beobachter*, 8/1 (1942). Quoted: Ertl, "NS-Euthanasie," 88.

40. *Völkischer Beobachter*, 8/1 (1942). Quoted: Ertl, "NS-Euthanasie," 88. Name: Heilpädagogische Klinik der Stadt Wien "Am Spiegelgrund."

41. Hubenstorf, "Tote," 418 (323).

42. Czech, Herwig, "Selektion und Kontrolle: 'Der Spiegelgrund' als zentrale Institution der

Wiener Fürsorge." In *Zwangssterilisierung zur Ermordung,* vol. 2, 165–88; 171; Czech, "Zuträger," 33; Koller, Birgit. "Die mediale Aufarbeitung der Opfer-Täter-Rolle in der Zweiten Republik dargestellt anhand des Spielfilms *Mein Mörder.*" University of Vienna, 2009, 69.

43. Thomas, Florian, Alana Beres, and Michael Shevell. " 'A Cold Wind Coming': Heinrich Gross and Child Euthanasia in Vienna." *JCN* 21 no. 4 (2006): 342–48; 344.

44. Hübener, Kristina, and Martin Heinze. *Brandenburgische Heil- und Pflegeanstalten in der NS-Zeit.* Berlin: Be.bra, 2002; Falk, Beatrice, and Friedrich Hauer. *Brandenburg-Görden: Geschichte eines psychiatrischen Krankenhauses.* Berlin-Brandenburg: Be.bra, 2007, 69–132. Gröger, Helmut, and Heinz Pfolz. "The Psychiatric Hospital Am Steinhof in Vienna in the Era of National Socialism." In *On the History of Psychiatry in Vienna,* edited by Eberhard Gabriel, Helmut Gröger, and Siegfried Kasper, 102–9. Vienna: Brandstätter, 1997, 106; Friedlander, *Origins,* 49.

45. Dahl, *Endstation,* 44.

46. Asperger, " 'Jugendpsychiatrie,' " 355.

47. Czech, "Abusive," 116. Also: Czech, Herwig. "Nazi Medical Crimes at the Psychiatric Hospital Gugging: Background

and Historical Context." Vienna: DÖW, 2008, 14–15; Neugebauer, Wolfgang. "Zur Rolle der Psychiatrie im Nationalsozialismus (am Beispiel Gugging)." In *Aufgabe, Gefährdungen und Versagen der Psychiatrie*, edited by Theodor Meißsel and Gerd Eichberger, 188–206. Linz: Edition pro mente, 1999.

48. Mühlberger, "Denken," 46; Czech, "Hans Asperger," 27; Hubenstorf, "Emigration," 172.

49. For example, the cases of Herman G., Johan Z., and Heinz P.; Malina, Peter. "Die Wiener städtische Erziehungsanstalt Biedermannsdorf als Institution der NS-Fürsorge—Quellenlage und Fallbeispiele." In *Verfolgte Kindheit*, 263–76; 267; Malina, "Geschichte," 171; Malina, "Fangnetz," 85.

50. Malina, "Erziehungsanstalt," 267.

51. Dahl, *Endstation*, 57.

52. Häupl, *Kinder*, 18; Ertl, "NS-Euthanasie," 101.

53. Ertl, "NS-Euthanasie," 99. Böhler, Regina. "Die Auswertung der Kinderkarteikarten des Geburtenjahrganges 1931 der Wiener Kinderübernahmestelle," 203–34; 226, 227, and Jandrisits, Vera. "Die Auswertung der Kinderkarteikarten des Geburtenjahrganges 1938 der Wiener Kinderübernahmestelle." 235–62, 250. Both in *Verfolgte Kindheit*.

54. Häupl, *Kinder*, 316–17.
55. Häupl, *Kinder*, 98–99. Photograph in alphabetical appendix.
56. Häupl, *Kinder*, 125–26.
57. Häupl, *Kinder*, 344–45.
58. Hager, "Hans Asperger." Ertl, "NS-Euthanasie," 100.
59. *Dr. Rohracher* (Signature), Univ. Kinderklinik in Wien, "Grohmann Elfriede, geb. 16.5.1930," 22 May 1944. WStLA 1.3.2.209.1.A47. HP: EG. Arche (Bezirkshauptmann) to Kinderübernahmsstelle, "Mj. Schaffer Margarete," 24 September 1941. WStLA 1.3.2.209.1.A47. B.H.2_B.J.A.2/B. HP: MS.
60. Häupl, *Kinder*, 496.
61. Donvan and Zucker, *Different*, 339, citing Herwig Czech.
62. Häupl, *Kinder*, 496–97. Herwig Czech also documents that Asperger transferred Herta Schreiber directly to Spiegelgrund. Czech, "Hans Asperger," 28.
63. Häupl, *Kinder*, 495–96.
64. Häupl, *Kinder*, 495–96; Czech, "Selektion und Auslese," 182.
65. Häupl, *Kinder*, 495–96; Czech, "Selektion und Auslese," 182.

1. Family history: Bezirkshauptmannschaft für den 24./25. Bezirk Wohlfahrtsamt, Dienstelle Liesing to heilpädagogische Abteilung der Kinderklinik, "Berka Christine," 30 May 1942; Univ.-Kinderklinik in Wien, "Berka, Christine"; both citations WStLA 1.3.2.209.1.A47 HP: CB.
2. Reichart and Weigt, K.L.D. - Lager, "Hotel Roter Hahn," to Wohlfahrtsamt Liesig, 30 May 1942. WStLA 1.3.2.209.1.A47. HP: CB.
3. Reichart and Weigt, 30 May 1942.
4. 24./25. Bezirk Wohlfahrtsamt, Dienstelle Liesing, 30 May 1942. Reichart and Weigt, 30 May 1942.
5. Handwritten notes; "Status," all WStLA 1.3.2.209.1.A47. HP: CB.
6. Berka, Christine, drawing. WStLA 1.3.2.209.1.A47. HP: CB.
7. Berka, Christine, statement, WStLA 1.3.2.209.1.A47. HP: CB.
8. "Nimm ein haarsieb und spare—auch mit Menschenseelen!" *Das Kleine Volksblatt*, 11 September 1940, 8.
9. Asperger, " 'Psychopathen,' " 76.
10. Asperger, Hans, "Berka Christine, 30.6.1928," 14 July 1942. WStLA 1.3.2.209.1.A47. HP: CB.

11. Asperger, Hans, Handwritten diagnosis. Also: Univ.-Kinderklinik in Wien, "Berka, Christine." Both WStLA 1.3.2.209.1.A47. HP: CB.

12. Asperger, Hans, "Berka Christine, 30.6.1928."

13. "Gutachten über Berka, Christine, geb. 30.6.1928," 21 May 1943 (183P 241/42). WStLA 1.3.2.209.1.A47. HP: CB.

14. Handwritten observation notes. WStLA 1.3.2.209.1.A47. HP: CB.

15. Kreissachbearbeiterin f. Jugendhilfe, NSDAP Gau Niederdonau, Kreisleitung Neunkirchen, Amt für Volkswohlfahrt, Abt. III Jugend to Dr. Aßberger, z. Hd. Frau Dr. Rohracher, allgemeine Krankenhaus Klinik, "Jgl. Elfriede Grohmann," 5 April 1944. WStLA 1.3.2.209.1.A47 WStLA 1.3.2.209.1.A47 HP: EG.

16. "Grohmann, Elfriede, geb. 16.5.1930," 22 May 1944. WStLA 1.3.2.209.1.A47 HP: EG; Kreissachbearbeiterin f. Jugendhilfe, Kreisleitung Neunkirchen, "Jgl. Elfriede Grohmann," 5 April 1944.

17. Kreissachbearbeiterin f. Jugendhilfe, Kreisleitung Neunkirchen, "Jgl. Elfriede Grohmann," 5 April 1944.

18. Handwritten report, "Grohmann Elfriede 13 ¾ J. aufg. am 11.IV.44."

19. Handwritten notes, "Status," 15 May 1944. WStLA 1.3.2.209.1.A47. HP: EG.

20. Kreissachbearbeiterin f. Jugendhilfe, Kreisleitung Neunkirchen, "Jgl. Elfriede Grohmann," 5 April 1944.
21. *Dr. Rohracher* (Signature), "Grohmann Elfriede," 22 May 1944. Kreissachbearbeiterin f. Jugendhilfe, Kreisleitung Neunkirchen, "Jgl. Elfriede Grohmann," 5 April 1944.
22. Rohracher, "Grohmann Elfriede," 22 May 1944.
23. Illing, "Gutachtliche Äusserung über Margarete Schaffer, geb. 13.10.1927," 9 March 1943. WStLA 1.3.2.209.1.A47. HP: MS.
24. Arche to Kinderübernahmsstelle, "Mj. Schaffer Margarete," 24 September 1941. Bezirkshauptmann (Arche) to Universitäts-Kinderklinik (Heilpädagogische-Abteilung), "Schaffer Margarete," 21 August 1941. B.H. 2-B.J.A. 2/L, WStLA 1.3.2.209.1.A47. HP: MS.
25. Arche, "Schaffer Margarete," 21 August 1941.
26. Penkler to Kinderübernahmsstelle, "Mj. Schaffer Margarete," 22 December 1942. WStLA 1.3.2.209.1.A47. B.H.2-B.J.A.2/L. HP: MS. Arche, "Schaffer Margarete," 21 August 1941.
27. Arche, "Schaffer Margarete," 21 August 1941.

28. Kreissachbearbeiterin f. Jugendhilfe, Kreisleitung Neunkirchen, "Jgl. Elfriede Grohmann," 5 April 1944. Arche, "Schaffer Margarete," 21 August 1941.

29. Gender roles in the Third Reich: Heineman, Elizabeth. *What Difference Does a Husband Make? Women and Marital Status in Nazi and Postwar Germany.* Berkeley: University of California Press, 1999; Stephenson, Jill. *Women in Nazi Germany.* Harlow; New York: Longman, 2001; Bridenthal, Renate, Atina Grossmann, and Marion Kaplan, eds. *When Biology Became Destiny: Women in Weimar and Nazi Germany.* New York: Monthly Review Press, 1984; Stibbe, Matthew. *Women in the Third Reich.* London; New York: Arnold, 2003. In Austria: Gehmacher, Johanna. *Völkische Frauenbewegung: deutschnationale und nationalsozialistische Geschlechterpolitik in Österreich.* Vienna: Döcker, 1998.

30. Asperger, " 'Psychopathen,' " 86 (40).

31. Asperger, " 'Psychopathen,' " 86 (39).

32. Asperger, " 'Psychopathen,' " 97 (51).

33. Asperger, " 'Psychopathen,' " 96 (51).

34. Asperger, " 'Psychopathen,' " 124, 121 (79, 77).

35. Asperger, " 'Psychopathen,' " 109, 92, 121 (65, 47, 77). Similar: 113 (69).

36. Asperger, " 'Psychopathen,' " 87, 88, 86 (43, 40).

37. Asperger, " 'Psychopathen,' " 90, 86 (46).
38. Asperger, " 'Psychopathen,' " 96 (51).
39. Asperger, " 'Psychopathen,' " 105, 104 (61, 59).
40. Asperger, " 'Psychopathen,' " 111, 109, 125, 121 (66, 65, 81, 77).
41. Pine, Lisa. *Nazi Family Policy, 1933–1945*. Oxford; New York: Berg, 1997, 117–46.
42. Asperger, " 'Psychopathen,' " 86, 87 (40, 41).
43. Asperger, " 'Psychopathen,' " 87, 112 (42, 68).
44. Asperger, " 'Psychopathen,' " 97 (51–52).
45. Asperger, " 'Psychopathen,' " 128–29 (84).
46. Asperger, " 'Psychopathen,' " 129 (84).
47. Asperger, " 'Psychopathen,' " 76.
48. Dr. R., Univ. Kinderklinik in Wien to Gaujugendamt Wien, Abt. F 2-Scha-5/44, "Schaffer Margarete, geb. 13.10.1927," 13 June 1944; Handwritten note, "Schaffer Margarete, geb. 13.10.1927," 18 April 1944; both WStLA 1.3.2.209.1.A47. HP: MS.
49. Dr. Rohracher, "Grohmann Elfriede," 22 May 1944. Handwritten notes, 1944. WStLA 1.3.2.209.1.A47; Handwritten notes, "Status," 15 May 1944. WStLA 1.3.2.209.1.A47; both HP: EG.
50. Asperger, " 'Psychopathen,' " 88, 91, 86, (43).
51. Asperger, " 'Psychopathen,' " 101, 102, 97 (56, 57, 52).

52. Asperger, " 'Psychopathen,' " 105, 111, 110 (61, 67, 66).

53. Asperger, " 'Psychopathen,' " 86 (40).

54. Asperger, " 'Psychopathen,' " 101, 97 (57, 51).

55. Rohracher, "Grohmann Elfriede," 22 May 1944. Handwritten report, "Grohmann Elfriede 13 ¾ J. aufg. am 11.IV.44," WStLA 1.3.2.209.1.A47. HP: EG. Illing, "Gutachtliche Äusserung," 9 March 1943.

56. Asperger, " 'Psychopathen,' " 88, 96 (43, 51).

57. Rohracher, "Grohmann Elfriede," 22 May 1944; Handwritten report, "Grohmann Elfriede 13 ¾ J. aufg. am 11.IV.44."

58. Luckesi and Asperger, Univ.-Kinderklinik, "Schaffer Margarete, geb. 13.10.1927." 23 August 1941; B.H. 2-B.J.A.2/L. WStLA 1.3.2.209.1.A47. HP: MS.

59. Asperger, " 'Psychopathen,' " 97, 124 (79).

60. Handwritten report, "Grohmann Elfriede 13 ¾ J. aufg. am 11.IV.44." Penkler, "Mj. Schaffer Margarete," 22 December 1942.

61. Handwritten report, "Grohmann Elfriede 13 ¾ J. aufg. am 11.IV.44." Handwritten notes, "Status," 15 May 1944.

62. Grohmann, Elfriede, to Katharina Grohmann; Grohmann, Elfriede, to Viktorine Zak. 5 May 1944. Both: WStLA 1.3.2.209.1.A47. HP: EG.

63. Handwritten report, "Grohmann Elfriede 13 ¾ J. aufg. am 11.IV.44."

64. Grohmann, Elfriede, to Dr. Auhlehner. WStLA 1.3.2.209.1.A47. HP: MS.

65. Handwritten report, "Grohmann Elfriede 13 ¾ J. aufg. am 11.IV.44."

66. Rohracher, "Grohmann Elfriede," 22 May 1944.

67. Rohracher, "Grohmann Elfriede," 22 May 1944.

68. Rohracher, "Grohmann Elfriede," 22 May 1944.

69. Grohmann, Elfriede, to Ferdinand [Grohmann]. WStLA 1.3.2.209.1.A47. HP: EG. Grohmann, Elfriede, to Katharina Grohmann.

70. Luckesi and Asperger, Univ.-Kinderklinik, "Schaffer Margarete, geb. 13.10.1927." 23 August 1941. Arche, "Mj. Schaffer Margarete," 24 September 1941; Luckesi and Asperger, "Schaffer Margarete, geb. 13.10.1927." 23 August 1941.

71. Arche, "Mj. Schaffer Margarete," 24 September 1941.

72. Dr. Margarete Hübsch, Anstaltsoberärtzin, and Dr. Helene Jockl, Abteilungsärztin, "Margarete Schaffer, geb.13.X.1927," Gutachtens der Wr. städt. Erziehungsanstalt am Spiegelgrund, 4 May 1942. WStLA 1.3.2.209.1.A47. HP: MS.

73. Hübsch and Jockl, "Margarete Schaffer, geb.13.X.1927," 4 May 1942; Direktor der Kinderübernahmsstelle to Direktion der Univ. Kinderklinik Wien Heilpäd. Station, 20 April 1944. WStLA 1.3.2.209.1.A47. HP: MS. Penkler, "Mj. Schaffer Margarete," 22 December 1942; Hübsch and Jockl, "Margarete Schaffer, geb.13.X.1927," 4 May 1942.

74. Hübsch and Jockl, "Margarete Schaffer, geb.13.X.1927," 4 May 1942. Sterilization at Steinhof: Spring, " 'Patient.' " Direktor der Kinderübernahmsstelle, 20 April 1944.

75. Penkler, "Mj. Schaffer Margarete," 22 December 1942.

76. Illing, "Gutachtliche Äusserung," 9 March 1943.

77. Direktor der Kinderübernahmsstelle, 20 April 1944. Handwritten note, "Schaffer Margarete," 18 April 1944.

78. R., Univ. Kinderklinik in Wien, "Schaffer Margarete," 13 June 1944.

79. Handwritten note, "Schaffer Margarete," 18 April 1944.

80. Schaffer, Margarete, to Schwester Neuenteufel [1944]. WStLA 1.3.2.209.1.A47. HP: MS.

81. Schaffer, Margarete, to Franz Schaffer, [1944]. WStLA 1.3.2.209.1.A47. HP: MS.

82. Schaffer, Margarete, Drawing. 19 April

1944. WStLA 1.3.2.209.1.A47. HP: MS.

83. R., Univ. Kinderklinik in Wien, "Schaffer Margarete," 13 June 1944. Handwritten note, "Schaffer Margarete," 18 April 1944.

84. R., Univ. Kinderklinik in Wien, "Schaffer Margarete," 13 June 1944. Winkelmayer, "Gutachten der Erziehungsberatung über Margarete Schaffer, geb. 13.10.1927, seit 23.3.44 Luisenheim," 29 March 1944. WStLA 1.3.2.209.1.A47. HP: MS.

85. R., Univ. Kinderklinik in Wien, "Schaffer Margarete," 13 June 1944. Universitäts-Kinderklinik in Wien, Biographical Information. WStLA 1.3.2.209.1.A47. HP: MS. R., Univ. Kinderklinik in Wien, "Schaffer Margarete," 13 June 1944. Also: Handwritten note, "Schaffer Margarete," 18 April 1944. Winkelmayer, "Gutachten der Erziehungsberatung," 29 March 1944.

86. Handwritten note, "Schaffer Margarete," 18 April 1944.

87. Asperger, " 'Psychopathen,' " 95–96, 94 (50, 49).

88. Asperger, " 'Psychopathen,' " 123, 103 (79, 58).

89. Asperger, " 'Psychopathen,' " 93.

90. Asperger, " 'Psychopathen,' " 90, 82–83. In this, Asperger was building upon his mentor Hamburger's idea of "thymogen automatism." Hamburger, Franz, *Die*

Neurosen des Kindesalters. Vienna: Urban & Schwarzenberg, 1939; Asperger, " 'Psychopathen,' " 93.

91. Asperger, " 'Psychopathen,' " 128, 130 (84, 85).
92. Asperger, " 'Psychopathen,' " 130, 129 (85, 84).
93. Asperger, " 'Psychopathen,' " 130 (85).
94. Asperger, " 'Psychopathen,' " 129 (85, 84).
95. Weygandt, Wilhelm. "Talentierte Schwachsinnige und ihre erbgesetzliche Bedeutung." *ZfNP* 161 no. 1 (1938): 532–34; 534; Tramer, "Einseitig"; Kirmsse, Max. *Talentierte Schwachsinnige: mit besonderer Berücksichtigung des Berner Gottfried Mind (Katzenraffael).* Bern: Sonder-Abdrück, 1911; Weygandt, Wilhelm. *Der jugendliche Schwachsinn: seine Erkennung, Behandlung und Ausmerzung.* Stuttgart: Enke, 1936, 94. Descriptions of "talented imbeciles": 88–94. Schmuhl, "Gehorsam," 1059.
96. Schaffer, Margarete, Dictation and handwriting sample. [1944] WStLA 1.3.2.209.1.A47. HP: MS.
97. Asperger, " 'Psychopathen,' " 106 (62).
98. Asperger, " 'Psychopathen,' " 115 (70–71).
99. Asperger, " 'Psychopathen,' " 89.
100. Asperger, " 'Psychopathen,' " 97–98, 99 (52, 54).
101. Asperger, " 'Psychopathen,' " 106, 115 (62, 71).

102. Handwritten note, "Schaffer Margarete," 18 April 1944. Hübsch and Jockl, "Margarete Schaffer," 4 May 1942.

103. R., Univ. Kinderklinik in Wien, "Schaffer Margarete," 13 June 1944. Handwritten note, "Schaffer Margarete," 18 April 1944.

104. Asperger, " 'Psychopathen,' " 86, 104, 97–98 (59, 52).

105. Asperger, " 'Psychopathen,' " 87–88, 97–98, 105 (42, 52, 60–61).

106. R., Univ. Kinderklinik in Wien, "Schaffer Margarete," 13 June 1944.

107. Asperger, " 'Psychopathen,' " 89 (45).

108. Asperger, " 'Psychopathen,' " 89, 90 (44, 45).

109. Asperger, " 'Psychopathen,' " 99 (53, 54).

110. Asperger, Hans, "Berka Christine," 14 July 1942.

111. Asperger, " 'Psychopathen,' " 117, 116 (74, 73).

112. Asperger, " 'Psychopathen,' " 116 (72–73).

113. Asperger, " 'Psychopathen,' " 111–12.

114. Asperger, " 'Psychopathen,' " 114 (70).

115. Asperger, " 'Psychopathen,' " 97, 87 (52, 42). Similar: Ernst: 105 (60).

116. Asperger, " 'Psychopathen,' " 111, 110 (67, 66, 65).

117. Asperger, " 'Psychopathen,' " 123, 97, 96 (79, 52, 51).

118. Asperger, " 'Psychopathen,' " 102 (57; 63).

119. Asperger, " 'Psychopathen,' " 89, 102, 96 (57, 63, 51). Similar: Hellmuth: 110 (66).

120. Asperger, " 'Psychopathen,' " 126 (82).

121. Asperger, " 'Psychopathen,' " 93, 112 (45–46, 68).

122. Asperger, " 'Psychopathen,' " 84 (37).

123. Asperger, " 'Psychopathen,' " 135 (89–90).

124. Asperger, " 'Psychopathen,' " 135 (90).

125. Hamburger, "Aussprache," 117.

126. Jekelius, "Grenzen," 386.

127. Asperger, " 'Psychopathen,' " 118 (74).

128. Asperger, " 'Psychopathen,' " 132, 133, 134 (87, 88, 89). Similar: 117 (74).

129. Asperger, " 'Psychopathen,' " 133 (88).

130. Asperger, " 'Psychopathen,' " 118, 134, 133 (74, 89, 88).

131. Asperger, " 'Psychopathen,' " 132, 108, 107 (87, 64, 62).

132. Asperger, " 'Psychopathen,' " 118 (75).

133. Asperger, " 'Psychopathen,' " 132 (87).

134. Asperger, " 'Psychopathen,' " 103, 108, 111 (58, 64, 67).

135. Asperger, " 'Psychopathen,' " 107 (63). "Asocials" in Vienna: Seliger, Maren. "Die Verfolgung normabweichenden Verhaltens im NS-System. Am Beispiel der Politik gegenüber 'Asozialen' in Wien." *Österreichische Zeitschrift für Politikwissenschaft.* (1991): 409–29.

1. Lehmann, Oliver, and Traudl Schmidt. *In den Fängen des Dr. Gross: das misshandelte Leben des Friedrich Zawrel.* Vienna: Czernin, 2001, 68.
2. Gedenkstätte Steinhof, *The War Against the "Inferior": On the History of Nazi Medicine in Vienna*, "Friedrich Zawrel." Interviews: http://gedenkstaettesteinhof.at/en/interview.
3. Ertl, "NS-Euthanasie," 85. Riegele, Brigitte, "Kindereuthanasie in Wien 1940–1945," In *Die ermordeten Kinder*, 25–46; 30. The "Book of the Dead" is available at the Viennese City and State Archive (WStLA) and accessible online at: http://gedenkstaette steinhof.at/en/BookoftheDead/book-dead.
4. Neugebauer, "Klinik," 302–303. Dahl, *Endstation*, 131.
5. Czech, "Zuträger," 29. Selection process: Ertl, "NS-Euthanasie," 97, 102–4.
6. Krenek, Hans. "Beitrag zur Methode der Erfassung von psychisch auffälligen Kindern und Jugendlichen." *AfK* 126 (1942): 72–84; 73.
7. Gedenkstätte Steinhof, "Alfred Grasel."
8. This was 60 percent of victims who had been transferred through Vienna. Dahl, *Endstation*, 57–58.

9. Dahl, *Endstation*, 55, 50–51.
10. Gedenkstätte Steinhof, "Ferdinand Schimatzek."
11. Gedenkstätte Steinhof, "Alois Kaufmann." See also, USC Shoah Foundation Institute testimony of Alois Kaufmann. VHA Interview Code: 45476. http://collections.ushmm.org/search/catalog/vha45476. Kaufmann, Alois. *Spiegelgrund, Pavillion 18: ein Kind im NS-Erziehungsheim.* Vienna: Gesellschaftskritik, 1993, and *Dass ich dich finde: Kind am Spiegelgrund; Gedichte.* Vienna: Theodor-Kramer, 2006; Kaufmann, Alois, Mechthild Podzeit-Lütjen, and Peter Malina. *Totenwagen: Kindheit am Spiegelgrund.* Vienna: Mandelbaum, 2007.
12. Gedenkstätte Steinhof, "Franz Pulkert."
13. Gedenkstätte Steinhof, "Karl Uher," Zawrel.
14. Czech, "Zuträger," 29; Ertl, "NS-Euthanasie," 102–4. Definitions of disability in Germany, Poore, *Disability,* 1–151. At least four children who died at Spiegelgrund were Jewish, but Jews were neither targets nor categories for elimination in the child euthanasia program. Neugebauer, Wolfgang. "Juden als Opfer der NS-Euthanasie in Wien 1940–1945." In *Zwangssterilisierung zur Ermordung,* vol. 2, 99–111; 105.
15. Gedenkstätte Steinhof, "Karl Jakubec."
16. Häupl, *Kinder,* 539.

487

17. The collection of survivor testimonies, "Spiegelgrund Survivors Speak Out," was conducted by the Documentation Centre of Austrian Resistance (DÖW) with support from the city of Vienna. The interviews are available in English at the Steinhof Memorial webpage. Gedenkstätte Steinhof, *The War Against the "Inferior": On the History of Nazi Medicine in Vienna.* "Spiegelgrund Survivors Speak Out." Translations are those of the organization, with very slight alterations. Other interviews are available in the documentary *Spiegelgrund*, directed by Angelika Schuster and Tristan Sindelgruber in 2000 (Vienna: Schnittpunkt).

18. In Mattias Dahl's sample of 312 children who were killed, 161 were girls and 151 were boys. Dahl, *Endstation*, 49.

19. Gedenkstätte Steinhof, Karger.

20. Gedenkstätte Steinhof, Pulkert. Gross, Johann. *Spiegelgrund: Leben in NS-Erziehungsanstalten.* Vienna: Ueberreuter, 2000, 62.

21. Gedenkstätte Steinhof, Pacher, Schimatzek.

22. Gedenkstätte Steinhof, Maier.

23. Gedenkstätte Steinhof, Pauer, Maier.

24. Gedenkstätte Steinhof, Kaufmann.

25. Gedenkstätte Steinhof, Pauer.

26. Gedenkstätte Steinhof, Maier, Karger.

27. Czech, "Abusive," 131.

28. Gross, *Spiegelgrund*, 69; also 96, 101.
29. Gross, *Spiegelgrund*, 80–81.
30. Lehmann and Schmidt, *Fängen*, 58.
31. Gedenkstätte Steinhof, Grasel.
32. Gedenkstätte Steinhof, "Karl Hamedler."
33. Gedenkstätte Steinhof, Pulkert, Pauer.
34. Gedenkstätte Steinhof, Karger.
35. Gedenkstätte Steinhof, Maier, Pauer.
36. Gedenkstätte Steinhof, Maier, Karger, Uher.
37. Gedenkstätte Steinhof, Kaufmann.
38. Gedenkstätte Steinhof, Pauer, Jakubec.
39. Gedenkstätte Steinhof, Uher, Kaufmann.
40. Gedenkstätte Steinhof, Zawrel.
41. Lehmann and Schmidt, *Fängen*, 68–9.
42. Gedenkstätte Steinhof, Grasel, Hamedler.
43. Gedenkstätte Steinhof, Karger.
44. Gedenkstätte Steinhof, Maier.
45. Häupl, *Kinder*, 330–33.
46. Häupl, *Kinder*, 385–87.
47. Häupl, *Kinder*, 526–27.
48. Czech, "Zuträger," 27–28.
49. During the first half of 1941, the average age of death at Spiegelgrund was around two and a half; in the second half of the year, the average age of death jumped to over seven. Czech, "Zuträger," 172.
50. Publications: Illing, Ernst. "Pathologisch-anatomisch kontrollierte Encephalographien bei tuberöser Sklerose." *ZfNP* 176 no. 1 (1943): 160–71, and "Erbbiologische

Erhebungen bei tuberöser Sklerose."
Zeitschrift für die gesamte Neurologie und Psychiatrie 165 no. 1 (1939): 340–45.

51. Czech, "Abusive," 112–20. Brain research on victims elsewhere in Germany: Karenberg, Axel. "Neurosciences and the Third Reich: Introduction." *Journal of the History of the Neurosciences* 15 no. 3 (2006): 168–72; 169–70.

52. Quoted: Thomas, Beres, and Shevell, "'Cold Wind," 344. Similar: Kaufmann, *Totenwagen*, 21–22.

53. Gedenkstätte Steinhof, Pacher, Karger.

54. Gedenkstätte Steinhof, Karger; Kaufmann, *Totenwagen*, 21.

55. Gross, *Spiegelgrund*, 75.

56. Gedenkstätte Steinhof, Pacher.

57. Gedenkstätte Steinhof, Jakubec.

58. Interrogation of Erwin Jekelius, 9 July 1948. Quoted: Ertl, "NS-Euthanasie," 128.

59. Interrogation of Marianne Türk, Landesgericht Wien, 16 October 1945. Quoted: Malina, "Fangnetz," 86.

60. Häupl, *Kinder*, 133.

61. Häupl, *Kinder*, 419–20.

62. Interrogation of Erwin Jekelius, 9 July 1948. Quoted: Ertl, "NS-Euthanasie," 151.

63. Interrogation of Anna Katschenka, 24 July 1946. Quoted: Dahl, *Endstation*, 39.

64. Statement by Anna Katschenka, 27 July

1948. Quoted: Neugebauer, "Klinik," 301.

65. Interrogation of Marianne Türk, 12 March 1946. Quoted: Dahl, *Endstation*, 43.

66. Interrogation of Ernst Illing, 22 October 1945. Quoted: Dahl, *Endstation*, 43.

67. Interrogation of Ernst Illing, 22 October 1945. Quoted: Dahl, *Endstation*, 41.

68. Häupl, "Einleitung," 14; Lehmann and Schmidt, *Fängen*, 79.

69. Häupl, "Einleitung," 14; Lehmann and Schmidt, *Fängen*, 79.

70. Interrogation of Marianne Türk, 12 March 1946. Quoted: Dahl, *Endstation*, 42.

71. Interrogation of Anna Katschenka, 24 July 1946. Quoted: Dahl, Matthias. "Die Tötung behinderter Kinder in der Anstalt 'Am Spiegelgrund' 1940 bis 1945." In *NS-Euthanasie in Wien*, vol. 1, 75–92; 79–80. Moral justification among euthanasia nurses: McFarland-Icke, Bronwyn Rebekah. *Nurses in Nazi Germany: Moral Choice in History*. Princeton, NJ: Princeton UP, 1999, 210–56. Nurses in euthanasia: Fürstler, Gerhard, and Peter Malina. *"Ich tat nur meinen Dienst": zur Geschichte der Krankenpflege in Österreich in der NS-Zeit*. Vienna: Facultas, 2004, including trial of Katschenka, 305–10.

72. Statement by Anna Katschenka, 27 July 1948. Quoted: Neugebauer, "Klinik," 301.

73. Butterweck, Hellmut. *Verurteilt und begnadigt: Österreich und seine NS-Straftäter.* Vienna: Czernin, 2003, 71–72.

74. Häupl, *Kinder*, 256–58.

75. Häupl, *Kinder*, 230–31.

76. *Österreichische Pflegezeitschrift*, 3/03, 25. Quoted: Ertl, "NS-Euthanasie," 106.

77. Testimony of Anny Wödl, 1 March 1946. Quoted: Totten, Samuel, William S. Parsons, and Israel W. Charny, eds. *Century of Genocide: Eyewitness Accounts and Critical Views.* New York: Routledge, 2013, 241.

78. Häupl, *Kinder*, 174–75.

79. Häupl, *Kinder*, 175.

80. Häupl, *Kinder*, 95–96.

81. Burleigh, *Death*, 101–3.

82. Burleigh, *Death*, 101–3; 11–42; 22–23; Meltzer, Ewald. *Das Problem der Abkürzung 'lebensunwerten' Lebens.* Halle: Marhold, 1925.

83. Häupl, *Kinder*, 496.

84. Dahl, *Endstation*, 106.

85. Häupl, *Kinder*, 406.

86. Interrogation of Marianne Türk, 12 March 1946. Quoted: Dahl, *Endstation*, 43.

87. Interrogation of Ernst Illing, 22 October 1945. Quoted: Dahl, *Endstation*, 43.

88. Häupl, *Kinder*, 494–95.

89. Häupl, *Kinder*, 106–8.

90. Häupl, *Kinder*, 439–40.

91. Häupl, *Kinder*, 227.
92. Gedenkstätte Steinhof, Maier.

CHAPTER 9—IN SERVICE TO THE *VOLK*

1. Austria lost around 385,000 people, almost 6 percent of its population. Of Austrian deaths, at least one in four, roughly 100,000, were due to Nazi persecution and the Holocaust. Around two thirds, or 261,000, were military deaths.
2. Steininger, Rolf. *Austria, Germany, and the Cold War: From the Anschluss to the State Treaty 1933–1955.* New York: Berghahn, 2008, 14–15.
3. Hubenstorf, "Emigration," 124–25, 122; Widhalm and Pollak, eds., *90 Jahre Universitäts-Kinderklinik*, 268–69. Throughout the University of Vienna Medical School: Ernst, "Leading," 790.
4. Löscher, *Eugenik,* 218.
5. Asperger, " 'Psychopathen,' " 128 (84).
6. Additional: Shepherd, Ben. *Terror in the Balkans: German Armies and Partisan Warfare.* Cambridge, MA: Harvard UP, 2012. Levy, Michele Frucht. " 'The Last Bullet for the Last Serb': The Ustaša Genocide against Serbs: 1941–1945." *Nationalities Papers* 37 no. 6 (2009): 807–37.
7. Felder, " 'Sehen,' " (2008), 108.

8. Felder, " 'Sehen,' " (2008), 108.
9. Felder, " 'Sehen,' " (2008), 108.
10. Felder, " 'Sehen,' " (2008), 108.
11. Felder, " 'Sehen,' " (2008), 108.
12. Felder, " 'Sehen,' " (2008), 108. Asperger, Hans. "Der Heilpädagogische Hort." *WkW* 57 no. 31/32 (1944): 392–93; "Postenzephalitische Persönlichkeitsstörungen." *MmW* 91 no. 9/10 (1944): 114–17; and " 'Psychopathen.' "
13. Asperger, "Das psychisch abnorme Kind." (1937), 1461; Asperger, "Das psychisch abnorme Kind." (1938), 1316; Asperger, "Zur Erziehungstherapie," 244; Asperger, " 'Psychopathen,' " 84 (38).
14. Asperger, "Der Heilpädagogische Hort," 393.
15. Asperger, "Zur Erziehungstherapie," 243–44.
16. Asperger, "Der Heilpädagogische Hort," 392.
17. Asperger, " 'Autistic Psychopathy' in Childhood," In *Autism and Asperger Syndrome*, edited and translated by Uta Frith, 37–92. The translation begins with the last paragraph of Asperger's "Presentation of the Problem" and moves to his section "Name and Concept."
18. Kretschmer, Ernst. *Körperbau und Charakter.* Berlin: Springer, 1928;

Klages, Ludwig. *Grundlagen*; Jung, Carl. *Psychologische Typen*. Zurich: Rascher, 1926. Stephen Haswell Todd situates Asperger within this intellectual context in his dissertation, "The Turn to the Self: A History of Autism, 1910–1944," University of Chicago, 2015.

19. Asperger, "Erwin Lazar—Mensch," 129.
20. Asperger, " 'Psychopathen,' " 78, 80.
21. Asperger, " 'Psychopathen,' " 80; Rudert, "Gemüt," 64, 65; Heinze, "Phänomenologie," 395.
22. Asperger, "Zur Erziehungstherapie," 246; " 'Jugendpsychiatrie,' " 355; "Das psychisch abnorme Kind," (1938), 1317.
23. Hamburger, Franz. "Psychisches Klima." *WkW* 55 no. 6 (1942): 105–8; 106, 108.
24. Asperger, "Das psychisch Abnorme Kind," (1938), 1317; " 'Jugendpsychiatrie,' " 354; Asperger, Hans. "Erlebnis und Persönlichkeit." *ZfK* 49 (1943): 201–23; 217.
25. Asperger, " 'Psychopathen,' " 128.
26. Villinger, Werner. "Charakterologische Beurteilung der schwererziehbaren Jugendlichen, insbesondere der jugendlichen Psychopathen." In *Bericht über den I. Internationalen Kongress*, edited by Hanselmann, 250, 248–49.
27. Panse, Friedrich. "Erbpathologie der

Psychopathen." In *Handbuch der Erbbiologie des Menschen*, vol. 2, edited by Günther Just, 1089–174. Berlin: Springer, 1939–1940, 1113, 1127, 1161.

28. Kujath, Gerhard. "Praktische Probleme der Jugendpsychiatrie und ihrer heilpädagogischen Auswirkungen." *MK* 38 (1942): 916–19; 917; Kujath, "Aufbau der Heim- und Sondererziehung im Rahmen der Jugendhilfe." *MK* 38 (1942): 1043–45; 1043, 1045; Hubenstorf, "Emigration," 173.

29. Kujath, "Probleme," 917.

30. Jekelius, "Grenzen," 385.

31. Ertl, "NS-Euthanasie," 133–34.

32. Illing, Ernst. "Characterkunde und Erbforschung, I." *DE* 11 (1943): 73–84; 78.

33. Illing, "Characterkunde," 79, 81, Illing, Ernst. "Characterkunde und Erbforschung, II." *DE* 11 (1943): 110–20; 113. Ideals: Bartov, Omer. *Hitler's Army: Soldiers, Nazis, and War in the Third Reich*. New York: Oxford UP, 1992.

34. Czech, "Selektion und Kontrolle," 177.

35. Koller, "Aufarbeitung," 84, 109.

36. Asperger, " 'Psychopathen,' " 80.

37. Asperger, " 'Psychopathen,' " 80–81.

38. Asperger, " 'Psychopathen,' " 81, 125.

39. Asperger, " 'Psychopathen,' " 116 (73); 88, 105 (43, 61); 125 (81).

40. Asperger, " 'Psychopathen,' " 125 (81).

41. Asperger, " 'Psychopathen,' " 122 (78).
42. Asperger, " 'Psychopathen,' " 120–21 (77, adapted); 122 (78).
43. Asperger, " 'Psychopathen,' " 136 (90). Asperger invoked Jung's "introverted type," Jung, *Psychologische Typen.*

CHAPTER 10—RECKONING

1. Gedenkstätte Steinhof, Pauer.
2. Gedenkstätte Steinhof, Kaufmann, Pacher.
3. Gedenkstätte Steinhof, Pacher. Helige, Barbara, Michael John, Helge Schmucker, and Gabriele Wörgötter. "Endbericht der Kommission Wilhelminenberg." Vienna: Institut für Rechts- und Kriminalsoziologie, 2013, 84.
4. Mayrhofer, Hemma. "Zwischen rigidem Kontrollregime und Kontrollversagen: Konturen eines Systems des Ruhighaltens, Schweigens und Wegschauens rund um das ehemalige Kinderheim Wilhelminenberg in den 1970er Jahren." Vienna: Institut für Rechts- und Kriminalsoziologie, 2013, 13; Sieder and Smioski, "Gewalt," 277 (164).
5. Brainin, Elisabeth, and Samy Teicher. "Terror von außen am Beispiel Spiegelgrund: Traumatische Erfahrungen in der Kindheit und deren Folgen." *PdKK* 58 no. 7 (2009):

530–52. Gedenkstätte Steinhof, Hamedler, Maier.

6. Gedenkstätte Steinhof, Grasel, Pacher.
7. Gedenkstätte Steinhof, Karger.
8. Gedenkstätte Steinhof, Zawrel. Koller, "Aufarbeitung," 84, 109.
9. "Die Kindermörder vom Steinhof auf der Anklagebank" (and "Die Kindermörder vom Steinhof vor Gericht"), *Neues Österreich*, 14 July 1946.
10. Haider, Claudia Kuretsidis. "Die Rezeption von NS Prozessen in Österreich durch Medien, Politik und Gesellschaft im ersten Nachkriegsjahrzehnt." In *NS-Prozesse und deutsche Öffentlichkeit: Besatzungszeit, frühe Bundesrepublik und DDR*, edited by Clemens Vollnhals, 403–30. Göttingen: Vandenhoeck & Ruprecht, 2012, 420. Excerpted testimony: Malina, "Fangnetz," 70–73. Vörös, "Kinder- und Jugendlicheneuthanasie," 70.
11. Excerpted testimony: Totten, Parsons, and Charny, *Century*, 239–42. Frankl, *Man's Search*, 134.
12. Hamburger's postwar activities: Seidler, ". . . vorausgesetzt," 52. Heinze was sentenced to seven years in prison in the Soviet Zone in Germany and served five, working as a camp doctor. After 1952 he was appointed director of the child and

adolescent psychiatry at Wunstorf hospital in Lower Saxony. Villinger's involvement in the T4 program was not known until 1961, the year he died, before which time he held numerous titles in psychiatric institutions and organizations. Other notorious perpetrators in Vienna who enjoyed successful postwar careers include Hans Krenek (director of the "educational" section of Spiegelgrund after 1942) and Hans Bertha (T4 "expert" and director of Steinhof from 1944–1945). Czech, "Zuträger der Vernichtung?" 30.

13. Hubenstorf, "Emigration," 174–81. English summaries: Angetter, Daniela. "Anatomical Science at University of Vienna 1938–45." *Lancet* 355 no. 9213 (2000): 1454–57; Hubenstorf, Michael. "Anatomical Science in Vienna, 1938–45." *Lancet* 355 no. 9213 (2000): 1385–86; Neugebauer, Wolfgang, and Georg Stacher. "Nazi Child 'Euthanasia' in Vienna and the Scientific Exploitation of its Victims before and after 1945." *Digestive Diseases* 17 no. 5–6 (1999): 279–85; Spann, Gustav, ed. *Untersuchungen zur Anatomischen Wissenschaft in Wien 1938–1945.* Vienna: Akademischer Senat der Universität Wien, 1998. Details: Czech, Herwig. "Forschen ohne Skrupel: die wissenschaftliche Verwertung von Opfern der NS-Psychiatriemorde in Wien." In

Zwangssterilisierung zur Ermordung, vol. 2, 143–64; 157–60.

14. Ronen, Gabriel, Brandon Meaney, Bernhard Dan, Fritz Zimprich, Walter Stögmann, and Wolfgang Neugebauer. "From Eugenic Euthanasia to Habilitation of 'Disabled' Children: Andreas Rett's Contribution." *JCN* 24 no. 1 (2009): 115–27; 120.

15. English summaries: Czech, "Abusive," 116–20; Seidelman, William. "Pathology of Memory: German Medical Science and the Crimes of the Third Reich." In *Medicine and Medical Ethics in Nazi Germany: Origins, Practices and Legacies*, 93–111. New York: Berghahn, 2002, 101–4. Timeline: Neugebauer, Wolfgang, and Peter Schwarz. *Der Wille zum aufrechten Gang*. Vienna: Czernin, 2005, 267–95.

16. It even led to a Canadian documentary, *Gray Matter*, directed by Joe Berlinger in 2004. Postwar attitudes: Neugebauer, Wolfgang. "Zum Umgang mit der NS-Euthanasie in Wien nach 1945." In *NS-Euthanasie in Wien*, vol. 1, 107–25; Neugebauer, Wolfgang, Herwig Czech, and Peter Schwarz. "Die Aufarbeitung der NS-Medizinverbrechen und der Beitrag des DÖW." In *Bewahren, Erforschen, Vermitteln: das Dokumentationsarchiv des österreichischen Widerstandes*, edited

by Christine Schindler, 109–24. Vienna: DÖW, 2008. Attitudes in Germany: Peiffer, Jürgen. "Phases in the Postwar German Reception of the 'Euthanasia Program' (1939–1945) Involving the Killing of the Mentally Disabled and its Exploitation by Neuroscientists." *Journal of the History of the Neurosciences* 15 no. 3 (2006): 210–44. Regarding other crimes of the Third Reich in Austria: Schulze, Heidrun, Gudrun Wolfgruber, and Gertraud Diendorfer, eds. *Wieder gut machen? Enteignung, Zwangsarbeit, Entschädigung, Restitution: Österreich 1938–1945/1945– 1999.* Innsbruck: Studien, 1999.

17. Hubenstorf, "Emigration," 183–86. Children's Hospital: Swoboda, W. "Die Nachkriegsperiode und die späteren Jahre." In *90 Jahre Universitäts-Kinderklinik,* 257–60.

18. Asperger, "Erwin Lazar—Mensch," 133. Felder, " 'Sehen,' " (2008), 109.

19. Hubenstorf, "Emigration," 193, 191–96. Overview: Berger, H. "Professor Dr. Hans Asperger zum 70. Geburtstag." *Pädiatrie und Pädagogik* 11 no. 1 (1976): 1–4; Oehme, Johannes. "Hans Asperger (1906–1980)." *Kinderkrankenschwester* 7 no. 1 (1988): 12; Asperger, *Heilpädagogik,* 1956, 1961, 1965, and 1968.

20. Sieder and Smioski, "Gewalt," 173, 274–75.
21. Sieder and Smioski, "Gewalt," 443. By the 1980s, the Curative Education clinic diagnosed around 2 percent of children with "dissociability," (compared to around 10 percent in the 1950s and 1960s). Staff diagnosed around 30 percent with "learning and achievement disorders," and 30 percent with "disciplinary disorders." Groh, Tatzer, and Weninger, "Krankengut," 108.
22. ORF Radio, Hans Asperger, 1974.
23. H. O. Glattauer, "Menschen hinter grossen Namen," Salzburg 1977, WStLA 3.13. A1-A: A; Olbing, "Eröffnungsansprache," 329; Topp, Sascha. *Geschichte als Argument in der Nachkriegsmedizin: Formen der Vergegenwärtigung der national-sozialistischen Euthanasie zwischen Politisierung und Historiographie.* Göttingen: Vandenhoeck & Ruprecht, 2013, 116.
24. ORF Radio, Hans Asperger, 1974.
25. ORF Radio, Hans Asperger, 1974; Löscher, *Eugenik*, 218.
26. H.O. Glattauer, "Menschen hinter grossen Namen," Salzburg 1977. WStLA 3.13.A1-A: A; Olbing, Herman. "Eröffnungsansprache zur 77. Tagung der DGfK." *MfK* 130 (1982): 325–29; 329; Topp, *Geschichte*, 116.
27. Löscher, *Eugenik*, 218.
28. Asperger, Hans. "Frühe seelische Vollendung

bei todgeweihten Kindern." *WkW* 81 (1969): 365–66; 366.

29. Asperger, Hans, "Das sterbende Kind." In *Befreiung zur Menschlichkeit: die Bedeutung des Emotionalen in der Erziehung*, edited by Hans Asperger and Franz Haider, 91–100. Vienna: Bundesverlag, 1976, 95.

30. Asperger, "Frühe seelische Vollendung," 366.

31. Wisdom of Solomon, 4:13, *Common English Bible,* "Früh vollendet, hat er viele Jahre erreicht;" Asperger, Hans. "Das sterbende Kind." *Internationale katholische Zeitschrift* 4 no. 6 (1975): 518–27; 522.

32. Asperger, "Frühe seelische Vollendung," 365.

33. Asperger, "Das sterbende Kind" (1976), 100.

34. Asperger, "Das sterbende Kind" (1975), 526.

35. e.g., Asperger, Hans. "Das Leibesbewusstsein des Menschen in der Technischen Welt." In *Erziehung angesichts der technischen Entwicklung*, edited by Leopold Prohaska, 58–69. Munich: Österreichischer Bundesverlag, 1965; "Personale Entfaltung in der Geschlechtlichkeit." In *Bedrohung der Privatsphäre: Erziehung oder Manipulation in einer offenen Gesellschaft*, edited by Hans Asperger and Franz Haider, 91–100. Salzburg: Selbstverlag der Internationalen Pädagogischen Werktagung Salzburg, 1977; Asperger and Haider, "Einleitung."

36. Asperger, Hans. "Die Psychopathologie der jugendlichen Kriminellen," In *Jugendkriminalität*, edited by Friedrich Schneider, 26–40. Salzburg: Otto Müller, 1952, 34; "Konstitution, Umwelt und Erlebnis in ihrer dynamischen Bedeutung für kriminelle Entwicklungen." *Österreichisches Wohlfahrtswesen* (1955): 1–4. For example, Asperger, "Determinanten," "Konstitution, Individualität und Freiheit." *Arzt und Christ* 4 (1958): 66–68; "Zur Einführung." In *Krise und Bewährung der Autorität*, edited by Hans Asperger and Franz Haider, 15–17. Vienna: Bundesverlag, 1972, 16. Relationship between religion and science: "Mensch und Tier." In *Ein Chor der Antworten: Glaube und Beruf*, edited by Hans Asperger, Charlotte Leitmaier, and Ferdinand Westphalen, 9–25. Vienna: Herold, 1969.

37. Asperger, Hans, and Franz Haider. "Einleitung." In *Das Werden sozialer Einstellungen in Familie, Schule und anderen Sozialformen*, 7–9. Vienna: Bundesverlag, 1974, 7–9; Asperger, "Der Student vor Fragen der Sexualität." *Universität und Christ; evangelische und katholische Besinnung zum 500jährigen Bestehen der Universität* (1960): 164–81; 174; Asperger, "Determinanten des Freien Willens: ein

naturwissenschaftlicher Befund." *Wort und Wahrheit* 3 no. 10 (1948), 256.

38. Asperger, "Determinanten," 255.

39. Bessel, Richard. *Nazism and War.* New York: Random House, 2009, 214.

40. Browning, Christopher. *Ordinary Men: Reserve Police Battalion 101 and the Final Solution in Poland.* New York: HarperCollins, 1993.

41. Gross, Jan. *Neighbors: The Destruction of the Jewish Community in Jedwabne, Poland.* Princeton, NJ: Princeton UP, 2001.

42. Levi, Primo. *The Drowned and the Saved.* New York: Summit, 1988.

43. Arendt, Hannah. *Eichmann in Jerusalem: A Report on the Banality of Evil.* New York: Penguin, 1963.

44. Most recently argued, respectively, in Silverman, *NeuroTribes*; Donvan and Zucker, *Different*; and by Herwig Czech in Hager, "Hans Asperger."

45. Hager, "Hans Asperger."

EPILOGUE

1. Due to the thematic focus of this book on autism, the notes do not represent the myriad subjects of Asperger's postwar articles.

2. Asperger, *Heilpädagogik*, 1952, 1956, 1961,

1965, and 1968. This page count is from the 1968 edition.

3. Asperger, Hans. "Zur die Differential-diagnose des kindlichen Autismus." *Acta Paedopsychiatrica* 35 no. 4 (1968): 136–45; "Formen des Autismus bei Kindern." *Deutsches Ärzteblatt* 71 no. 14 (1974): 1010–12; "Frühkindlicher Autismus"; *Probleme des kindlichen Autismus*; "Problems of Infantile Autism," 48. Arranged posthumously by Franz Wurst: Asperger, "Kindlicher Autismus, Typ Asperger," 293–301, and "Kindlicher Autismus, Typ Kanner," 286–92. Both in *Psychotherapie und Heilpädagogik bei Kindern*, edited by Hans Asperger and Franz Wurst, 293–301. Munich: Urban & Schwarzenberg, 1982.

4. Asperger, *Probleme des kindlichen Autismus*, 2. Asperger did invoke "autistic" as an adjective in some postwar publications, as one of a series of attributes, rather than as a psychopathy, e.g., "Heimweh des Erlebnis des Verlassenseins bei autistischen Kinder." In *Psychologie et traitement pédagogique du sentiment d'abandon*, 17–22. Leuven: Société internationale de l'orthopédagogie, 1962, 122; "Konstitution, Individualität," 3; "Die Psychopathologie"; "Seelische Abwegigkeiten als Ursachen der Jugendverwahrlosung." In *Die Jugend-*

verwahrlosung und ihre Bekämpfung, edited by Friedrich Schneider, 21–36. Salzburg: Otto Müller, 1950.

5. Asperger, "Heimweh," 18.

6. Asperger does invoke *Gemüt* in terms of "thymotropic therapy," which had been Franz Hamburger's idea of treating children with empathy; he does not cite Hamburger in these references. e.g., "Suggestivtherapie." In *Psychotherapie und Heilpädagogik bei Kindern*, edited by Hans Asperger and Franz Wurst, 74–79. Munich: Urban & Schwarzenberg, 1982.

7. Asperger's own translation of the repeated passage, Asperger, "Problems of Infantile Autism," 48; also: Asperger, "Formen des Autismus," 1010; *Probleme des kindlichen Autismus*, 6.

8. Asperger, "Kindlicher Autismus," 287; Asperger, "Formen des Autismus," 1010.

9. e.g., Asperger, "Problems of Infantile Autism," 50–51, *Probleme des kindlichen Autismus*, 10, "Kindlicher Autismus," 286–92.

10. e.g., Asperger, "Formen des Autismus," 1012.

11. Asperger, Hans. "Typische kindliche Fehlentwicklungen in der Stadt und auf dem Lande." In *Das Landkind heute und morgen: Gegenwartsfragen der Landjugend*, edited by Franz Wurst, 85–94. Vienna:

Österreichischer Bundesverlag, 1963, 86, 89.

12. Asperger, *Heilpädagogik* (1968), 199. Also: Asperger, "Kindlicher Autismus," 298.
13. van Krevelen, Dirk Arn. "Early Infantile Autism and Autistic Psychopathy." *Journal of Autism and Childhood Schizophrenia* 1.1 (1971): 82–86.
14. Wing, Lorna. "Reflections on Opening Pandora's Box." *Journal of Autism and Developmental Disorders* 35 no. 2 (2005): 197–203; 198. Asperger, "Problems of Infantile Autism," 48. Asperger and Kanner's definitions: Eyal, Gil, et al. *The Autism Matrix: The Social Origins of the Autism Epidemic.* Cambridge, UK: Polity, 2010, 214–21.
15. Wing, Lorna. "Asperger's Syndrome: A Clinical Account." *Psychological Medicine* 11.1 (1981): 115–29; "Reflections."
16. Wing, "Asperger's Syndrome," 115. Eghigian, "Drifting," 296–300.
17. Frith, ed., *Autism and Asperger Syndrome.*
18. Vajda, F. J. E., S. M. Davis, and E. Byrne, "Names of Infamy: Tainted Eponyms," *Journal of Clinical Neuroscience* 22 no. 4 (2015): 642–44. e.g., Reiter syndrome, Wegener's granulomatosis, Van Bogaert-Scherer-Epstein Syndrome, Cauchois–Eppinger–Frugoni syndrome, Hallervorden-

Spatz disease, Seitlberger disease, the "Clara cell," and the Spatz-Stiefler reaction. The ethics of eponymous diagnoses and the Third Reich: Strous and Edelman, "Eponyms and the Nazi Era: Time to Remember and Time for Change," *Israel Medical Association Journal* 9 no. 3 (2007): 207–14.

19. American Psychiatric Association, *DSM-5*, "Autism Spectrum Disorder," 299.00 (F 84.0).

20. Quoted: Feinstein, *History,* 204.

21. World Health Organization, ICD-10, "Asperger's Syndrome," Diagnosis code 84.5.

22. Hacking, Ian. "Kinds of People: Moving Targets." British Academy Lecture. London, 11 April 2006; Sontag, Susan. *Illness as Metaphor*. New York: Farrar, Straus and Giroux, 1978.

23. Term: Kaplan, Marion A. *Between Dignity and Despair: Jewish Life in Nazi Germany*. New York: Oxford UP, 1998.

24. Social influences on the autism diagnosis: Nadesan, Majia Holmer. *Constructing Autism: Unravelling the 'Truth' and Understanding the Social*. London: Routledge, 2013; Hacking, Ian. *The Social Construction of What?* Cambridge, MA: Harvard UP, 1999.

25. Asperger, " 'Psychopathen,' " 129, 130 (84, 85); Baron-Cohen, Simon. "The Extreme

Male Brain Theory of Autism." *Trends in Cognitive Sciences* 6 no. 6 (2002): 248–54.

26. And up to 97 percent for fifteen-year-olds. Polyak, Andrew, Richard M. Kubina, and Santhosh Girirajan. "Comorbidity of Intellectual Disability Confounds Ascertainment of Autism: Implications for Genetic Diagnosis." *American Journal of Medical Genetics, Part B: Neuropsychiatric Genetics* (2015): Part B 9999, 1–9; 3. Eyal et al. *Autism Matrix,* 46–58.

27. Gilman, Sander. *Hysteria beyond Freud.* Berkeley: University of California Press, 1993; Goldstein, Jan E. *Console and Classify: The French Psychiatric Profession in the Nineteenth Century.* Chicago: University of Chicago Press, 2002; Arnaud, Sabine. *On Hysteria: The Invention of a Medical Category between 1670 and 1820.* Chicago: University of Chicago Press, 2015.

Illustration Credits

44 The University of Vienna Children's Hospital, Vienna. ANL/Vienna, no. 12849041.

46 University Children's Hospital, Vienna: children on deck chairs and wicker beds in the roof garden. Photograph, 1921. Wellcome Library no. 28603i.

48 University Children's Hospital, Vienna: the play area. Photograph, 1921. Wellcome Library no. 28455i.

109 Propaganda for the plebiscite. ANL/Vienna, no. 1072942.

114 Dean Eduard Pernkopf lectures at the University of Vienna Medical School, April 26, 1938. ANL/Vienna, no. 12851777.

152 Arial view of Steinhof. Walter Mittelholzer/ ETH-Bibliothek.

352 Portrait of Hans Asperger (1906–1980), 1956. ANL/Vienna, no. 8081531 - Pf 27300:C (1).

Books are produced in the United States using U.S.-based materials

Books are printed using a revolutionary new process called THINKtech™ that lowers energy usage by 70% and increases overall quality

Books are durable and flexible because of Smyth-sewing

Paper is sourced using environmentally responsible foresting methods and the paper is acid-free

Center Point Large Print
600 Brooks Road / PO Box 1
Thorndike, ME 04986-0001 USA

(207) 568-3717

US & Canada:
1 800 929-9108
www.centerpointlargeprint.com